"THE BELIEVER'S WEALTH, WALK, AND WARFARE"

Commentary on Ephesians

W. Max Alderman

Printed
March 2024

Copyright © 2024

For additional copies of this book or
other titles by Dr. Max Alderman, write:

(In the United States)
"Strengthen the Things Which Remain" Ministries
Evangelist W. Max Alderman
406 Myrtle Crossing Lane
Statesboro, Georgia, 30458
912-601-2137
Email Philipministry@gmail.com

(In Canada)
Bethel Baptist Church,
4212 Campbell St. N.,
London, Ont. N6P 1A6
1-866-295-4143 (Toll Free) • 519-652-2619 (voice)
info@bethelbaptist.ca (e-mail)

Printed in Canada by
Bethel Baptist Print Ministry

TABLE OF CONTENTS

Forward 7
Prologue 8
Introduction 10
The Book Summarized 12
The Setting of the Book 17

Chapter One: A Divine Nature Planned by His Sovereignty. (1:1-6) 22

Verse Summaries Vv. 1-6 22
The Writer and His Audience (Vv. 1-6) 24
Paul's Audience 27
The Way His Plan Blesses Us (1:3) 34
The Way His Plan Benefits Us (1:4-6) 39

Chapter Two: A Divine Nature Purchased by His Son (1:7-14) 46

Verse Summaries 1:7-14 46
The Great Price of the Purchase was Remitted (1:7) 48
To Manifest His Rich Grace Perpetually (1:8) 52
The Great Purpose of the Purchase was Revealed (1:9-12) 54
To Reveal the Great Mysteries of God (1:9-10) 54
To Reveal the Great Mercies of God (1:11-12) 57
A Divine Nature Protected by His Spirit (1:13-14) 60
The Holy Spirit Promises Protection (1:13b-14) 62

Chapter Three: The Truth of the Revelation (1:15-23) 67

Verse Summaries 1:15-23 67
Paul had an Interest in Them (vs. 15-23) ... 69
Paul Prayed for Them (Vs 16-19) 72

He Prayed that God's Power Might be Recognized by Them (V. 19) 80

The Triumph of the Resurrection of Christ (Vs. 20-21) 83

The Telling of the Exaltation of Christ (Vs. 22-23)   84

Chapter Four: The Miracle, Mercy, and the Manifestation of a Different Life (2:1-10) 88

Verse Summaries (2:1-10) 88

The Beginning of the Commentary, (2:1-10)90

But God....(V 4) 96

The Way Grace Works 101

Chapter Five: Remember Your Past Relationship (2:11-22) 104

Verse Summaries (2:11-22) 104

The Beginning of the Commentary, (Vv 11-22)   107

Things the Gentiles were Without 109

The Wall Broken Down 113

The Hostility Removed 119

Chapter Six: The Mystries Revealed to the Church(3:1-9) 124

Verse Summaries (3:1-9) 124

The Beginning of the Commentary (3:1-9)126

The Mystery Revealed to the Church 129

Paul was Used to Reveal the Mystery........135

Chapter Seven: The Churches Special Role (3:10-21) 139

Verse Summaries (3:10-21) 139

The Beginning of the Commentary, (3:10-21)141

The Prayer Resumes 147

Chapter 8: The Conditions for the Believer's

Walk(4:1-6)................................155

Verse Summaries (4:1-6) 155

The Beginning of the Commentary (4:1-6)156

Walking with Gratitude 156

Notice the One's in This Section 162

Chapter 9: The Way the Church Operates (4:7 –16) 166

Verse Summaries: (4:7-16)........................166

The Beginning of the Commentary (4:7-16)168

To Everyone Given 169

The Different Ministries of the Church 173

The Unity of Faith and Knowledge............179

Chapter 10: (4:17-5:6) 183

Verse Summaries: (4:17-5:6).....................183

The Beginning of the Commentary (4:17-32; 5:1-6)   188

The Challenge to a Different Walk............188

Put on the New Man..................................196

Put Away Some Things 203

The Charity in the Believer's Walk 206

Chapter 11: Beware! Watch Who You Hang Out With (5:7-19) 213

Verse Summaries: (5:7-19) 213

The Beginning of the Commentary (Vv. 7-19)215

Light and Darkness....................................215

The Spirit-Filled Life 219

The Results of Spirit-Filled Life.................223

Chapter 12: Love and Submission (5:20-33) 229

Verse Summaries: (Vv. 5:20-33) 229

The Beginning of the Commentary (Vv. 5:20-33)   232

5

    Wives in Submission to Their Husbands..232

    Husbands Love Your Wives 238

    Christ our Example 245

Chapter 13: (6:1-24) 252

    Verse Summaries: (6:1-24) 252

    Commentary for Chapter (6:1-24) 257

    Children, Parents-Masters, Servants 257

    The Believers Warfare (6:10-17) 266

    The Believer's Armor 271

    Loins Girt About with Truth 272

    The Breastplate of Righteousness 276

    Feet Shood with the Preparation of the Gospel of Peace 278

    The Shield of Faith 279

    Conclusion to the Ephesian Letter 282

BIBLIOGRAPHY 285

FOREWORD

The book of Ephesians has often been compared with the Old Testament Book of Joshua. As the Israelites were blessed with all material blessings in the land of Canaan, a land flowing with milk and honey, God's people in the New Testament – as well as today's Christians – are blessed with all Spiritual blessings in heavenly places in Christ Jesus. The Lord God is the giver; it is His to give, and it can be ours to receive if we have the desire.

Dr. W. Max Alderman is a tremendously gifted writer and has been blessed by the Lord to be able to bring out great scriptures on Christian living in this Commentary on Ephesians and make the scriptures so understandable and practical to everyday living. This book on Ephesians is all about **"Wealth, Walk, Warfare In the Spirit."** Christian living depends on Christian learning; duty is always founded on doctrine, and if Satan can keep a Christian ignorant, he can keep him impotent (powerless). By the way, how can we practice what we do not know? Reading this book will help you to walk this kind of life. This book tells the truth! And it is the truth that is presented that will set you free!

I know no man more qualified to write on this subject than Dr. W. Max Alderman, who was my pastor for over twenty years. It is a great honor to recommend Dr. W. Max Alderman's book on Ephesians as one of his greatest accomplishments.

Evangelist Ray Brown, Philippians 4:19
Young Harris, Georgia

PROLOGUE

Many years ago, I became acquainted with the writings of Ruth Paxson. Her book on Ephesians grabbed my attention when I discovered how she divided the Book of Ephesians into three parts. Chapters 1-3, "The Wealth of the Christian"; Chapters 4 and 5, called "The Walk of the Christian," and in chapter 6, she said it shows "The Warfare of the Christian." This description fits the Book of Ephesians so naturally. In honor of her perception in recognizing and naming it as she did, I have chosen to call this book similar to hers in her honor: "The Believer's Wealth, Walk, and Warfare." It is written as an excellent tribute to the Apostle Paul, who wrote Ephesians to encourage the church to be in harmony with one another. One theologian said: The theme may be stated pragmatically as "Christians, get along with each other!" (Daniel Wallace). Maintain the unity practically which Christ has affected positionally by his death." (Another central theme in Ephesians is keeping Christ's body (that is, the Church) pure and holy, as suggested by it being presented as "a glorious church without spot or wrinkle.

Since I am giving tribute to her, it would be appropriate to say some things about her grasp of what is happening in Paul's lofty Letter. She likened it initially to the "Grand Canyon of the Scriptures." She said so after having seen the Grand Canyon but once, which was 28 years earlier, and she also said it was as fresh in her mind as the day she saw it. Paxton said: A well-known Bible teacher says, "In this epistle, we enter the Holy of Holies in Paul's writings." Dr. A. C. Gaebelein writes, "This epistle is God's highest and best. Even God cannot say more than He has said in this filling-full of His Word." (Paxson)

To study this excellent book in Paul's Prison Epistles, do

so not as only a venture but as an adventure while we carefully ascend into the sterling pages of God's Holy Writ. May we be careful as we take each step, ensuring we do not leave one pebble of God's Word unturned. The rich nuggets of God's Word are there for our finding! May we prospect well... To help the reader do just that, each verse will be given in the summary form to help provide an overview of what is being said. Then, that same summary statement is repeated as an introduction to each verse in the commentary section. Once each verse is explained, an exegetical commentary will be given using King James English rather than Greek, except occasionally for a critical explanation of some words to gain further understanding, as expected in studying the etymology of a word. For a more prosperous and deeper study, extensive explanation will be given as warranted. It, of course, would contain more information that would not be readily available without intensive research to capture the culture, the geography, the meaning of the words, etc., as used in the narrative of the Scriptures in the Letter to Ephesus. (Dr. W. Max Alderman)

INTRODUCTION

There have been many ways of describing the Book of Ephesians. F. F. Bruce, a noted New Testament scholar, calls Ephesians "the quintessence of Paulinism." C. H. Dodd called Ephesians "the crown of Paulinism." According to William Hendriksen, Ephesians has been called "the distilled essence of the Christian religion," "the most authoritative and most consummate compendium of the Christian faith," and "full to the brim with thoughts and doctrines sublime and momentous." (Deffinbaugh). W. O. Carver described the Book of Ephesians as "the greatest piece of writing in all history." Then, English poet Samuel Taylor Coleridge called it "the most divine composition of man." Ephesians has been described as "the Switzerland of the New Testament," "the crown and climax of Pauline theology." Then, as mentioned in the Prologue, Ruth Paxson called it the Grand Canyon of the Bible, and G. Campbell Morgan called it "The Alps of the Bible."

From these, we learn that there is much respect among theologians as to the value and the quality of this sublime Prison Epistle. Another exciting aspect of this Epistle is that it contains the longest sentence in the Bible. In the original Greek, verses 3 through 13 form one long sentence. Teachers of English have stated that 30 words are about all one can adequately place in one sentence and keep it fluent, yet in Greek, there are over 260 words in this one sentence. Through confluent inspiration, the Lord took what would have been a confusing jangle of words and turned it into that which is loftily inspired Truth. The Book of Ephesians is neatly divided into two parts, with Chapters 1-3 being about Doctrines and Chapters 4-6 having to do with Duty. Then, Ruth Paxson further divides it into The Wealth of the Christian (Chapters 1-3), The Walk of the Christian

(Chapters 4-5), and Chapter 6 considers "The Warfare of the Christian beginning in verse 10." Next to the Book of Romans, Ephesians has been said to be the most helpful for the teachings about soteriology or salvation.

The Book Summarized

There are six chapters in the Book of Ephesians, each with a theme (as I named them for this study). The first Chapter addresses the subject of *redemption* and how it pertains to one's salvation. The verse that this theme hinges on is verse 7: "In whom we have redemption through his blood, the forgiveness of sins, according to the riches of his grace;" This chapter speaks of the method of His choosing, and when the choosing took place, (verse 4); It tells us how He "predestinated us unto the adoption of children by Jesus Christ himself." (Verse 5). In the first Chapter, we are "enlightened by Him making known to us "the mystery of his will." (And that being through the Apostle Paul.) (verse 9). This Chapter also enlightens us to how we are guaranteed an inheritance by being "sealed with that holy Spirit of promise." (Verse 13). This verse also shows the three ingredients necessary for one's conversion. One's conversion involves the call of the Gospel, the belief of the Truth, and the Sanctification of the Spirit, as defined in 2 Thessalonians 2:13,14 and also stated here. With our salvation, we are granted "The spirit of wisdom and revelation in the knowledge of him." (Verse 17). We also are shown "the greatness of His power to us-ward who believe." (Verse 19). The Chapter closes with His power or authority being announced with Him being overall. (Verses 20-23) which is attributed to Him being raised from the dead or His resurrection from the dead. (Verse 20).

The second Chapter Emphasizes *"The Grace Given."* As the first verse states, one must be quickened or made alive to walk in Him. Dead people do not walk. Verse 2 teaches us that the believer's walk contrasts how he was before he was quickened or made alive. Upon one's conversion, we have been raised to "sit together in heavenly places in Christ

Jesus." (Verse 6) Our being raised from the dead is attributed to Christ's raising us from Spiritual death unto Spiritual life. That life is in Him alone. All is made possible by God's grace (Verses 7-9), for it is a gift of God. We are shown in chapter two that we are His workmanship, created in Christ Jesus unto good works, "which God hath before ordained that we should walk in them." (Verse 10).

Verses 11 and 12 indicate that Paul is writing primarily to a Gentile audience as he describes them as being aliens from "the commonwealth of Israel and strangers from the covenants of promise." They enjoyed the nearness not only because of Christ's resurrection but they "were made nigh by the blood of Christ." (Verse13) Verse 19 clearly states that those saved were no longer aliens, "no more strangers and foreigners but fellowcitizens with the saints, and of the household of God." Paul closes Chapter Two by saying they were "builded together for an habitation of God through the Spirit.

The suggested theme of Chapter Three is *"The Mystery Given."* In verses three and four, Paul wants his readers to know the source of the mystery and the intent of the mystery being given. He also wanted the mystery to be understood by the reader, as verse four states. "Whereby, when ye read, ye may understand my knowledge in the mystery of Christ," Paul told them the mystery was previously hidden, showing how and why it is called a mystery. It can be stated that what was previously unknown and concealed was a mystery. Upon it being revealed, it no longer is. Paul was chosen to be the steward of the mystery mentioned here and other mysteries. The Incarnation and the Church mystery is revealed to Paul, who then reveals it to Christendom. It was unimaginable that the Jews and the Gentiles would be fellow heirs and partakers of his promises in Christ by the gospel. (Verse 6). One of the aspects of the mystery is the fellowship of the mystery, which previously was unknown. (Verse 9) Verse 10 is a tremendous statement of Truth when it says God reveals His mind to the Church through the Word of God as delivered by the Apostle Paul. The way that Paul reveals Christ's mystery is so very uplifting to know that "the whole family in heaven and earth is named." (Verse15) Then, he told the Church at Ephesus that Christ would grant unto the believers, according to the riches of his glory, (that they would) be strengthened with might by his Spirit in the inner man." (Verse 16). The greatest benefit of this mystery is knowing "that Christ may dwell in our hearts by faith." (Verse 19-21).

The suggested theme of Chapter Four is *"Walking Worthy."* The chapter begins with the thought of walking with much gratitude, understanding that the invitation given was an invitation to eternal life (salvation). One of the main reasons for Ephesians being written is a call "to keep the unity of the Spirit in the bond of peace." One's walk cannot be effective when turmoil involves the body of Christ. (Verse 3). The chapter continues by showing a list of those whom God has used and still uses to strengthen and perfect the saints for the work of the ministry while the body of Christ is being edified. (Verses 11-12). Paul stresses the cooperative harmony of the church working together to accomplish those things that are Spiritual, ensuring that life reflects the radical change that occurred at salvation and continues to occur with Spiritual growth or with the perfecting of the saints. (Verses 22-32) Paul names some things to be put off that would hinder the church and each individual from having a Godly testimony.

The theme for Chapter Five is *"The Spirit-Filled Walk."* This chapter continues the subject of the believer's walk. Paul labeled those things offensive to having a sterling Christian walk while knowing that the root problem of the church is not living in harmony or unity, which could be attributed to those things mentioned along with the warnings given. Sometimes, Paul is seen trying to head off something harmful without saying it is happening. His Epistle to the Church at Colossi showed that kind of warning. There seems to be more than just a warning here; some may have been committing some of the things spoken of here. (Verse 14) He said, "Awake thou that sleepest, and arise from the dead, and Christ shall give thee light." Paul is stressing Godliness to help ensure having a relation to the Lord, described as "being filled with the Spirit." (Verse 18) Then, Paul gives the evidence of what constitutes one being Spirit-filled. (Verses 19-21) He speaks concerning all relationships as he addresses the wife and husband, the children and parents, and the employee and employer. (Slave, master).

The closing theme beginning in verse 10 of Chapter 6 is *"Fighting a Good Fight."* Paul very carefully and orderly includes every part of the believer's armor to protect against Satanic intrusion and attack. Peter emphasized resisting the devil in his letters, and Paul emphasized being equipped to defend oneself from the onslaught of the devil, which included one offensive weapon: the Word of God. We cannot stand against Satan unless we put on the whole armor of God and have the Word of God for a forceable attack. The power is vested in the Word of God.

THE SETTING OF THE BOOK

True Bible believers who accept the Canon of Truth, the Bible, would also accept the words written therein. For that reason, Paul is stated as the author God used under divine and confluent inspiration to pen the words of his Epistle. There have been those who say it was written by someone else as a forgery. Those receiving the Letter and Paul, who wrote it within its historical context, would have recognized such in their lifetime. No such thing is stated historically by Paul or the Church to suggest that it was a forgery; Paul would have quickly exposed it if it were. Also, those providentially involved in compiling the Canon would have disqualified it as a forgery if it genuinely was. Some also suggest that his letter was written by one of his students as a pseudonym. Because Paul unequivocally stated that he was the writer, such notions or suggestions are also unacceptable. Paul says who he is and is the author by stating that he is "an apostle of Jesus Christ by the will of God (writing) to the saints…" The evidence seems to suggest that he wrote this Epistle around 60 AD. The Book of Acts showed that Paul had a relationship with the Church for about three years before he moved on. (Acts 20:17-38). His Letter was written from a prison in Rome, and for this reason, it is referred to as a Prison Epistle. Even though the Romans had bound him, he referred to himself as a Prisoner of Christ. The Letter is similar to the Letter he wrote to the Church at Colossi, which causes many to suggest that it was written near the time he wrote to the Church at Colossi. There is nothing stated to suggest that is the case; it is mostly thought so by its similarity to the Letter to the Colossians.

Paul identified the church in Ephesus as the one he was writing to. Ephesus was the capital city of the Roman province of Asia, which corresponds roughly to the modern region known as Asia Minor and modern-day Turkey. During the first century, it was one of the most populous and important port cities in the Roman Empire, serving as a gateway between the Eastern and Western worlds. Geographically, it lay on the coast of the Aegean Sea, not too far north of the Meander River. We know from Acts 19 that during Paul's time in Ephesus, he had great conflict with worshippers of the pagan goddess Artemis and with many of the occult practices in the city. Correspondingly, Paul wrote in Ephesians 5:11 that Christians should "have no part in the unfruitful works of darkness" — a reference to the immoral practices of pagan idolatry. In Ephesians 6:12, he taught that Christians are in a battle "against the rulers of the darkness of this world against spiritual wickedness in high places." Archaeological research shows that Artemis was considered the nurturer of Ephesus and was said to have made Ephesus the most glorious city in the province of Asia. Indeed, Paul was mindful of this and redirected the church's thinking to the true Nurturer of their souls. In Ephesians 5:27-29, Paul described the relationship between Christ and his church using the Greek words *ektrephō*, meaning to "nourish" or "nurture," and *endoxos*, meaning "held in honor" or "glorious." This seems to relate to Artemis's impact on Ephesus and the surrounding area, which could have led to Paul addressing them in this manner. (Kidd).

We know that the primary recipients of Paul's Letter are the Church at Ephesus, which could have included many "house churches." Also, when Paul wrote to the Church at Colossi, he stated that he wanted to include other churches in the Lycus Valley in his readership as indicated by Colossians 4:12,13: 12, *"Epaphras, who is one of you, a servant of Christ, saluteth you, always labouring fervently for you in prayers, that ye may stand perfect and complete in all the will of God."*

13 *For I bear him record, that he hath a great zeal for you, and them that are in Laodicea, and them in Hierapolis.* With this being so, the Letter to the Church at Ephesus became a shared Letter. This is indicated by the fact that it addresses similar needs relevant to each church. The import and magnitude of these Letters, which Paul wrote from the prison in Rome, were helpful to the Churches directly addressed as well as to all known believers by being included in the Canon of Truth.

Paul seems to be addressing three major concerns as it involves the church at Ephesus. The first had to do with addressing their sinful nature, as they mostly were new converts. Though they were saved believers, they needed to be aware of how they still had their flesh to contend with, along with the world and the devil. They would question what was expected of them now that they were believers and new converts. Paul gave a sample list of sins and sinful practices that should no longer characterize who they now were. I say sample because I do not believe it would be the entire gamut of sins. He expressed, "In time past ye walked according to the course of the world," but he reminded them that was "the spirit that now worketh in the children of disobedience." (Chapter 2:2-3). Paul also dealt with racial tensions that would naturally be a concern since the church had both Jews and Gentiles, with it being mostly Gentiles. The Bible defines three ethnic groups: the Jew, the Gentile, and the Church. Once one becomes a believer, he is no longer referred to as either Jew or Gentile but as the Church. (Chapter 2:11-22). Before Abraham introduced the Jew, there was only one classification, and that being Gentile. Then, until the cross, there were Jew and Gentile, but after the veil was wrent in twain, there came into existence the Church, which graciously allowed both Jew and Gentile to come boldly to the throne of Grace while becoming one as the Church. (I Corinthians 10:32; Ephesians 2:11-22).

The third concern was the part Satan plays in the scheme of things. Beginning in Chapter 6 and verse 10, the church is instructed to outfit themselves for Spiritual warfare. The heathen philosophies, with many originating in Athens, were taking their toll on the Roman world. The main element describing their attitudes was that there was no God to answer to and no afterlife existence. That is one reason they could be either stoic or epicurean in their thinking and belief. The stoics seemed to believe everything was god in a pantheistic way, while the Epicureans were content to "eat, drink, and be merry" as they thought this life was all there was. These were reasons they did not feel accountable. With such thinking, Satan already had them. So, Satan seems to invest his energies in the new believers who are significantly impacting their world and their surroundings. The new converts were vital targets for Satan to hinder or disrupt their potential to live for Christ and Him alone. Paul knew this and, therefore, instructed them to equip themselves so that they could resist the attacks of Satan continuously. In the final portion of the Letter, he gives specifics on how to accomplish their resistance against Satan's attacks.

Paul's Letter to the Church at Ephesus is less polemical or controversial in tone compared to Romans, Galatians, or the Corinthian Letters. A more positive manner may have been necessary to encourage those engaged in Spiritual battles. This also could contribute to how well it is received in an inspirational way, as shown by its lofty manner of being described in the Prologue and the introduction of this commentary.

THE BELIEVER'S WEALTH, WALK, AND WARFARE
Beginning the Commentary Section Of the Book

CHAPTER ONE

A Divine Nature Planned by His Sovereignty. (1:1-6)

For the believer to enjoy the incredible wealth that originates in the Father through the Son, by the Spirit, he needs to begin by understanding the sovereignty of God. God is Sovereign and is in complete control of all that is, as Philippians teaches us when it says, it is by Him that all things consist. Paul reveals so much in this wonderful Book of the workings of God and just how marvelous it is. One cannot help but read Ephesians discovering as he does the way he is being captivated by the intense movement of God constantly revealing Himself to the Christian. And just like climbing the Alps, each step reveals more of His Splendor, only pausing to look down, seeing that the Grand Canyon of God's Word is revealed clearly to you as you climb. Whether you look up or down or to either side, it is all God! Paul shows us that God planned all of this for His infinite Glory. Please allow these verse summaries to introduce you to the commentary to follow.

VERSE SUMMARIES 1:1-6

1 *Paul, an apostle of Jesus Christ by the will of God, to the* *saints which are at Ephesus, and to the faithful in Christ Jesus:* This is Paul's way of introducing in his salutation to whom he is writing and perhaps his attitude and reason as a writer. Sometimes, he refers to himself as a servant as he did in his Letter to the Church at Philippi. By doing that, he identified with Christ as the One who came to serve humanity. In Philemon, he referred to himself as a "prisoner of Jesus Christ," which related to Philemon's run-way slave Onesimus, whom Paul met in Prison. When he wrote Philemon, Paul emphasized that he was in prison not as a criminal for having broken the Roman law but as a prisoner of and for the Lord Jesus Christ.

2 *Grace be to you, and peace, from God our Father, and from the Lord Jesus Christ.* The magnitude of the word grace never had the meaning it now does, which began with Christ. He is the One who makes grace so amazing. The grace given proceeds the peace that follows. Grace and peace were words associated with the Jews and the Gentile's form of greeting.

3 *Blessed be the God and Father of our Lord Jesus Christ, who hath blessed us with all spiritual blessings in heavenly places in Christ:* Paul is worshiping Deity in his salutation. There is praise on his lips and "praise on his pen as he writes." He gives a eulogy to God, who he recognizes as God and Father of Jesus Christ. At a funeral, we are said to eulogize or praise the deceased. Here, Paul is eulogizing One who lives and will never die!

4 *According as he hath chosen us in him before the foundation of the world, that we should be holy and without blame before him in love:* There is a lot of Theology in these verses and requires comparative studies to get the precise meaning that Paul spoke. It involves an entire discipline of Theology that has been debated for several millennia.

5 *Having predestinated us unto the adoption of children by Jesus Christ to himself, according to the good pleasure of his* *will*. The words predestinated, adoption, and children all in the same verse are ways of saying the same thing about His own and the next verse tells what it results in by it being so.

6 *To the praise of the glory of his grace, wherein he hath made us accepted in the beloved.* The reason for praise is based upon what His grace accomplishes in us by Him making us accepted. We are not accepted in and of ourselves but in Him, Christ Jesus, alone.

The Beginning of the Commentary Vv. 1-6

The Writer and His Audience

1 *Paul, an apostle of Jesus Christ by the will of God, to the saints which are at Ephesus, and to the faithful in Christ Jesus:* This great book opens with the writer being identified. Indeed, it must be understood that God is the Author, but Paul is the writer whom God chose to exercise what we refer to in theology as *confluent inspiration as he wrote*. The term *confluent inspiration* means that the Lord used the personality of Paul and then blew His holy breath into his writing personality with the result of Paul being used by God to deliver the inspired, infallible Word of God. The truth was not at all compromised when God did this. The writers of the Word of God were incredibly protected, but even more than that, the Word of God was protected. Paul states his name first, who Commissioned him, and to whom he is writing.

This is Paul's way of introducing himself in his salutation, to whom he is writing, and perhaps his attitude and reason as a writer. Sometimes, he refers to himself as a servant as he did in his Letter to the Church at Philippi. By doing that, he identified with Christ as the One who came to serve humanity. In Philemon, he referred to himself as a "prisoner of Jesus Christ," which related to Philemon's run-way slave Onesimus, whom Paul met in Prison. When he wrote Philemon, Paul emphasized that he was in prison not as a criminal for having broken the Roman law but as a prisoner of and for the Lord Jesus Christ.

The name Paul means "little." Saul was the name he was known by when he was leveling his persecution against the Church. Saul is his Hebrew name, whereas Paul is his Roman name. His name was changed in Acts 13:9, and Paul is the name that is primarily used in the New Testament. *Saul* begins by introducing himself with his name, *Paul*, which became common after Acts 13:9. In Hebrew, his name was Sha'ul, and Paul is the English word for the Roman (Latin) name "Paulus." Sha'ul (Saul) seemly decided to start using his Roman name, Paulus (Paul), only after going to the Gentiles and encountering the Roman proconsul of Cyprus, Sergius Paulus (one of the top officials in the Roman Empire). This may be why Sha'ul took the last name (Paulus) of the prominent man who was his first convert. By using the Roman name Paulus, possibly even at the suggestion of Sergius Paulus, Sha'ul now had more accessible access to the Romans he was trying to tell the good news of Jesus to. We know from the study of Acts that Paul spent the rest of his life wanting to go to Rome to preach the gospel – often to the highest Roman authorities. The name Paulus undoubtedly helped him gain access to Roman circles.

Paul introduces himself as an apostle. Paul refers to himself as ἀπόστολος Ἰησοῦ Χριστοῦ, "apostle of Jesus Christ." The term ἀπόστολος, "apostle," is used in classical Greek primarily for ships being sent out for cargo or military expeditions. Infrequently, it refers to a single person as an envoy or emissary. It appears only once in the Alexandrinus text of the LXX (1 Kgs 14:6) where שׁלוּחַ, the passive participle of שׁ.ל.ח, is rendered "to send" or "to send forth." (Hoecher). The title apostle had three meanings in the New Testament. In John 13:16, the word apostle is used primarily to describe *a messenger*. The term was also used to describe *missionaries*, men sent by the church to preach the Gospel. In this sense, Paul and Barnabas are called apostles, Acts 14:4, 14 and probably Andronicus and Junias, Romans 16:7. The third way that the term is used, and in a stricter sense, is when those selected men were chosen directly by the Lord Jesus Christ to serve a particular function. Their commission was given by all authority, and with this commission, they also had the apostolic gifts for authenticating the Gospel to the unbelieving Jews and doing the extraordinary work of the Church during its infancy to all groups of people. This work was done during the Apostolic Age or the Age of the Apostles. This level of Apostleship no longer exists. As was true of the personal call of the 12 Apostles, Paul's claim to apostleship was likewise based on the divine call of Christ (Rom 1:1; Col 1:1; Galatians 1:1, 15; 1 Corinthians. 1:1; Ephesians. 1:1; Col. 1:1; 1 Tim. 1:1; 2 Tim. 1:1; Titus 1:1). His call was unique to the other apostles, in the way he was called after the death, burial, and the resurrection of the Lord Jesus Christ. His call took place on the road to Damascus. His authority for being an apostle is based upon the truth that he was "not of men, neither by man, but by Jesus Christ, and God the Father, who raised him from the dead" (Gal 1:1). His encounter with the resurrected Christ served as the basis for his unique claim to be an "apostle of the Gentiles" (Rom 11:13) and; not by him being commissioned by some clergy, or religious group. Paul bases his apostleship on the grace of God, not on some charismatic or ecstatic gifts or one having the signs of an apostle (2 Cor. 12). His apostolic commission was to serve God primarily through the preaching of the gospel (Rom 1:9; 15:19; 1 Col 1:17). (Alderman)

Paul certainly knew that he was called to be an apostle, and this confirmed his commission by how he identified himself in his opening salutation. He referred to himself in this manner, "Paul, an apostle of Jesus Christ by the will of God." He understood that Christ had called him while on the road to Damascus and that this call was according to the will of God. This call was a supernatural call in that Christ revealed Himself to Saul from Heaven. That is what qualified him to be an apostle.

PAUL'S AUDIENCE

In the opening salutation, Paul writes to two groups: those described as *saints in Ephesus* and the *faithful in Christ Jesus*. The saints are commonly addressed in Paul's writings. This Letter is being written to those who make up the redeemed, the born-again ones called saints by having been sanctified at the moment of their conversion. The word Saint can have an adjective quality in a descriptive sense and a noun quality in stating who they are as being redeemed. He further signifies that they are not only saints but also faithful brethren. This does not assume that all the church members were saints and faithful in Christ Jesus, but as the letter's author, he let them know to whom his letter was intended.

The word "saint" comes from the Greek word *hagios*, which means "consecrated to God, holy, sacred, pious." It is almost always used in the plural, "saints." "Then Ananias answered, Lord, I have heard by many of this man, how much evil he hath done to thy saints at Jerusalem:" (Acts 9:13). "And it came to pass, as Peter passed throughout all *quarters*, he came down also to the saints which dwelt at

Lydda." (Acts 9:32). "Which thing I also did in Jerusalem: and many of the saints did I shut up in prison, having received authority from the chief priests; and when they were put to death, I gave my voice against *them*." (Acts 26:10). There is only one instance of the singular use, and that is Salute every saint in Christ Jesus. The brethren which are with me greet you. (Philippians 4:21). In Scripture, there are 67 uses of the plural "saints" compared to only one use of the singular word "saint." Even in that one instance, a plurality of saints is in view: "Salute every saint in Christ Jesus. The brethren which are with me greet you." (Philippians 4:21). The idea of the word "saints" is a group of people set apart for the Lord and His kingdom. Three references refer to the godly character of saints: "That ye receive her in the Lord, as becometh saints, and that ye assist her in whatsoever business she hath need of you: for she hath been a succourer of many, and of myself also." (Romans 16:2). "For the perfecting of the saints, for the work of the ministry, for the edifying of the body of Christ:" (Ephesians 4:12). "But fornication, and all uncleanness, or covetousness, let it not be once named among you, as becometh saints;" (Ephesians 5:3). (Got Questions)

In using the term "saint" (ἅγιος), Paul appropriates for all believers (including Gentiles) a term that was commonly used by the old covenant people of God (Exodus 22:31 [22:30]; Psalms 16:3 [15:3]; 34:9 [33:10]; Daniel 7:18, 21, 22, 25). They were called "holy ones" because God had chosen and consecrated them to him as his people. God called them to reflect his purity and integrity in their lives (Lev 11:45; 19:2). This descriptive expression became a common way of referring to the new covenant people of God in the early church (see Acts 9:13; Hebrews 3:1; Jude 3; Rev 5:8), but Paul particularly favored it. He uses this term numerous times in speaking of the believing readers of his letters and addresses most of his letters "to the saints" (Rom 1:7; 1 Cor 1:2; 2 Cor 1:1; Phil 1:1; Col 1:2). (C.E. Arnold) "Under the old dispensation, the Israelites were called *saints* because they were separated from other nations and consecrated to God. In the New Testament, the word is applied to believers, not merely as externally consecrated but as reconciled to God and inwardly purified. The Greek word from which the word 'saint' is derived signifies 'to cleanse,' either from guilt by a propitiatory sacrifice, as in Hebrews 2:11 and 9:10, 14, or from inward pollution, and also to consecrate. Hence, saints are those who are cleansed by the blood of Christ, and by the renewing of the Holy Spirit, and thus separated from the world and consecrated to God."— Commentary on Ephesians.

When writing the Letter to the Church at Ephesus naming the saints and those faithful in Christ Jesus, he included those who were believers in the total area surrounding Ephesus, which included up to a quarter of a million people who lived there with them also being included as believers. This indicates an indefinite number of people. Then, when including the sister Churches that could have read this Letter, it could comprise many more people. Now, with the Book of Ephesians being a part of the Canon or the Bible, that one singular Book has been read and loved for around two millennia. The preaching of Paul and the other preachers God had used means many had received Christ when this Letter was written. I am sure it contributed to much of the martyrdom during the age of persecution, which included nearly all of the Apostles and even the Apostle Paul.

2 *Grace be to you, and peace, from God our Father, and from the Lord Jesus Christ.* The strength of the word grace never had the meaning it now does, which began with Christ. He is the One who makes grace so amazing. The grace given proceeds the peace that follows. Grace and peace were words associated with the Jews and the Gentile's form of greeting.

This opening salutation is given with both the Greek and the Hebrew considered but expands beyond that. Paul used this greeting in each of his letters. In addition to the church, Paul spoke to two distinct ethnic groups that comprised the church body: the Jew and the Gentile. The word "grace" is the Greek word charis, which means grace but also carries the idea of favor. So when a person greeted someone with this salutation, it was the equivalent of him saying, "I greet you with grace and favor." But Paul wasn't only addressing the Greek world. As a Jew himself, he also wanted to greet the Jewish world that would be reading his epistles. When the Jews met, their customary way of greeting one another was to say, "Shalom!" This is still the traditional greeting exchanged between Jews in Israel today. The Greek equivalent for the Hebrew word shalom is the word eirene, which is the word for peace. (Milner) *"Grace be to you, and peace, from God our Father, and the Lord Jesus Christ"* (V. 2). Paul will show the mystery of how the Jew and the Gentile can come together as the Church, where there is neither Jew nor Gentile. It appears that Paul is addressing the two ethnic groups that comprise the church. The Greek salutation or greeting would be "grace," whereas the Hebrew greeting would be "peace." Paul identifies with both racial groups as he begins this letter by using words that are familiar to both the Jew and the Gentile. As truth is expounded, he will show the mystery of how these two groups unite together to become one in the church.

Here, he used both. The first word, grace, in redemptive order, comes first, for there can never be peace without first there being grace. It is commonly understood and stated that "grace" must always proceed with "peace" in order. Two things may be said about this being so, and also the words being used. Grace is the word that speaks of the unmerited favor God bestows upon the believer. The gentile was undoubtedly aware he had no merit in and of himself. He recognized he truly needed the grace of God upon his life if he were in any way to be found acceptable unto God. And following grace (Ephesians 2:8,9), there could be incredible peace. The word peace is used over 200 times in the Bible, but Paul used it to describe being reconciled to God and having his favor. In John 14:27, "Jesus said, Peace, I leave with you, my peace I give unto you: not as the world giveth, give I unto you. Let not your heart be troubled, neither let it be afraid." Indeed, the peace spoken of here can only come from God.

Then, there are two main ways of describing peace. One way is "peace with God." This peace can only come with conversion or salvation. Before salvation occurs, the unconverted is an enemy of and to God. It may be true that he is not an enemy in a harmful or malicious sense, but legally and judicially, it is so. God cannot give the natural or unregenerate person peace with Himself until he is saved. He cannot be saved until he receives the blood payment for his sins by faith because, without the "shedding of blood, there is no remission of sin." "then Peter said unto them, Repent, and be baptized every one of you in the name of Jesus Christ for the remission of sins and ye shall receive the gift of the Holy Ghost." (Acts 2:38). I Corinthians 2:14 also teaches us the lost person cannot receive things from God or have a relationship with God: "But the natural man receiveth not the things of the Spirit of God: for they are foolishness unto him: neither can he know them, because they are spiritually discerned."

God took the initiative to pursue peace with us by sending His Son to earth. Jesus lived a perfect life; His crucifixion paid for the sins of all who would trust in Him (Hebrews 4:15; 2 Corinthians 5:21), and His resurrection guarantees our justification before God (Romans 4:25). Jesus is the Prince of Peace (Isaiah 9:6). He is the One who gives us peace with God. That's why the message of salvation in Christ is called the "gospel of peace" (Ephesians 6:15).

The "peace of God" comes from having an ongoing relationship with God based upon one's living obediently to the Word of God. The Holy Spirit comforts our hearts by giving us a tranquil spirit that helps us face our trials and troubles and have a right relationship with God. He comforts us so there may be joy even while experiencing the challenging circumstances in our lives. The kind we would much rather not be involved in. We certainly do not put those tough times on our calendar with joyful anticipation, yet even so, with the peace of God, we can have the joy this Epistle speaks. Sadly, so many desire the peace of God without meeting God's requirements for having such peace. It would behoove us to carefully examine our relationship with God concerning the Word of God. Anytime we disobey the Truth, we cannot expect God to grant us the full extent of God's peace. (The Joy Book; Alderman)

The Way His Plan Blesses Us. (1:3)

3 *Blessed be the God and Father of our Lord Jesus Christ, who hath blessed us with all spiritual blessings in heavenly places in Christ:* Before considering how His plan blesses us, it would be appropriate to consider how we are to bless God. Paul is worshiping Deity in his salutation. There is praise on his lips and "praise on his pen as he writes." He gives a eulogy to God, who he recognizes as God and Father of Jesus Christ. At a funeral, we are said to eulogize or praise the deceased. Here, Paul is eulogizing One who lives and will never die!

Verse three begins in this manner: *"Blessed be the God and Father of our Lord Jesus Christ."* Using the word blessed as applied to God means we honor and praise Him. The Greek word *eulogetos* is the word from which we get our English word eulogy. God is the One to Whom we should eulogize and give praise and honor. Then, as we honor Him, He will return a blessing to us by giving us His favor, making us happy, or causing us to prosper spiritually. In our text, however, the benefit is in the past tense, which signifies that God has already blessed us according to His plan and purpose. He *"hath blessed us with all spiritual blessings in heavenly places in Christ: According as he hath chosen us in him before the foundation of the world, that we should be holy and without blame before him in love."* (Vv. 3b-4).

God developed a plan based upon His fore-knowledge that allows the blessing to originate in the heavenly places to minister to us in an earthly setting. 2 Thessalonians 2:13-17 gives valuable insight into how the blessing comes upon the Gentile. *But we are bound to give thanks alway to God for you, brethren beloved of the Lord, because God hath from the beginning chosen you to salvation through sanctification of the Spirit and belief of the truth: Whereunto he called you by our gospel, to the obtaining of the glory of our Lord Jesus Christ. Therefore, brethren, stand fast, and hold the traditions which ye have been taught, whether by word, or our epistle. Now our Lord Jesus Christ himself, and God, even our Father, which hath loved us, and hath given us everlasting consolation and good hope through grace, Comfort your hearts, and stablish you in every good word and work.* (2 Thessalonians 2:13-17)

There are three notable parts to the blessing available to the one who believes. First, we are told that "God hath from the beginning chosen you to salvation..." The time frame for the blessing to originate in heavenly places was from the beginning. The beginning that is spoken of is known only to God. The starting point for this "beginning" seems to be when God revealed the elements that pertain to one's conversion. First, there is a part that belongs to God alone. This involves His choosing. Just exactly how did He choose? For such a question, He answers. He began with the Gospel call: *Whereunto he called you by our gospel.* Some are convinced that the Gospel is unnecessary for one to be saved. They will tell you there is no need for either missionaries or Gospel preachers. Yet, God tells us in this portion of Scripture that "God hath from the beginning chosen you to salvation." This means that from the beginning, He had a plan; in this plan, the first necessary part was the call of the Gospel. The second is the "belief of the truth." Once the Gospel witness declares the Gospel, the hearer is responsible for accepting and believing the truth. Some might argue that those who believe will believe the truth without any personal exercising of the will. Those who take this position disregard that man is responsible to God, including the operation of his will. The third necessary and notable part of conversion is the "sanctification of the Spirit." This act of *consecration* can only be done by the Heavenly Father. John 6:44 illustrates this truth: *No man can come to me, except the Father which hath sent me draw him: and I will raise him up at the last day* (John 6:44).

The formula for God's choosing will appear each time a salvation plan is given. An example of this is shown in the first chapter of Ephesians. In verse 13, notice, "*In whom ye also trusted, after that ye heard the word of truth, the gospel of your salvation: in whom also after that ye believed, ye were sealed with that holy Spirit of promise.*" In this verse, the call of the Gospel considers the first part of the verse that says, *"After that, ye heard the word of truth, the gospel of your salvation."* The believing of the truth is identified this way, "ye believed," and then the sanctification of the Spirit is shown this way, *"ye were sealed with that holy Spirit of promise."* Again, any time Scripture is given relative to conversion, it will contain these three necessary parts.

The theme for the book of Ephesians could very well be "applied grace" or putting that grace to work. The first three verses show us the source of the mentioned grace that allows God to have a plan for redemption and how redemption is implemented. The first 14 verses summarize what is being said in the first four chapters. We must remind ourselves that when Paul wrote this letter, he was writing it as a mystery. He was privileged to reveal this mystery, which, mainly through him, was also delivered to the other apostles and prophets in the New Testament economy.

Historically, this church letter served an immediate purpose as it ministered to a particular people group that made up the saints of Ephesus. Still, as viewed in time, it was a letter written to include all of the faithful in Christ Jesus. This could be why this book met the qualifications of being in the sacred Canon of Truth. Paul emphasizes that what was written was according to the will of God; this letter is not a product of human genius but God speaking through human instrumentality as He chose to reveal Himself through human vessels. God reveals Himself to the Jew and the Gentile as the great One who blesses. According to Gill, God graciously made His blessings available as the only one who could genuinely bless. Notice what Gill says: "God is the author and giver of all blessings; and he blesses his people with them, as he is the God and Father of Christ, and as he is their covenant God and Father in Christ; and he only can bless; if he blesses not, none can; and if he blesses, they are blessed indeed: the "us" that are blessed are such who deserve, according to the tenor of the law, to be cursed; and are not all men, but some distinct from others; and who are before described as saints, and faithful in Christ Jesus; and include both Jews and Gentiles, who belong to the election of grace. And the blessings such are blessed with are spiritual, so called to distinguish them from temporal blessings" (Gill).

All the benefits and plans of redeeming grace that Paul considers in this Ephesians study have Christ as its strength. Christ is the source of power, whether it is the legal strength necessary to make His covenant binding or the strength to keep us saved eternally. The covenant of grace would not be of any force or power if it were not for Christ, and indeed, we could not enjoy enduring eternal salvation if it were not for Him being the Strong One. This, which we are referring to, has the throne room as its origin. The terms *"Heavenly place," "the heavenlies,"* or the reference to it appear five times in this book (1:3, 1:20, 2:6, 3:10, 6:12), reminding us that not only is Heaven the place that our blessings originate, but that it is something to be enjoyed now; not just in the future, and is available with much power. This study will emphasize the benefits of justification, sanctification, new birth, eternal life, peace, nearness, reconciliation, the gift of the Spirit, etc.

"These things are available now while we are pilgrims upon this earth. Israel was promised temporal blessings in earthly places on condition of obedience to the law. But all of their attempted works have gained them nothing. But God has given, on the ground of His grace alone and by the infinitely valuable sacrifice of His Son, every spiritual blessing in heavenly places to all who receive His Son in this day of His grace. This verse entitles us to claim every Old or New Testament spiritual blessing. We cannot claim the temporal blessings promised to Israel, but what is spiritual is ours" (Grant).

We may summarize these blessings in the following manner as we recognize that three things are indicated here in our text. First, they are *spiritual*, not material, as were Israel's blessings. Then, they are *heavenly* and not earthly, realizing that every good and perfect gift comes from above (so says James in his Epistle). And thirdly, these blessings are in Christ. That marks the crowning jewel of these beautiful blessings that God, our Heavenly Father, makes available to us. It all comes from His Son to us.

The Way His Plan Benefits Us. (1:4-6)

4 *According as he hath chosen us in him before the foundation of the world, that we should be holy and without blame before him in love*: There is a lot of Theology in these verses and requires comparative studies to get the precise meaning that Paul spoke. It involves an entire discipline of Theology that has been debated for several millennia. This fourth verse in our first chapter reveals how God preplanned our existence and redemption. God must explain things to us relative to His attributes and strengths. He is undoubtedly omnipotent, having no limits to His power. Another attribute of God is that He is omnipresent, meaning that by His Spirit, He is everywhere. He is also omniscient in that there is nothing that he does not know. He has perfect comprehension. Thus, this verse is to be understood, *According as he hath chosen us in him before the foundation of the world, that we should be holy and without blame before him in love:* (Ephesians 1:4).

It was in "eternity past" that God chose us "in him," as indicated by the formula given to us in 2 Thessalonians 2:13-

17. God's choosing was predicated upon His foreknowledge. Having perfect and complete knowledge, He also had the competence to develop a plan that would require *work* on the part of God and a *responsibility* on the part of man. This in no way takes away from the grace of God; it only permits God to exercise His sovereignty according to His purposes. The Scriptures indicate that God created man with both a will and a responsibility. This verse suggests His divine intention to bring us to full maturity. "When the Spirit's work in us has completed, including the quickening of our mortal bodies at the first resurrection, we shall be landed in heaven. We shall then be marked by perfect holiness of nature and perfect freedom from all blame of conduct. We shall be forever in the presence of the God and Father of our Lord Jesus Christ in an atmosphere of perfect love. That will be heaven, indeed. Thus, verse 4 begins in a past eternity and ends in a future eternity." (Hole)

During the believer's lifetime, the Lord is doing an ongoing work of grace to get the believer to where he can be presented as a part of the Church without "spot or wrinkle." The book of Ephesians gives us insight as to how God accomplishes this. There has been much debate in the realm of theology regarding the teachings of foreknowledge, election, and predestination. Much of the instructions will continue with ongoing discussion as it has for centuries. Charles Spurgeon wrestled with the teachings as they involved man's free will concerning how God elects men to salvation. He wisely recognized that these two doctrines are like two rails on a railroad track. They run side by side, never seeming to touch but never spreading apart. Much about the way God chooses is mysterious, and it will continue to be that way, perhaps because man by nature is lazy, and this helps prompt men to "dig a little deeper." I certainly know that because all of the teachings that pertain to this subject are not revealed to me, I have had to study diligently, whereas otherwise, I may not have done so.

One of the main reasons that much debate has gone on as it pertains to verses like this is that we are so prone to think only in human terms. We have no omnipotence, omnipresence, or omniscience in our makeup. We have to move with respect to time. We can make plans, but not with the benefit of omniscience as God can. Because God does enjoy these attributes, He can plan and elect with perfect knowledge as He pleases. "As he pleases" is the difference. He could choose from the beginning, but He was also pleased to let mankind have the responsibility of believing the Gospel. As God did with Lydia, so He does with us. He opens our hearts of unbelief so that we can receive the Gospel. Again, this does not at all take away from His grace. It allows man to come to repentance, demonstrating that He is not willing that anyone should perish but that all should come to repentance regarding his predestination.

5 *Having predestinated us unto the adoption of children by Jesus Christ to himself, according to the good pleasure of his will.* The term predestination, as it is used in our text, means that God predetermined ahead of time that the saved would be adopted into the family of God as mature or adult sons. He could have saved us without adopting us, but He did not. That means that we have the incredible privilege of enjoying the rights of sonship with all of its blessings immediately upon our being saved. What is so remarkable is that the Lord did it according to His will. He was not forced to do this; He did it with pleasure. Before we examine this aspect of his predestination, we can further investigate the act of His doing so for adoption. "In the NT, adoption means placing a believer in the family of God as a mature, adult son with all the privileges and responsibilities of sonship (Gal. 4:4–7). The Spirit of adoption plants within the believer the instinct to address God as Father (Rom. 8:15). Our adoption as sons is by Jesus Christ. God could never have brought us into this position of nearness and dearness to Himself as long as we were in our sins. So the Lord Jesus came to earth, and by His death, burial, and resurrection, He settled the sin question to God's satisfaction. The infinite value of His sacrifice on Calvary provides a righteous basis on which God can adopt us as sons." (McDonald) Adoption is a metaphor that shows or illustrates what is going on as one is saved using the Roman example: "Adoption was a significant and common practice in the Roman world. Today, we can write a will and leave our wealth and property to anyone we want, male or female. In the Roman world, with few exceptions, a man had to pass his wealth on to his son(s). If a man had no sons or felt that his sons were incapable of managing his wealth or were unworthy of it, he would have to adopt someone who would make a worthy son. These adoptions were not infant adoptions as is common today. Older boys and adult men were formally adopted. Sometimes, the adoptee might even be older than the man adopting him. When the adoption was legally approved, the adoptee would have all his debts canceled, and he would receive a new name. He would be the legal son of his adoptive father and entitled to all the rights and benefits of a son. A father could disown his natural-born son, but an adoption was irreversible. (Grudem)

The term predestination should not frighten those of us who are in the faith. It is simply a term that can only be accurately used by one with foreknowledge. With this ability, God predestinates His children to be like His Son, Christ Jesus. Romans 8:28-29 teaches us this: "And we know that all things work together for good to them that love God, to them who are the called according to his purpose. For whom he did foreknow, he also did predestinate to be conformed to the image of his Son, that he might be the firstborn among many brethren."

Some may have you believe that the word pleasure, as used herein "according to the good pleasure of his will" (verse 5), is a strict hedonistic term and that God is incapable of enjoying pleasure of any kind. This is certainly not so, for God finds great joy in bringing many sons unto glory, as Hebrews speaks of. This is the demonstrated purpose of God's electing grace. He plans to have a large family, which pleases Him. It was He who made us "accepted in the beloved." He did this to bring glory to Himself through the redemptive graces of His Son, Jesus Christ. During the early 1900s, J. Armitage Robinson, D.D. understood this truth as he stated, "To sum up verses three through six, the blessing, for which we bless God, is spiritual, in the heavenly sphere, in the exalted Christ. It is by an eternal choice whereby God has selected us in Christ. So far as we are concerned, its goal is the fullness of all virtues, and that is love. It includes an adoption through Jesus Christ to a Divine sonship. Its motive lies far back in the will of God. Its contemplated issue in the Divine counsel is that God's grace freely bestowed on us in His Well-beloved, should be gloriously manifested and eternally praised."

6 *To the praise of the glory of his grace, wherein he hath made us accepted in the beloved.* The reason for praise is based upon what His grace accomplishes in us by Him making us accepted. We are not accepted in and of ourselves but in Him, Christ Jesus, alone. We should remain mindful that any grace we enjoy as members of the redeemed family originates in Christ Jesus. The Father did not need more sons (children), for He had All He needed in His beloved Son, Jesus. There was nothing wrong with Him, and to have us meant ultimately to have sinners for children who were so unworthy. For Him to have us meant He willingly had us, even though He knew our future downfall beginning with

Adam. Yet, He had us anyway. This is why the expression, *To the praise of the glory of his grace*, is found in this verse. With all of our known failures, He had us anyway! For this reason, He made us "accepted in the beloved" (on the merit of His Son), and by Him having done this, it grants us the legal right through adoption to enjoy that which also brought pleasure to Him and then to praise Him.

In the New Testament, the word praise is used eleven times. It is used nine times by Paul and twice by Peter. It is used four times for people's praise of others and of God (Rom 13:3; 2 Cor 8:18; Phil 4:8; 1 Pet 2:14). Two of the times, God praises human beings (Rom 2:29; 1 Cor 4:5), and then five times human beings are seen praising God. (Eph 1:6, 12, 14; Phil 1:11; 1 Pet 1:7). In our Text, the believers praise God. We can praise Him because of His grace work, and that work He did on us and in us was sufficient to make us accepted by Him. Remembering it is not what we offer in and of ourselves that God is pleased with; Abel is an Old Testament example of one offering his best, and it came up woefully short. He was refused because he did not serve or offer obediently what God required of Him; it would be like him wanting to please or impress God with his offering or his own righteousness instead of God's. Abel may have thought His offering superior to God's; that is what pride will do. God's work is a spiritual work involving Him, putting His righteousness in us with nothing we can offer. The song that says, "Nothing in my hands do I bring…simply to the cross I cling" says it so well.

CHAPTER TWO

A Divine Nature Purchased By His Son. (1:7-14)

The following verses help us understand how our redemption was graciously accomplished. It emphasizes no work of our own, but all glory be unto Christ as stated. The redemption payment was his blood, which included forgiving our sins, graciously accomplished even when we did not deserve it. He gave us wisdom and prudence to understand the previously unknown mysteries about Christ, bringing together all in one in Christ. The most gracious aspect is that what He does for us allows us to bring Him pleasure, glory, and honor. Upon being saved, He seals us with "that holy Spirit of Promise." He makes us accepted!

VERSE SUMMARIES 1:7-14

7 *In whom we have redemption through his blood, the forgiveness of sins, according to the riches of his grace;* Redemption is a most lovely word used to describe what happened and is initiated upon one's conversion. The Lord redeemed us as described here by *the redemption through his blood*. It is wonderful because we could not have the forgiveness of sins without it. For Christ to do so is to do it according to *the riches of his grace*, as stated so eloquently in this verse. For one to be a recipient of His redeeming grace, there must be belief.

8 *Wherein he hath abounded toward us in all wisdom and prudence;* The word abounded is His graciously rendering to us for time and eternity all that pertains to His well-planned Salvation. The wisdom and prudence of God embeds all that is, and the only flaws are not of His but a result of the awful sin curse that befell humanity and all of the creation, thus necessitating making all things new as Revelation 21:1-5 declares.

9 *Having made known unto us the mystery of his will, according to his good pleasure which he hath purposed in himself:* The fact that God made known through Paul and the others by His own choosing did not mean it was because humanity demanded it. It was because God chose to exercise His own Sovereign prerogative according to His own pleasure and satisfaction, based on the premise that God does all things well.

10 *That in the dispensation of the fulness of times he might gather together in one all things in Christ, both which are in heaven, and which are on earth; even in him:* The word dispensation is a way of describing the workings of God. How He operates according to His plan with the ultimate purpose of bringing together all things under his control that were voluntarily relinquished after the curse fell upon the earth and all that there is.

11 *In whom also we have obtained an inheritance, being predestinated according to the purpose of him who worketh all things after the counsel of his own will:* This verse emphasizes the sovereignty of God and the way He exercises that sovereignty to accomplish His purpose and intent. He does not haphazardly do anything by chance. He does not need the workings of *chance* to accomplish His plan.

12 *That we should be to the praise of his glory, who first trusted in Christ.* This verse shows that God changes us, and people recognize that the change had to come from Him. It is much more than turning over a new leaf. It is being made a new creature.

13 *In whom ye also trusted, after that ye heard the word of truth, the gospel of your salvation: in whom also after that ye* *believed, ye were sealed with that holy Spirit of promise.* Again, glory comes to the Father when He saves the person who hears the Gospel, believes the Gospel, and is sealed or Saved by the Spirit of God, who makes us alive in Him.

14 *Which is the earnest of our inheritance until the redemption of the purchased possession, unto the praise of his glory.* The Holy Spirit, upon our being sealed, after quickening us, we can enjoy the promise of everlasting life.

The Beginning of the Commentary Vv. 7-14

The Great Price of the Purchase was Remitted. (1:7)

7 *In whom we have redemption through his blood, the forgiveness of sins, according to the riches of his grace;* Redemption is a most lovely word used to describe what happened and is initiated upon one's conversion. The Lord redeemed us as described here by the redemption through his blood. It is wonderful because we could not have the forgiveness of sins without it. For Christ to do so is to do it according to the riches of his grace, as stated so eloquently in this verse. For one to be a recipient of His redeeming grace, there must be belief. Redemption, as it reflected Paul's Jewish training, referred first to how God redeemed the nation of Israel during the Exodus. This was a national redemption that involved "God's chosen people" being set free from Egyptian bondage. God is often spoken of in the New Testament as the Redeemer of His people, Israel. The second redemption brings about the liberty of the *New People*. Jesus has once and for all provided redemption for those in the New Testament economy by shedding His blood. In doing so, He has put off His anger toward us, who are only at the best, wicked and defiled sinners. We have no merit, state, or rank in and of ourselves. Yet, when God commended his love toward us while we were yet sinners, He was able to do all that was required to bring us to a state of repentance and then to a state of being redeemed. The wrath of God is no longer against us; instead, we have the free pardon of sin. At such moment we become *New People* or a *New Creature in Christ.* (2 Corinthians 5:17)

John Gill certainly knew how to summarize this great truth when he wrote the following: "That redemption by Christ is such a deliverance, as that it is setting persons quite free and at entire liberty; such who are dead to sin by Christ are freed from it, from the damning power of it, and its dominion and tyranny; and though, not as yet, from the being of it; yet, ere long, they will be; when, with the rest of the members of the church, they will be presented glorious, without spot or wrinkle, or any such thing: and such are free from the law; though not from obedience to it, yet from the bondage of it; they are delivered from it, and are no longer held in it, as in prison; but are directed and exhorted to stand fast in the liberty from it, with which Christ has made them free; and this will have its full completion on all accounts when the saints shall be delivered from every degree of bondage into the glorious liberty of the children of God." (Gill)

Redemption could not have happened without Christ shedding His precious blood (else, He would not have shed it). Also, it should not be overlooked He had to be willing and able to do so just as required by the Kinsman Redeemer Law. The payment of His perfect blood was essential for the justice of God to be served and then for Him to be satisfied. His blood was perfect, as He was also perfect, meaning no blemish or defect was found in His sacrifice for redemption. The lamb, offered in the Old Testament without blemish, was only a crude type (in comparison) to the offering of Himself. The redemption was also provided for reconciliation so that the reconciled could be at peace with God. Having the "peace of God, which passeth all understanding" (Philippians 4:7) is undoubtedly the great result of redemption found only in Christ Jesus.

Another purpose of redemption by Christ is that the redeemed might enjoy the blessing of adoption; so it is said that God sent his Son "To redeem them that were under the law, that we might receive the adoption of sons" (Gal. 4:6-7). One of the great benefits of adoption is in verse 6,7: *"And because ye are sons, God hath sent forth the Spirit of his Son into your hearts, crying, Abba, Father. 7 Wherefore thou art no more a servant, but a son; and if a son, then an heir of God through Christ."* We who are redeemed receive an inheritance through Christ and may enjoy the full benefits and blessings of that inheritance for all eternity. This is true because, just as the Roman law stated, even though a freeborn could be cut out of his inheritance, an adopted child could not. The same is also true of those spiritually adopted. No more so than he can be unborn.

The sanctification of God's elect is another benefit of redemption by Christ; *"Who gave himself for us, that he might redeem us from all iniquity, and purify unto himself a peculiar people, zealous of good works"* (Titus 2:14), and again, Christ loves the Church and gave himself for it, a ransom price, *"that he might sanctify and cleanse it"* (Eph. 5:25-26). The redeemed are redeemed by his blood *"from a vain conversation"* (1 Pet. 1:18). Then, as a result of redemption by Christ, the Spirit of Christ begins a work of sanctification and carries on that work in the souls of God's people; and by applying the grace and benefit of redemption,

He places them under the highest obligation to the holiness of life and conversation; see Galatians 3:14. Just in knowing that by God's Spirit, He is doing an ongoing work of sanctification so that we might be presented as a glorious Church, without "spot or wrinkle," should cause us to strive to be more like Him.

Another great gift of redemption is being set free from every enemy, including Satan. The very definition of redemption demands that the redeemed person be set free and is never again subject to bondage. Our freedom should be claimed even now while we breathe and have our being. The saved will never face Hell or the Lake of Fire and all the torments associated with those places. "Redeemed, O How I love to proclaim it!" If enough has not been said regarding our redemption, we also will forever enjoy all of the eternal benefits of salvation. God will reveal Himself and these benefits as "eternity rolls."

To manifest His rich grace perpetually. (1:8)

8 *Wherein he hath abounded toward us in all wisdom and prudence*; (Vv. 7-8)

The word abounded is His graciously rendering to us for time and eternity all that pertains to His well-planned Salvation. The wisdom and prudence of God embed all that is, and the only flaws are not of His but a result of the awful sin curse that befell humanity and all of the creation, thus necessitating making all things new as Revelation 21:1-5 declares. The church should operate in a wise manner as the Word of God gives it its purpose and direction. With this being said, the Lord has extended that capability by abounding towards the church with all wisdom and prudence. Prudence indicates the wise application of reason or the ability to govern and discipline oneself using knowledge. The church's strength is then characterized in relationship to its understanding of and applying truth. Ephesians will teach us how this is accomplished in chapters three and four. We do not have to be tossed "two and fro" by every wind and doctrine. When it operates properly, the church will exercise and perform its ministry very efficiently in its doctrine and its duty. Though the church will constantly face attack from Satan when it is working as it should, it will have the ability to do its ministry and its warfare with wisdom and prudence. The same wisdom and prudence that God had inherent to Himself, He makes available through His perfect Word to His own. In the Epistle of James, we have been instructed that if anyone lacks wisdom, they may ask of God (James 1:5). This is another benefit for those redeemed in Christ Jesus.

Understanding how God lavishly abounded towards us in wisdom and prudence requires that we understand that He used much wisdom and prudence by His sovereign right and ability to have the necessary blueprint for our redemption. Paul showed it was not a haphazard or ill-considered action when God lavished his grace upon his people. Just as God chose his people before the foundation of the world (v. 4), (by His Own wise plan) predetermined that he would adopt them as his children (v. 5a), and did so in joyous agreement with his considered purpose (v. 5b), so also his decision to lavish his grace upon his people by paying the cost of their redemption by the death of his Beloved Son was in accord with his infinite capacity for wisdom and understanding. Once again, Paul emphasizes that God's graciousness to his people is not a marginal or occasional characteristic of his dealings with them but is integral to his character and, thus, to the way He is as very God. (Thielman) God does and accomplishes according to His purpose and intent.

Properly defined, this kind of wisdom is the kind that belongs to God. It is supreme intelligence that has as its example the creation of all that there is and the salvation of all who would be saved. Those two examples show that both of those creations could have only been accomplished by God Himself. Prudence indicates the insight that shows how such wisdom is applied.

The Great Purpose of the Purchase was Revealed. (1:9-12

To reveal the great mysteries of God. (1:9-10)

9 *Having made known unto us the mystery of his will, according to his good pleasure which he hath purposed in himself:* We might understand how the word mystery is used in the Scriptures and defined here in our immediate text; we will make these observations. The word mystery does not necessarily mean something wholly hidden and not alluded to previously, but rather, it means something that is not entirely understood. Thayer's Greek lexicon says that mystery is "in the Scriptures, a hidden or secret thing, not obvious to the understanding." Thayer also points out that in rabbinic writings, "it denotes the mystic or hidden sense: of an OT saying, Eph. 5:32." The word mystery merely implies something enigmatic, contained in the Old Testament Scriptures in cryptic language, but the meaning withheld until Christ revealed it to His disciples. We learn that this mystery, as it pertained to the Church, was revealed to Paul and the Apostles, but then Paul revealed it to us through the church letters. In effect, Paul was the steward of these mysteries related to the Church, just as they involved the Gentiles and Jews coming together as the Church.

The mysteries referred to in the New Testament are truths revealed in time when God pleases. Many concepts were initiated in the Old Testament, such as those related to the first and the second coming of Christ, the doctrine of the resurrection, atonement, and even salvation, that were clarified in the New Testament. It was as though a veil was placed over certain doctrinal truths, only to be revealed at God's discretion and at the particular time of His choosing. Since many of the local religions had mystery rites, it was important for Paul to clarify that he was referring to another mystery different from their pagan ideas. Many of the readers of this letter had perhaps once been initiated into the mystery rites of Artemis, Isis, Cybele, Dionysus, or any of several pagan gods. They thought these secret rituals brought the initiates into a deeper connection with the deity that promised the impartation of spiritual power and insight. (Arnold). But Paul had to take these ways of understanding mysteries as used by the heathen and show how God revealed unto him the Truths that are part of the Canon of Truth we know as the Bible.

The New Testament uses the word "mystery" in reference to eight concepts or spiritual truths that are intimated but not fully revealed by the Old Testament. Five mysteries are associated with the Church: one of Israel in the Church Age, one of the Tribulation, and one of the Kingdom. (Verse by Verse Ministry)

These mysteries are named in the New Testament explicitly and explained as:

- The mystery of the Kingdom, specifically, the development and timing of the Kingdom program (Matthew 13)

- The mystery of the seven stars and seven golden lampstands (Revelation 1)
- The mystery of the body of Christ (Ephesians 3)
- The mystery of the indwelling of the Spirit and the incarnation (Colossians 1, Romans 8, Ephesians 1)
- The mystery of the Bride of Christ (Ephesians 5)
- The mystery of the Rapture of believers (1Corinthians 15)
- The mystery of Israel's hardening (Romans 11)
- The mystery of the seven climactic judgments to end the age (i.e., Tribulation) (Revelation 15-18)

10 *That in the dispensation of the fulness of times he might gather together in one all things in Christ, both which are in heaven, and which are on earth; even in him:* The word dispensation is a way of describing the workings of God. How He operates according to His plan with the ultimate purpose of bringing together all things under his control that were voluntarily relinquished after the curse fell upon the earth and all that here is. The idea behind the word dispensation also is a plan or a strategy. "the plan which the master of a family, or his steward, has established for the management of the family… it signifies, also, a plan for the management of any sort of business." (Clarke) God began unfolding his plan of salvation with the coming of Messiah because that represented "the fullness of time" (τὸ πλήρωμα τῶν καιρῶν). This precise expression occurs no other time in biblical literature. Still, its closest counterpart occurs in Gal 4:4–5: "But when [lit.] the fullness of time (τὸ πλήρωμα τοῦ χρόνου) was come, God sent forth his Son, made of a woman, made under the law, to redeem them that were under the law, that we might receive the adoption of sons." This passage highlights many of the same themes as here: the coming of Messiah, redemption, and adoption. The church still lives in the fullness of times, but they will not be completely fulfilled until the day of redemption (4:30). (Exegetical Commentary).

The term *dispensation* and the expression *dispensation of the fullness of times* describe all His *administration* (the way God deals in different ways) for time and eternity, including the full effects of sin. Sin did havoc on all creation, including heaven itself, with the fall of Lucifer. There is an eschatological aspect of what Paul is speaking, and by using the Name Christ, it has to do beginning with glorification and the ascension of Christ to be followed with all that Christ will do harmoniously with the Father in bringing all under His authority in heaven and in earth. The name Christ is used of Him when He had performed His priestly work of offering His blood at the Heavenly Mercy Seat (or place where the blood is deposited) in Heaven, which satisfied once and for all the payment for sins. One of the aspects of this being true is how all things are gathered into one in Christ, That in the dispensation of the fulness of times, he might gather together in one all things in Christ, both which are in heaven, and which are on earth; even in him: The fulness of times shows what happens when Christ begins at the millennium and goes into eternity bliss where there will be no more sin or curse.

To reveal the great mercies of God. (1:11-12)

11 *In whom also we have obtained an inheritance, being predestinated according to the purpose of him who worketh all things after the counsel of his own will:* This verse emphasizes the sovereignty of God and the way He exercises that sovereignty to accomplish His purpose and intent. He does not haphazardly do anything by chance. He does not need the workings of chance to accomplish His plan. Paul is carefully stating that eternal benefits are available as an inheritance according to the Father's pleasure and purpose, having worked it out in such a manner "after the counsel of his own will." This was a design that began in the mind of God according to His sovereign purpose. He predestined it, and Paul worded it to be so "to the praise of his glory, who first trusted in Christ." The Scriptures clearly state that these benefits come only to those who trust Christ. In this particular case, Paul is referring to the Jews who were converted and became a part of the church, to be followed by the Gentiles. The Scriptures also teach us that there is an overriding counsel and purpose at work regarding God's creation. Some say that every lightning bolt is purposely lit by Him, every butterfly lights upon a particular leaf according to His purpose, and every leaf falls to the earth when He wants it to. I do not believe this is the case, though it would be no effort. Instead, I think God put specific laws that govern the universe into effect. He provides the design and the energy to create and sustain His creation. He lets His creation operate according to His prescribed laws. The leaves fall to the ground at their specified time according to the seasons He put into effect. These laws must work concerning each other. This further shows God's efficiency and how He does everything decently and in order.

An example of this is that if you jump off of a building, there is a law called gravity that will let you fall at a consistent rate until you meet what has been described in physics as resistance. There is another law called inertia, which says that an object tends to stay at rest until acted upon otherwise, or an object tends to remain in motion until acted upon otherwise. The ground will stop the falling body while changing the falling body's inertia at the same time.

These are laws that God put into effect. If God wanted to spontaneously superintend every action upon the earth, He certainly could have done so, but I believe He is much more efficient than that.

In the same way, God was able to put laws into effect as He governs the universe efficiently; he also has rules for our human existence and laws that govern our accountability back to Him. He has laws as it pertains to salvation. Using that term may not be technically correct, but God scoped out the plan of salvation within the counsel of the Trinity, according to his plan or dispensation. This plan was implemented at the beginning according to His purpose. He did not go into counsel with His creation to devise a plan, for He needed no other but Himself as the Triune God. This plan benefited the Jew first and then the Gentile. Paul will further explain this aspect of the mystery.

12 *That we should be to the praise of his glory, who first trusted in Christ.* This verse shows that God changes us, and people recognize that the change had to come from Him. It is much more than turning over a new leaf. It is being made a new creature. I can relate to how this must feel in human terms as I would pastor the people God gave me. Nothing was more thrilling than to see people come to the Lord and then go on in the faith and radiate the goodness of God in their lives. It was refreshing to the entire church body as well. God saves us not for our glory but for His glory. Though all glory ultimately goes to God, he lets us enjoy the benefits of His plan in a church and a pastoral sense. When we see the maturity of the saints that God has let us have a part in their spiritual development, it gives satisfaction unlike any other. When we realize what he does for us who endeavor to please Him, it brings satisfaction in knowing that God is doing a work in us to make us more mature in the faith. We then find joy in saying to God be the glory! Can you imagine how He finds pleasure in those radically changed upon becoming a new creature in Christ? The Church at Ephesus was told in the first three chapters how much wealth they had in Christ. Their eternal wealth could be enjoyed, as is true with all believers on earth.

As used here, the word trusted is also associated with faith and hope. All three of these words rest upon the Word of God. To trust in Christ is to have spiritual confidence in Him and believe Him by first trusting the Word of God to be true. Having that belief is also the hope that projects to the future with absolute confidence. There is even an eschatological confidence in "the things to come" for the believer.

III. A Divine Nature Protected by His Spirit. (1:13-14)

13 *In whom ye also trusted, after that ye heard the word of truth, the gospel of your salvation: in whom also after that ye believed, ye were sealed with that holy Spirit of promise.* Again, glory comes to the Father when He saves the person who hears the Gospel, believes the Gospel, and is sealed or Saved by the Spirit of God, who makes us alive in Him. Again, we recognize the formula for one's conversion in verse 13. There is the call of the Gospel, "the gospel of your salvation." Then there is the believing of the truth, "in whom also after that ye believed," to be followed by the sanctification of the Spirit: "ye were sealed with that holy Spirit of promise." Just as it was within the purposes of God to bring all into one body, it began with the Jew, and here, the same privilege is extended to the Gentile as well. In this chapter, we are introduced to the work of the Trinity. We have already seen the Father's part in the great work of redemption. Remember in verses three and four, Blessed be the God and Father of our Lord Jesus Christ, who hath blessed us with all spiritual blessings in heavenly places in Christ: According as he hath chosen us in him before the foundation of the world, that we should be holy and without blame before him in love: (Ephesians 1:3-4). These verses remind us of the Father's work, and verse five shows us the work of the Son: Having predestinated us unto the adoption of children by Jesus Christ to himself, according to the good pleasure of his will. (Ephesians 1:5).

The third ingredient to one's conversion is the Holy Spirit's work. We have referred to this work, as 2 Thessalonians does, as the sanctification of the Spirit. Salvation involves blending the supernatural, which involves God, and the human, which involves man. Man can be involved as a witness, as Paul recognized when he said: *I have planted, Apollos watered; but God gave the increase. So then neither is he that planteth any thing, neither he that watereth; but God that giveth the increase. Now he that planteth and he that watereth are one: and every man shall receive his reward according to his labor. For we are labourers together with God: ye are God's husbandry, ye are God's building.* (1 Corinthians 3:6-9). As much as man is involved, much more is God. When we are told that it was God that "giveth the increase," this means that there is a part that only He can do. This is the work of the Holy Spirit that has been described in different ways, such as: "the new birth," "Sanctification of the Spirit," "the indwelling of the Spirit," and "conversion." In each of these cases, the Holy Spirit is involved. The miraculous part of conversion requires the Holy Spirit to do His work; otherwise, there will be no conversion. The eternal soul can only find protection and escape the horrors of Hell by trusting in the Lord Jesus Christ and being sanctified by the Spirit. Upon one's conversion, that person is also sealed or protected against ever being lost again.

B. The Holy Spirit Promises Protection. (1:13b-14)

Most have heard the expression "Signed, sealed, and delivered." The Seal was used metaphorically, describing the Holy Spirit making a promise that the transaction is complete. Even from ancient times, it is commonly understood that there are several common uses for a seal. Some of these are:

1. To authenticate or confirm as genuine.
2. To mark as one's property.
3. To make secure.

These three things apply as it involves salvation and how the Spirit seals us. The work of grace is undoubtedly genuine. In Christ Jesus, our salvation is real. The Holy Spirit, as He seals us, confirms it as true. Then, we are identified by carrying the mark. Does he mark you? When you are marked, you are assured by the earnest "until the redemption of the purchased possession" takes place. The ancient commentator John Gill wrote this about the sealing of the Holy Spirit: "...the Spirit of God continues still as a sealer of his people, and as an earnest and pledge of their inheritance until the day of redemption; but it is to be understood of the confirming, certifying, and assuring the saints, as to their interest in the favour of God, and in the blessings of grace, of every kind, and their right and title to the heavenly glory; See Gill on "2 Co 1:22," and the seal of these things is not circumcision, nor baptism, nor the Lord's supper, nor even the graces of the Spirit; but the Spirit himself, who witnesses to the spirits of believers the truth of these things, and that as a "spirit of promise": so called, both because he is the Spirit promised, as the Syriac and Ethiopic versions render it, whom the Father and Christ had promised, and who was sent by them; and because he usually seals, or certifies believers of the truth of the above things, by opening and applying a word of promise to them: and which he does also, as the "Holy" Spirit; for this sealing work of his leaves a greater impress of holiness upon the soul, and engages more to acts of holiness; wherefore the doctrine of assurance is no licentious doctrine; no persons are so holy as those who are truly possessed of that grace; and as for such who pretend unto it, and live in sin, it is a certain thing that they in reality know nothing of it." (Gill)

An interesting and correct aspect of the sealing is, as Harold Hoehner shows that God seals the believers in Christ with the promised Holy Spirit when they have heard and believed the gospel of salvation. The sealing with the Spirit must not be confused with the other ministries of the Spirit. The indwelling of the Spirit refers to his residence in every believer (Rom 8:9; 1 John 2:27). The baptizing ministry of the Spirit places believers into the body of Christ (1 Cor 12:13). The filling by the Spirit is the control of the Spirit over believers 'lives (Eph 5:18). The sealing ministry of the Spirit is to identify believers as God's own and thus give them the security that they belong to him (Eph 1:13; 4:30; 2 Cor 1:22). The very fact that the Spirit indwells believers is a seal of God's ownership of them. Fee says it well: "the Spirit, and the Spirit alone, marks off the people of God as his own possession in the present eschatological age." One further note is that the indwelling, baptizing, and sealing ministries of the Spirit are bestowed on every believer at the moment of conversion. There are no injunctions because they are integral to the gift of salvation. This is not to be confused with the exhortation to believers to be repeatedly filled by the Spirit from the moment of their conversion to the end of their lives here on earth. To summarize, the believers are sealed with the Spirit at the moment of conversion, indicating God's ownership of them. (Hoehner)

A seal is an instrument of stone, metal, or other hard substance (sometimes set in a ring), on which is engraved some device or figure and is used for making an impression on some soft substance, such as clay or wax, affixed to a document or other object, in token of authenticity. One of the most important uses of sealing in antiquity was to give proof of authenticity and authority to letters, royal commands, etc. It served the purpose of a modern signature when the art of writing was known to only a few. Thus, Jezebel "wrote letters in Ahab's name, and sealed them with his seal" (1 Kings 21:8); the written commands of Ahasuerus were "sealed with the king's ring," "for the writing which is written in the king's name, and sealed with the king's ring, may no man reverse" (Esther 8:8,10; 3:12). (1) One of the most important uses of sealing in antiquity was to give proof of authenticity and authority to letters, royal commands, etc. It served the purpose of a modern signature when the art of writing was known to only a few. Thus, Jezebel "wrote letters in Ahab's name, and sealed them with his seal" (1 Kings 21:8); the written commands of Ahasuerus were "sealed with the king's ring," "for the writing which is written in the king's name, and sealed with the king's ring, may no man reverse" (Esther 8:8,10; 3:12). (D. Miall Edwards)

14 *Which is the earnest of our inheritance until the redemption of the purchased possession, unto the praise of his glory.* The Holy Spirit, upon our being sealed, after quickening us, we can enjoy the promise of everlasting life. Understanding the fuller meaning of this verse requires understanding the word earnest. Found three times in the

New Testament:

The "earnest of our inheritance" (Ephesians 1:14); "the earnest of the Spirit" (2 Corinthians 1:22; 5:5).

It is equivalent in Hebrew `erabhon (found in Genesis 38:17,18,20), in Latin arrabo, French arrhes and the Old English arles. The term is mercantile and comes originally from the Phoenicians. Its general meaning is a pledge or token given as the assurance of fulfilling a bargain or promise. It also carries the idea of forfeit, which is now common in land deals, only from the obverse side. In other words, the one promising to convey property, wages, or blessing binds the promise with an advance gift or pledge, partaking of the quality of the benefit to be bestowed. If the agreement is about wages, then a part of the wages is advanced; if it is about land, then a clod given to the purchaser or beneficiary may stand as the pledge of final and complete conveyance of the property.

Figurative:

In the spiritual sense, as used in the passages above, the reference is to the work of the Spirit of God in our hearts being a token and pledge of perfect redemption and a heavenly inheritance. There is more than the idea of security in the word as used, for it implies the continuity and identity of the blessing. (C. E. Schenk; ISBE)

Using this word as a metaphor and explaining in such simple yet profound terms, the Lord meant business and still does as signified by giving an *earnest*. The quality and the worth of our inheritance, as expressed in the offer of an earnest, is not diminished. We enjoy the total worth of our salvation at conversion, which guarantees not greater or more perfect quality but greater quantity as the ages roll.

CHAPTER THREE
Ephesians 1:15-23

The Truth of the Revelation of Christ

VERSE SUMMARIES 1:15-23

Paul is letting the Church and the Christians around Ephesus know he has heard a very good and encouraging report and is praying for them. The things in the immediate context of his praying begin in verse 16 and include "thanksgiving." His praying continues through verse number 18, and not only is he praying, but he is letting them know the greatness of God, who is the Reason for answered prayers. Paul desires that they not only know about God but wisely know His Word and how it applies to who they are. The Word of God is not just for Theological Truth; it is for practical Truth to guide and protect the believers.

15 *Wherefore I also, after I heard of your faith in the Lord Jesus, and love unto all the saints.* News travels fast... it is so wonderful when that news is good news. Paul heard very good news about those in Ephesus who were a part of the church there and serving God. Their faith was heard about. Coupled with their faith in the Lord Jesus was their love unto all the saints. There is enough in this 15th verse for churches to model after. Some churches seem to have love, but their faith is weak, and others seem to have their orthodoxy and faith but no indication of having love. It is admired when a church has faith and love working together. And even better if, like the Church at Thessalonica, it had faith, hope, and Charity in its description.

16 *Cease not to give thanks for you, making mention of you in my prayers;* Paul knew how to show thankfulness as shown in each of his letters, with it being no exception here. He gave thanks for them in his prayers.

17 *That the God of our Lord Jesus Christ, the Father of glory, may give unto you the spirit of wisdom and revelation in the knowledge of him:* God, the Father of glory, is where one should find wisdom and revelation. Both these terms are divinely given and not otherwise.

18 The eyes of your understanding being enlightened; that ye may know what is the hope of his calling, and what the riches of the glory of his inheritance in the saints, Even as Paul taught the Corinthians that the natural or unregenerate person could not understand or even comprehend the things of God because they were Spiritually discerned shows that kind of discernment is Spiritual and thus grants one the opportunity to know things, and in this instance, it is the hope of his calling and the glory of His inheritance in the saints.

19 *And what is the exceeding greatness of his power to us-ward who believe, according to the working of his mighty power.* God intends that believers enjoy the exceeding greatness of His power.

20 *Which he wrought in Christ, when he raised him from the dead, and set him at his own right hand in the heavenly places;* verses such as this allow the believer to understand Spiritual authority and how God orders His government. All such power requires the resurrected Savior's power to be demonstrated and reckoned.

21 *Far above all principality, and power, and might, and dominion, and every name that is named, not only in this world, but also in that which is to come:* There is no comparison when comparing His power to all others. Theirs, in contrast, would be miniscule.

22 *And hath put all things under his feet, and gave him to be the head over all things to the church.* This is another way of describing how all will be in submission to Him who has omnipotence or all power.

23 *Which is his body, the fulness of him that filleth all in all.* Paul is telling the church in Ephesus that not only does Christ have a body of believers, but that body of believers is the church. In and by the Church, Christ is to be seen and revealed to the world and all parts of that world in which they come in contact.

The Beginning of the Commentary Vv. 15-23

Paul had an interest in them. (Vs. 15-23)

15 *Wherefore I also, after I heard of your faith in the Lord Jesus, and love unto all the saints.* As mentioned news travels fast… it is so wonderful when that news is good news. Paul heard very good news about those in Ephesus who were a part of the church there and serving God. Their faith was heard about. Coupled with their faith in the Lord Jesus was their love unto all the saints. There is enough in this 15th verse for churches to model after. Some churches seem to have love, but their faith is weak, and others seem to have their orthodoxy and faith but no indication of having love. It is admired when a church has faith and loves working together. And even better if, like the Church at Thessalonica, it had faith, hope, and Charity in its description.

Paul had spent three quality years in Ephesus, and from

this statement found in verse 15, he seemed to be time removed from them and had not heard from the church for an extended period. Now that he has heard of their "faith in the Lord Jesus, and love unto all the saints," he wants them to know how much it meant to him. Ephesians 20 tells us of the very emotional time when Paul had to leave the Church at Ephesus to continue his ministry elsewhere. It was difficult because Paul told them they would see his face no more. Since this study involves the Church at Ephesus, it will be appropriate to include this "Goodbye" by Paul as he was leaving Ephesus. It is this recorded departure of Paul that gives us such great insight into the way that Paul related to this church. Before we look at these verses, please observe what Barnes had to say about this most tender departure: "And when they were come to him. The following discourse is one of the tenderest, affectionate, and eloquent anywhere to be found. It is strikingly descriptive of the apostle's manner of life while with them; evinces his deep concern for their welfare; is full of tender and kind admonition; expresses the firm purpose of his soul to live to the glory of God, and his expectation to be persecuted still; and is a most affectionate and solemn farewell. No man can read it without being convinced that it came from a heart full of love and kindness and that it manifests a great and noble purpose to be entirely employed in one great aim and object—the promotion of the glory of God in the face of danger and of death." Barnes' Notes on the New Testament)

17 *"And from Miletus he sent to Ephesus and called the elders of the church.* **18** *And when they were come to him, he said unto them, Ye know, from the first day that I came into Asia, after what manner I have been with you at all seasons,* **19** *Serving the Lord with all humility of mind, and with many tears, and temptations, which befell me by the lying in wait of the Jews:* **20** *And how I kept back nothing that was* *profitable unto you, but have shewed you, and have taught you publickly, and from house to house,* **21** *Testifying both to the Jews, and also to the Greeks, repentance toward God, and faith toward our Lord Jesus Christ.* **22** *And now, behold, I go bound in the spirit unto Jerusalem, not knowing the things that shall befall me there:* **23** *Save that the Holy Ghost witnesseth in every city, saying that bonds and afflictions abide me.* **24** *But none of these things move me, neither count I my life dear unto myself, so that I might finish my course with joy, and the ministry, which I have received of the Lord Jesus, to testify the gospel of the grace of God.* **25** *And now, behold, I know that ye all, among whom I have gone preaching the kingdom of God, shall see my face no more.* **26** *Wherefore I take you to record this day, that I am pure from the blood of all men.* **27** *For I have not shunned to declare unto you all the counsel of God.* **28** *Take heed therefore unto yourselves, and to all the flock, over the which the Holy Ghost hath made you overseers, to feed the church of God, which he hath purchased with his own blood.* **29** *For I know this, that after my departing shall grievous wolves enter in among you, not sparing the flock.* **30** *Also of your own selves shall men arise, speaking perverse things, to draw away disciples after them.* **31** *Therefore watch, and remember, that by the space of three years I ceased not to warn every one night and day with tears.* **32** *And now, brethren, I commend you to God, and to the word of his grace, which is able to build you up and to give you an inheritance among all them which are sanctified.* **33** *I have coveted no man's silver, or gold, or apparel.* **34** *Yea, ye yourselves know, that these hands have ministered unto my necessities, and to them that were with me.* **35** *I have shewed you all things, how that so labouring ye ought to support the weak, and to remember the words of the Lord Jesus, how he said,* ***It is more blessed to give than to receive.****"* (Acts

20:17-35)

Paul's love for the church is indeed indicated in the above Scriptures, indicating the reason for Paul's praying as he did for this particular church. Now, he is writing them, letting them know that even as he loved them, they are doing likewise. We must remember that what we learn about the Church at Ephesus, as recorded in the Book of Ephesians, had happened before the seven letters were written in Revelation describing how Ephesus had left its first love.

Paul prayed for them. (Vs. 16-19)

16 *Cease not to give thanks for you, making mention of you in my prayers;* Paul knew how to show thankfulness as shown in each of his letters, with it being no exception here. He gave thanks for them in his prayers. Paul did not just pray for them and then forget them; he prayed for them without ceasing. When he ceased not to pray for them, that meant that he did not leave off praying for them. He prayed for them whether it was convenient or not. Paul prayed as he did because he genuinely cared for those he had labored with for "the space of three years." Indeed, we should acquire from this study the value of praying for others for the prayer of intercession. Paul certainly set a good example as he prayed. Prayer allows us to work with God on the behalf of others. God only works in partnership with us when we pray. Too often, we attempt to do the impossible with only what we can do with the arm of the flesh instead of depending upon God through prayer. The blessing of hearing how God was prospering the church at Ephesus could be attributed to the way Paul was praying for them. He also petitioned for them. (vs. 16, cf. 17-19)

I use the word petition while describing Paul's praying because the petition is a prayer word that means: "asking."

Paul was asking not for himself but for those dear souls at Ephesus. While he was asking, he also was interceding on their behalf. First, may we examine the way one makes his petition? Then, we will look at the word intercede and see how both the prayer of petition and intercessory prayer were used in the two prayers that Paul prayed in the Book of Ephesians. The petition focuses on our personal needs. When we go into the presence of our Heavenly Father, we must feel our total helplessness. Dr. J. Oswald Sanders has this interesting remark on the word *petition*: "The picture behind the word is that of a beggar sitting at the side of the road, begging for the king's help as he passes by. It expresses destitution and inadequacy, inability to meet one's needs, and total dependence on another. It is a need expressed in a cry." We are the beggars, and our Heavenly Father is the King.

As we see our lack, inadequacy, and inability, we hear Him calling us, "Let us then come boldly unto the throne of grace that we may obtain mercy and find grace to help in time of need." The petition is a heartfelt cry that communicates a sense of urgency. More than fifty passages in the Psalms describe this type of need. They include expressions like Cleanse me, help me, or strengthen me. In his book "How Can God Answer Prayer?" Dr. William Edward Biederwolf gives an exciting insight into the meaning of the word petition. "Apart from the fact that the primary meaning of the word prayer is a petition, apart also from the fact that one hundred and two times in the New Testament (to say nothing of the numerous instances of the Old Testament) are foreign words whose primary meaning is also petition translated prayer, thirty-three times in the New Testament and thirty-nine in the Old Testament we find the simple word ask (which is the exact translation of its foreign equivalents) used to describe the act of going to God in prayer. As we consider this, we wonder if we are not wasting words and time in proving that prayer means primarily petition. Of course, it means petition, and when the great prayer Teacher said, "Ask and ye shall receive," He most assuredly meant that we were to obtain something through our asking." (Bilderwolf)

As indicated, Paul demonstrated the importance of prayer and praying by his excellent example, which certainly included petition. In chapter three, Paul is seen bowing (Ephesians 3:14). When he does this, he intercedes on their behalf. "It is in intercession," said Andrew Murray, "that the Church is to find and wield her highest power. It is the root and strength of all church work." If the local church practiced intercessory prayer, as did Paul, the church could enjoy an ongoing revival. When one intercedes on behalf of someone else, it is interesting to note that the acts of interceding and mediating are very similar. To illustrate this truth, Dr. William Wallace Horner made this observation in his book, "Let Us Pray": "There is a very striking similarity between the words, Mediator and Intercessor. Mediator means the one between, and when applied to Christ, He stood between an angry God and a guilty sinner. For the Son of God to perform the role of a Mediator between God and man, He needed to be clothed with human nature. Therefore, He had to be born of a virgin, as was foretold by the Prophet Isaiah: *"Therefore the Lord Himself shall give you a sign: Behold a virgin shall conceive, and bear a Son, and shall call His name Immanuel"*, Isa. 714, which being interpreted means God with us—The God-Man. Christ was a man who 'was in all points tempted like as we are, yet without sin.' He was very God, for He said: 'I and the Father are one.' As a Mediator, He reached down and took the hand of repenting and trusting sinner and reaching up, He took the hand of an angry God, and when Christ died, through the blood of the atonement, God grasped the hand of the sinner, and they were made one in Christ. The intercessor occupies a similar but different position before God. In prayer, he lifts the guilty sinner into the presence of the Holy Ghost, and through the mediating work of Jesus Christ, the sinner is saved with everlasting salvation. The intercessor becomes the priest of God, who pours out the blood of Christ upon the mercy seat as "the lamb of God, slain from the foundation of the world," and "taketh away the sins of the world." (Horner)

17 *That the God of our Lord Jesus Christ, the Father of glory, may give unto you the spirit of wisdom and revelation in the knowledge of him:* God, the Father of glory, is where one should find wisdom and revelation. Both these terms are divinely given and not otherwise. Having Purpose should characterize us as we pray. We ought to pray on purpose and also with purpose. In the Psalms, David knew the value of having a definite purpose when he prayed. *"My voice shalt thou hear in the morning, O LORD; in the morning will I direct my prayer unto thee, and will look up."* (Psalms 5:3). When David indicated that he would direct his prayers towards God, he was saying that he would order his prayers in such a manner that there would be a definite purpose in his praying. Someone described how David directed his prayers as being likened to a priest who carefully orders the sacrifice he is to offer by making careful and deliberate cuts with his knife. He would not chop his meat as a butcher would; he would sever it very carefully as prescribed by God. The word direct has also been used to describe an archer who takes careful and deliberate aim before he releases his arrow, ensuring he is aiming for the target. Each time we pray, our prayers should strike the target just as the arrow does when released by the skillful archer.

When Paul was praying for the Church at Ephesus, he had specific things he was praying for with carefulness and precision. He prayed that God would give them "the spirit of wisdom and revelation in the knowledge of him." Nothing will be more helpful to the church than to know who He is... "Oh, to know Him". Having an intimate relationship with the Father, through the Son, by the Holy Spirit will greatly strengthen the church, and Paul knew as much. Using the word revelation alludes to the Mystery that was received by Paul regarding the church and the incarnation of Christ. In Chapter 3, beginning in verse 3, Paul talks more about the revelation of the mystery and how it was for and certainly included the Gentiles. Paul wanted to teach them these truths, and they were able to teach others. It was for this reason that he prayed as he did. What Paul is asking for the Church at Ephesus is that they may be wise about God as learned from the Word. He mentioned Jesus, who is God because there was much confusion during the time that Paul was writing this with the Gnostic teachings, what was known as the Colossian Heresy, and those others who believed Jesus was begotten of God instead of being co-existent with God eternally. At His birth, He finally came into existence; they reasoned falsely. Paul is saying it is the purpose of the church to know Him rather than know somewhat about Him. And he wants them to have the spirit of wisdom and Revelation. He is making a distinction between their spirit and His Spirit when speaking to the Ephesians, knowing that Revelation and wisdom must come from the Lord, and upon having His Spirit, it should radically affect our spirit; our spirit is affected by His Spirit!

Paul was also aware of the Athenians' and the Romans' ideas and their treatment of wisdom, as the Greeks were especially known for being *knowledge seekers*. Their teachings and influence invaded the churches and spilled over into their reasoning, which meant the Ephesians had to constantly clarify and purify their minds with the Truth and have their spirit thinking rightly about who Christ is, and so should we. This is what Paul is warning them of when he says that God was the One to give them a spirit of wisdom and revelation in the knowledge of Him.

18 *The eyes of your understanding being enlightened; that ye may know what is the hope of his calling, and what the riches of the glory of his inheritance in the saints.* Even as Paul taught the Corinthians that the natural or unregenerate person could not understand or even comprehend the things of God because they were Spiritually discerned shows that kind of discernment is Spiritual and thus grants one the opportunity to know things, and in this instance, it is the hope of his calling and the glory of His inheritance in the saints. Paul personifies the word *understanding* by using the word *eyes*, which conveys what Paul was saying unto them regarding their understanding with the expression "The eyes of your understanding being enlightened." This kind of enlightenment comes from the Lord and He alone by His Spirit and Word. The eye is metaphorically the avenue through which light flows to the heart or mind. In all literature καρδία, "heart" refers to the physical organ, but more frequently, it is used figuratively to refer to the seat of the moral and intellectual life. In classical literature καρδία, "heart" is used to refer to the physical organ of humans and beasts. Still, more frequently, it refers to the seat of feelings and emotions, of will or volition, and of thought and understanding. In nature, it is used in the middle or core of a plant. (Hoehner) καρδία (kardia) is the Greek word from which we get the English word cardio, and it appears 157 times in the New Testament. The understanding capability, as spoken here, is not only regarding one's intellect, which involves the capacity of the brain to reason, think, and process information, but on a much more noble plane to Spiritually discern the Truths of God, specifically His Word.

Paul wants the Church at Ephesus to have a Spiritual understanding of what their salvation or conversion ultimately means, as it involves Spiritual inheritance. Such enlightenment occurred at their conversion, but Paul wants them to know that it does not stop there. It is to be built upon with hope or faith, both of the same essence. In addition to their eyes being opened, this involves the hope of his calling and the riches of the glory of his inheritances.

Paul is not emphasizing the saints' inheritance here, but Christ's inheritance by Him possessing the saints the Father gave Him in *bringing many sons unto glory.* (Hebrews 2:10, *For it became him, for whom are all things, and by whom are all things, in bringing many sons unto glory, to make the captain of their salvation perfect through sufferings.*) Everything said here is built upon the work of redemption accomplished by Christ, including the work of the cross. However, as used here, hope is the grand expectation of what Christ promises in His Word, the absolute certainty that God will do what He promises. Paul says this was all accomplished by His intent and purpose in His predestination and election. Paul emphasizes the intimacy one should have in Christ in verse 17, which should result in what he is speaking about beginning in verse 18.

He prayed that God's power might be recognized by them. (V. 19)

19 *And what is the exceeding greatness of his power to usward who believe, according to the working of his mighty power.* God intends that believers enjoy the exceeding greatness of His power. There is the present power that we need practically down here to do the good work of the Lord. Paul wants the church to know "the exceeding greatness of his power." Too often, as we make up the church, we operate anemically. It is as though we do not believe that the Lord has the available power to make the church function as it ought. Everything that we are involved in, as it relates to the church, we should do with the awareness that God strengthens us. The church at Sardis was instructed while in its weakened state to "strengthen the things which remain." The Lord is the one who grants the power for such a strengthening. The prescription for the Sardis's recovery was to "strengthen those things which remain." This prescription is both simple and yet it is also profound. Please, let me explain… For several years, I used this prescription to help our churches. Even in our churches, we have been guilty of not seeing the forest for the trees.

When the Lord gave the instructions to strengthen the things, He did not say, "Strengthen the thing (singular) which remains," but He said, "Strengthen the things (plural) which remain." The ability to exercise that strength comes from God. The church's ministry has many things within its composite or body besides the people who make up the church. Examining ourselves personally should cause us to be mindful that even as Paul prayed, an exceeding great power is available to make us stronger. We should look at ourselves and think of ways to strengthen ourselves within Christ's body by claiming His strength. In a practical sense, we might look at ourselves physically. Remember, God has only given us one body for a lifetime. If we have allowed ourselves to become weakened by constant abuse, we should examine ourselves and determine how we can make ourselves either healthier or stronger. Many have abused their bodies with their sinful habits. These addictions will take a gradual lifetime toll on the user's body, causing them to become extremely weakened by such abuse. The longer it takes for corrective action, the longer it takes for recovery.

The exact parallel is also found in the church. The longer the church tolerates things that will handicap or hinder it, the more difficult it becomes for the church to recover.

To strengthen the things which remain means that there should be an examination. This examination requires giving close attention to the whole by first giving attention to its parts. The church should examine each part separately as it functions concerning all its ministries. Consider it this way: the pastor has his things, such as Sunday school, choir, Christian day school, visitation, printing ministry, mission program, etc. The pastor looks at all of these things to strengthen them. To strengthen the things that remain, he will go to the principal and tell the principal that the school is one of the things that he wants to strengthen as a pastor. He will tell the principal that he has many things that make up the school, which may be strengthened. An example of what his things would be: teachers, curriculum, students, finances, and scheduling. To strengthen those things, the principal should consider how the Lord can empower him to strengthen the school. He will look at everything that comprises the school and then make those things relative to the school stronger. We can expect to become stronger using this approach throughout the church. In doing the Lord's work, there is a practical and Spiritual part; in some ways, the two seem to overlap.

In addition to addressing practical things, we should also look closely at the church's members. Paul wanted the church to claim what could be theirs by claiming the power in Christ. The same Paul that speaks of "the exceeding greatness of his power" (V. 19) also says *"that in the ages to come he might shew the exceeding riches of his grace in his kindness toward us through Christ Jesus"* (2:7). We should recognize that God intends that we be empowered to do what is required of us in the ministry. God grants us the power to be saved, the ability to stand during conflict, the power to serve, and even the power to shout or worship. Nothing strengthens the church more than having His power and knowing it.

Paul also wanted the Church to know the future power ongoing that began at the resurrection and continued at His coronation. When Christ is described with His throne, it represents a recognizable throne and His seat of authority (another kind of power) and the power, which speaks of His strength (further indicated by Him being seated on the right hand of God, which symbolizes that strength. This verse also indicates that His power works or is efficient. It is a power of meekness, a strength also under control, like a strong stallion that can be bridled. The 20th verse speaks of Jesus being seated at God's right hand.

The Triumph of the Resurrection of Christ. (Vs. 20-21)

20 *Which he wrought in Christ, when he raised him from the dead, and set him at his own right hand in the heavenly places.* Verses such as this allow the believer to understand Spiritual authority and how God orders His government. All such power requires the resurrected Savior to be demonstrated and reckoned. **21** *Far above all principality, and power, and might, and dominion, and every name that is named, not only in this world, but also in that which is to come*: (Eph 1:20-21)

What more excellent way to express or demonstrate the power of God than to do it regarding His bodily resurrection? We must reject the teaching that allows Christ to remain upon a cross symbolically. The cross of Christ is necessary, but we do not focus on Him remaining upon the cross; instead, we focus on the resurrected Christ, seated in power on the Father's right hand. The resurrection generously provided an incredible display of His power. Also, it served as a witness to the available power to raise a poor lost sinner from his lost state. The Book of Ephesians tells us that we are seated in heavenly places when we are raised. Considering that the power was available for raising Christ from the dead, then that same power is also available to raise the lost soul and the perishing soul from the dead.

The Telling of the Exaltation of Christ. (Vs. 22-23)

22 *And hath put all things under his feet, and gave him to be the head over all things to the church.* There is no comparison when comparing His power to all others. Theirs, in contrast, would be miniscule.

23 *Which is his body, the fulness of him that filleth all in all.* Paul is telling the church in Ephesus that not only does Christ have a body of believers, but that body of believers is the church. In the Church, Christ is to be seen and revealed to the world and all parts of that world in which they come in contact. The resurrection of Christ, followed by the exaltation of Christ, grants Christ the legal right to be over all His creation. He who was greatly humbled in his kenosis is greatly exalted in His ascension to the throne. The words, *head over all things* signify this. God the Father placed His Son in the place of respectful honor as the King of Kings and the Lord of Lords, to be fully revealed when Christ returns on a white horse to fight the battle of Armageddon and prepare to usher in the Millennium.

We see how the church serves within the economy of God and is carefully placed within the economy of all. The church has a parallel influence upon all of God's creation. It is God's will for the church to influence the world rather than the world to influence the church. The Church is an organism rather than an organization, though it is to do all things decently and in order. The word *head* is a metaphor that shows that the church's intelligence is to be derived from God alone. Just as the human body requires the head and brain for all functions, so does the church body. The word *body* is also a metaphor that assists us in understanding how the church functions by comparing it to the human body. The word body is used several times when describing the church.

When describing the church body, we recognize that each member is distinct in that it has its particular functioning members who serve in a local sense, with Christ being its Head or its Government. The similarities of the different churches are attributed to the fact that we all have the Word of God to lead and direct us by His Spirit. Some try to connect all the churches as one loosely, but understanding that the word church is described functionally as an assembly, it is impossible to assemble all in one place in this manner; that will only take place in glory when there is the assembly of the Church of the First Born. In a practical sense, the church is local, with Him still being the Head. Just as the Lord can inhabit each believer as their personal Savior, He can inhabit us collectively as the church. There is no reason that we must accept the teachings that the church is universal. There will be churches with similar characteristics, but our relationship on a universal scale is that we belong to His kingdom. Only the saved or the redeemed make us His kingdom. However, as we consider the local church, its membership can be saved or lost even as wheat and tares, known only by God in the ultimate sense.

These last two verses in this chapter describe the church's relationship with Christ and the world. To show this relationship and the spirit of this relationship, Joseph Benson has this to say with a universal lean but sill show Christ's total domain: *And hath put* —Greek, *upetaxen, hath subjected; all things under his feet* —this is said in allusion to Psa. Cx. 1, *Till I make thine enemies thy footstool.* The psalm is a prophecy, not only of Christ's exaltation to universal dominion in human nature (1 Cor. xv. 27) but also of the entire subjection of all his enemies, 1 Cor. xv. 25. For in ancient times conquerors put their feet on the necks of their enemies in token of their subjection, Josh. x. 23, 24. *And gave him to be head over all things to the church* —As it is here declared that Christ is raised to universal dominion for the sake of his church, that is, for the noble purpose of erecting and establishing it, and uniting the angels who are in heaven, and all the good men, who have lived and are to live on earth, in one harmonious society, that they may worship and serve God together, and be happy in one another's society to all eternity, it was necessary for accomplishing this grand purpose, that the evil angels should be subjected to him; and even that the material fabric of the world, with everything it contains, should be under his direction, that he might order all the events befalling his people, in such a manner as to promote their holiness, and prepare them for heaven who would be saved. Add to this, he is in such a sense made *head over all things to his church* as to cause even its enemies, however not designed by them and unwillingly, to serve its interests; and all events, whether prosperous or adverse and all persons and things, *to work together for* the *good* of its members. To these, he is a head, not merely of government, but likewise of guidance, life, and influence, as is implied in the following clause. *Which is his body* —The church is called the body of Christ to signify that the true and living members thereof are united to and animated by him, that they are under his direction and the objects of his care, and that they are united to one another in love, after the manner of the members of the human body, which are governed by the head, and united to one another by various joints, ligaments, nerves, arteries, veins, and other vessels of communication and intercourse. *The fulness of him that filleth all in all* —this expression may mean that his church, that is, the spiritual part of it, is *completed*, or *filled* by him, with all sorts of gifts and graces. So Locke understands it. Thus, believers are said to receive out of Christ's fullness, *grace for*, or *upon grace*. Macknight, however, takes the clause in a different sense, observing that by calling the church to the *pleroma, the fulness of Christ*, the apostle intimates that he who is universal Lord would want a principal part of his subjects if the church among men on earth were not united and subjected to him as its head. *Who filleth all in all* —That is, who filleth all his members with all their spiritual gifts and graces, according to the place and office in his body which he hath assigned them" (Benson).

Though what Benson said described a universal church position, he did show the proper relationship of Christ, being the Head, to His body. And each church, when properly operating, will recognize His Headship as though it should be rightly so, universally, in all churches. Much confusion erupts if one tries to unite all together in a universal sense without regard for the practical carrying on of the church in its intended local sense.

CHAPTER FOUR
Ephesians 2:1-10

The Miracle, Mercy, and the Manifestation of a Different Life

In this beautiful grace chapter, Paul begins by showing the Church at Colossi and all Christendom just how unworthy we are of receiving God's marvelous grace. In his beloved song, John Newton started his song Amazing Grace with these wonderful and true words, Amazing Grace, how sweet the sound that saved a wretch like me. These verses highlight the wretched state of man and show man's awful condition and how depraved he is. Paul is offering this as he prepares the reader for the great statement involving saving grace. The great doctrine of grace is displayed here, but a careful and focused study will reveal that grace and God's favor are seen throughout the Scriptures. It is also true that one can see "The Grace Hand of God" in a day-by-day existence...which should cause us also to say, "Amazing Grace, how sweet the sound."

VERSE SUMMARIES 2:1-10

1 *And you hath he quickened, who were dead in trespasses and sins;* To be quickened or made alive is something only God the originator of life can do; for he is Life. This verse is more than a metamorphosis; it is a work of creation as those saved become new creatures in Christ.

2 *Wherein in time past ye walked according to the course of this world, according to the prince of the power of the air, the spirit that now worketh in the children of disobedience:*

What a remarkable change takes place upon one's conversion. Paul is saying, "This is the way you were," as though he wanted them not to forget the magnitude of such saving grace and how much love that performed it.

3 *Among whom also we all had our conversation in times past in the lusts of our flesh, fulfilling the desires of the flesh and of the mind; and were by nature the children of wrath, even as others.* Paul reminds them that their conversation (conduct) before their new birth was flesh-driven and also due to their corrupt minds following the god of this world, Satan. They were described in such a state as *the children of wrath.*

4 *But God, who is rich in mercy, for his great love wherewith he loved us.* The expression "But God" changes everything. He is rich in mercy and has such great love. Imagine how lost we would be if there had been no "But God" statement.

5 *Even when we were dead in sins, hath quickened us together with Christ, (by grace ye are saved;)* In such a depraved state having such need, without life He gives us that are in Christ His life.

6 *And hath raised us up together, and made us sit together in heavenly places in Christ Jesus:* This is a parallel statement that shows Him being raised from the dead in His flesh, and we being raised from a Spiritual death and together able to be joined together in heavenly places in Christ Jesus.

7 *That in the ages to come he might shew the exceeding riches of his grace in his kindness toward us through Christ Jesus.* There should be continual rejoicing in knowing that His grace will not be terminated for any reason that involves His kindness proportioned to the power of His omnipotence.

8 *For by grace are ye saved through faith; and that not of yourselves: it is the gift of God.* The outstanding words in this verse are grace, faith, and gift. It is by grace, God's part; through faith, man's part to believe.

9 *Not of works, lest any man should boast.* The nature and the origin of such grace take away any opportunity for boasting.

10 *For we are his workmanship, created in Christ Jesus unto good works, which God hath before ordained that we should walk in them.* He chose to reveal the magnitude of His grace by His own design. That said, we can be called "His trophies of grace" knowing well that all glory belongs to Him.

The Beginning of the Commentary (2:1-10)

1 *And you hath he quickened, who were dead in trespasses and sins;* To be quickened or made alive is something only God the originator of life can do; for he is Life. This verse shows more than a metamorphosis; it is a work of creation as those saved become new creatures in Christ. Speaking to the Church at Ephesus, Paul made a powerful statement involving *contrast*, a potent literary tool to draw attention to word meanings. The distinction Paul makes is when he tells them they have been radically changed from eternal death to an eternal state of life. Paul is saying, "You hath he quickened." This word first appeared in the 1400s to describe life or liveliness. When God quickens us, He makes us alive. God's quickening in our lives can affect us in many ways. By the power of God, we can be quickened or revived from sickness, discouragement, fear, and, of course, death. *Jesus is the Life* (John 14:6), and He can grant life to us: "*For as the Father raiseth up the dead, and quickeneth them; even so the Son quickeneth whom he will*" (John 5:21). *The Holy Spirit also gives life: "It is the spirit that quickeneth; the flesh profiteth nothing"* (John 6:63).

Some of the ways God quickens us according to His

Word is described in (Psalm 119:154) as according to His lovingkindness (Psalm 119:88); His quickening is associated with His tender mercy (Psalm 119:156), His righteousness (Psalm 119:40), and our joy (Psalm 85:6). He quickens us to keep us on the godly path: "turn away mine eyes from beholding vanity; and quicken thou me in thy way" (Psalm 119:37), and to preserve a people who call upon Him: "Quicken us, and we will call upon thy name" (Psalm 80:18). We ask the Lord to quicken our thoughts and the fervor we once had for Him (Psalm 42:11). We cry out for Him to quicken us when we are depressed (Psalm 119:25). We ask that He quicken our hearts when we are pulled by the enticements of the world so that we remain faithful to His Word (Psalm 80:18). Believers in Christ are spiritually *quickened* by God at the moment of salvation: "And you hath he quickened, who were dead in trespasses and sins" (Ephesians 2:1). And believers look forward to being *physically* quickened after death at the resurrection: "If the Spirit of him that raised up Jesus from the dead dwell in you, he that raised up Christ from the dead shall also quicken your mortal bodies by his Spirit that dwelleth in you" (Romans 8:11). (Got Questions)

   In contrast to being quickened or made alive, Paul uses the word dead or death to indicate not a literal physical death but metaphorically a Spiritual death. Romans 6:23 shows how it is used, *"The wages of sin is death."* Colossians 2:13 *And you, being dead in your sins and the uncircumcision of your flesh, hath he quickened together with him, having forgiven you all trespasses*; Dead and made alive, such contrast and such a difference. These two words show the change Paul speaks of in 2 Corinthians 5:17. "Therefore if any man be in Christ, he is a new creature: old things are passed away; behold, all things are become new." Romans 5:12-14 offers a clear understanding of the origin, the degree, fashion, and state of this kind of death: **12** *"Wherefore, as by one man sin entered into the world, and death by sin; and so death passed upon all men, for that all have sinned:* **13** *(For until the law sin was in the world: but sin is not imputed when there is no law.* **14** *Nevertheless, death reigned from Adam to Moses, even over them that had not sinned after the similitude of Adam's transgression, who is the figure of him that was to come."* While being in this Spiritually terminal death, their manner of living was so corrupted. They had no relationship to God, and "their foolish hearts were darkened," as Romans chapter one teaches.

2 *Wherein in time past ye walked according to the course of this world, according to the prince of the power of the air, the spirit that now worketh in the children of disobedience:* What a remarkable change takes place upon one's conversion. Paul is saying, "This is the way you were," as though he wanted them not to forget the magnitude of such saving grace and how much love that performed it. Paul calls upon the Church at Ephesus to compare how they were and how they had become because of the gracious work of Christ. He is describing their wicked state before their conversion and just how needy they were for God's wonderful grace, which this chapter speaks of. This is one of the most lofty portions of the Scriptures, showing how extraordinary grace is in this second chapter. Paul identified their manner of walk, a Jewish way of describing everything about them, and we similarly use that expression today. My dad challenged me to "walk right" by saying, "Son, you need to walk your talk." I knew what he meant!

To walk "according to the course of this world" shows a contrast in how a person walks differently, as shown beginning in Chapter Four, upon his conversion. The course is the Greek word *aeon, αἰών*, which is used to describe age or time. During Paul's lifetime, when he was writing to the Church at Ephesus, it was a time of moral declension or decline. The wicked philosophies coming out of Athens were taking their toll on Rome, and Rome had enough wickedness and evil of its own to be included. Paul is telling them they once walked wickedly to the same degree. Their walk was prescribed by the prince of the power of the air (Satan). Paul tells them that what controlled them then is now leading the *children of disobedience* as they walk according to the course of the world.

Usually, it is translated as "course," but it could be translated as "age" or "era," in its current meaning depicting a span of time or period. The following term κόσμος, "world," is used to describe the created material world as in 1:4, but it can also refer to the ethical world, which is the satanically organized system that hates and opposes all that is godly (cf. John 15:18, 23; 18:36; 1 Cor 3:19). The second sense fits best with the present context. The genitive could be attributive, "this worldly age or era," but it is more likely descriptive, "age of this world," meaning the era characterized by this ungodly world in contrast to the age to come, which will be of a different character. Some interpret the present age as "the era of the Fall." In other words, the unregenerate are found "conforming to the standards of the present world order." They go along with what is fashionable and acceptable and are not out of step with the rest of the world. Hence, they embrace temporal values. They are concerned only with activities and matters of the present age, not with God and eternal values or the judgment to come. (Hoehner)

3 *Among whom also we all had our conversation in times past in the lusts of our flesh, fulfilling the desires of the flesh and of the mind; and were by nature the children of wrath, even as others.* Paul reminds them that their conversation (conduct) before their conversion was flesh-driven and also due to their corrupt minds following the god of this world, Satan. They were described in such a state as *the children of wrath*. Paul does not blame their prior ungodliness on the corrupt world order only but on their conversation (conduct, walk) satisfying the lusts and desires of their flesh, including their mind constantly conforming to the world. Their inherited sinful nature lets them easily be children of wrath no different than the others. They are now surrounded by the pagans and the unbelievers that they once were a part of, and now Paul is encouraging the church to learn to live in such a society as believers who witness their change after their conversion. They also were to get along with fellow believers. They are being reminded in this verse how things were with them before their conversion. This reminder also challenges them not to let their flesh control them since they no longer naturally serve their flesh as children of wrath.

The *flesh* speaks of the material part of our bodies; we also refer to it as our physical body. Spiritually, it refers to the appetite associated with the sin curse. If we indeed have a new nature, we should exemplify that nature. Paul names some of these activities done according to the flesh rather than the Spirit to help us make a Spiritual and legal distinction. Paul is not saying he will no longer have the flesh to contend with upon one's conversion, but it should not describe our overall conduct. The more spiritual we are, the more we should personally abhor those things associated with the flesh.

Many scholars have seen the Jewish concept of the "evil inclination" (yēṣer hārā ʿ) behind Paul's view of the flesh. The idea that every person struggles with an inner propensity toward evil was central to Jewish thinking among the rabbis at the time of Paul. This impulse resulted in a struggle with each individual's good impulse, the yēṣer hāṭôb. The evil impulse inclined people to engage in every manner of sin. For the rabbis, studying the Torah was the only way to battle the evil inclination. For Paul, however, it is the new covenant blessing of the Holy Spirit, God's empowering presence to overcome this tendency. (Zondervan; Ephesians)

But God...

4 *But God, who is rich in mercy, for his great love wherewith he loved us.* The expression "But God" changes everything. He is rich in mercy and has such great love. Imagine how lost we would be if there had been no "But God" statement. Paul must always think of himself as he was before his conversion when he considers the goodness of God. In writing to the Romans he said: **24** *O wretched man that I am! who shall deliver me from the body of this death?* **25** *I thank God through Jesus Christ our Lord. So then with the mind I myself serve the law of God; but with the flesh the law of sin.* The following verses expound on His greatness and how He makes us alive according to His great love with no tribute to be given to ourselves but to God alone. Paul's writings often show a semantic connection between grace, mercy, and love. Though grace and mercy are not exact synonyms, they function similarly. One often requires or includes the other. In this chapter, these three walk together in function and agreement. When God offers His grace, it is because He loves us enough to do so, and it is an act of mercy. Mercy is defined as kindness or goodwill towards the miserable and the afflicted, joined with a desire to help. In meaning, it includes compassion. Metaphorically, it describes God providing in a bountiful way those being helped abundantly. The magnitude of this happening is based upon His great *love for us*.

When God revealed Himself at Mount Sinai, He declared in Exodus 34:6,7b, *The Lord, The Lord God, merciful and gracious, longsuffering, and abundant in goodness and truth,* **7** *Keeping mercy for thousands, forgiving iniquity and transgression and sin;* God showed His great mercy in delivering Israel and forgiving them of their sins, and Paul assured the Church at Ephesus that God is still that kind of God.

5 *Even when we were dead in sins, hath quickened us together with Christ, (by grace ye are saved;)* In such a depraved state having such need, without life He gives us that are in Christ His life. Considering the original contrasting description of the saved and the lost, verse five uses the phrase "dead in sins" to describe one devoid and depraved, having no Spiritual life, and the words *quickened us together with Christ* were used as thrilling words to describe the magnitude of our having life; His life! He did not turn from us when we were woeful sinners; instead, He made us alive with the life in Christ and flows from Christ. Our life is based on the premise that we have His life imparted as an *everlasting life* with no contribution from ourselves to make it so. Paul is telling them that Christ did not come to us only when we had improved our state to the extent of meeting a level of requirement that would merit us an opportunity to be saved for our having achieved such. No, a thousand times no! It was based upon the fact that as the song "Rock of Ages" teaches us, "There was nothing in my hands that I could bring, but simply to the cross I cling."(Toplady; 1776)

A significant aspect of being quickened together with Christ is that there is enough Theology in our Text to remind us that we are together with Christ (Colossians 3:3) and in Christ (2 Corinthians 5:17), Who is also in us (Colossians 1:27-29). A Christ relationship is defined as how Christ works in us, through us, and with us while we are simultaneously in Him. These four relationship aspects reveal an excellent way of His bestowing mercy and grace to us; there is no reason to justify such even happening apart from His great love.

He came to us *even when we were* in such a miserable and deplorable state, totally helpless and with no hope, and through redemption, set us free from the bondage of sin to live eternally with Him. Verse 5, the emphasis is on hath quickened us together *with Christ*. Verse 6 emphasizes making us sit together in heavenly places *in* Christ Jesus. In verse 7, he might shew the exceeding riches of his grace in his kindness toward us *through* Christ Jesus. These prepositions have connecting and interpretational values used to explain Christ's workings, which Paul wisely used and thus are revealed in this wondrous Book or Letter to the Church at Ephesus.

6 *And hath raised us up together, and made us sit together in heavenly places in Christ Jesus:* This is a parallel statement that shows Him being raised from the dead in His flesh, and we being raised from a Spiritual death and together able to be joined together in heavenly places in Christ Jesus. In verse five, we who are in Christ are quickened together, so as in verse 6, raised together, and then He made us sit together. We are seated in the heavens with Christ because we are in him. Our union with Christ gives us the right to be in the heavenly places. Although we are in the *heavenlies* positionally, we remain on earth to live a resurrected life in connection with having a resurrected Christ. God, who has benefited us with every spiritual blessing (1:3), enables us. Ephesians 2:10 states that the believer is created for good works here on earth. The idea of being seated in the heavenlies is not from a Gnostic concept of salvation as Paul taught those at Colossi. (Hoehner)

When thinking of Christ as being our High Priest who is seated in the heavenlies, or heavenly places, after having paid the offering of His precious blood on the mercy seat, carries in His heart in a representative manner the souls of men even as the earthly priest carried the stones upon his chest, representing the twelve sons of Jacob and their dependents who were atoned for on the Day of Atonement. In that representative manner, full legal benefits ensure the protective salvation of all the redeemed. Aaron was the first high priest of the temple at Jerusalem to have worn the priestly breastplate several centuries before Christ, which foreshadowed Him. Later, it was worn by the High Priest when he was presented in the Holy Place in the name of the Children of Israel. This was all done in a predictive or prophetic manner to picture Christ, which offers a better Priesthood. Interestingly, the Old Testament priest had so many external requirements that, in some way, depicted Christ and His holiness, and the stones of the breastplate were no exception. The stones of the breastplate appear as one of three lists of gems in the Bible. In Ezekiel 28:13, Revelations 21:19–20, and Exodus 28:17–20, there are lists of the 12 foundation stones. The authorized list is (1) red jasper (sardius), (2) citrine quartz (topaz), (3) emerald, (4) ruby (carbuncle), (5) lapis lazuli (sapphire), (6) rock crystal (diamond), (7) golden sapphire (ligure), (8) blue sapphire (agate), (9) amethyst, (10) yellow jasper (chrysolite), (11) golden beryl (onyx), (12) chrysoprase (jasper). The Hebrew names of these 12 stones are (1) Odem, (2) Pitdah, (3) Bareketh, (4) Nophek, (5) Sappir, (6) Yahalom, (7) Leshem, (8) Shebo, (9) Ahlamah, (10) Tarshish, (11) Shalom, (12) Yashpheh. It was also called <u>Aaron's Breastplate</u> which the High Priest wore.

    Christ hath raised us with him as the better Priesthood (comp. Philippians 3:10) so that we no longer walk *"according to the course of this world,"* but according to the life of Christ; we walk *"in newness of life."* And seated us with him in the heavenly places in Christ Jesus. Even as God placed Jesus at his right hand in heaven, *so he has placed his people with him in heavenly places, i.e., places where the privileges of heaven are dispensed, where the air of heaven is breathed, where the fellowship and the enjoyment of heaven are known, where an elevation of spirit is experienced as if heaven were begun.* Such was the case of the three disciples on the Mount of Transfiguration, of the two on the way to Emmaus, when their heart burned within them; of the beloved disciple when he was "in the Spirit on the Lord's day," of many at the Holy Supper, or in fervent communion with brother and sister believers, when they seem at the very gate of heaven. This is sometimes the experience at conversion, but the vividness of the feeling does not always abide. The repetition of "in Christ Jesus" in this connection emphasizes that this gracious proceeding of God towards us is in immediate connection with the work and person of Christ. As one with Christ Jesus, all this raising comes to us. (Pulpit)

The Way Grace Works

7 *That in the ages to come he might shew the exceeding riches of his grace in his kindness toward us through Christ Jesus.* There should be continual rejoicing in knowing that His grace will not be terminated for any reason that involves His kindness proportioned to the power of His omnipotence. Paul is letting the Church know that the work of the Father, Christ Jesus, and the Holy Spirit is an eternal and indeed a good work as the exceeding riches of His grace are revealed with kindness (in the ages to come). One commentator tries to word the significance of the expression *exceeding riches* by using "filthy rich" to describe such generosity. I see this in absolute contradistinction to His riches, for there is nothing filthy about the purest gift and giver. For He is the altogether lovely One. The riches are not only exceeding but also extraordinary in value, incomprehensibly; there is no way to measure such value. *In the ages to come*, the expression is Paul's way of saying you have the immediate benefit of one's salvation and the ongoing help that goes beyond the parousia (the Second Coming or the second advent) for all eternity. His riches will not give out or diminish, for God is inexhaustible. We are told that it is accomplished through Christ Jesus.

8 *For by grace are ye saved through faith; and that not of yourselves: it is the gift of God.* The outstanding words in this verse are grace, faith, and gift. It is by grace, God's part; through faith, man's part to believe. For by grace have ye been saved, through faith. Therefore, on the part of God, salvation is by grace; on the part of man, it is through faith. It does not come to us by an involuntary act, as light falls on our eyes, sounds on our ears, or air enters our lungs (Pulpit). When we are so far enlightened as to understand it, there must be a personal reception of salvation by us, and that is by faith. Faith immediately believes in the good news of free salvation through Christ and accepts Christ as the Savior; this is only possible when one believes the saving Gospel and God opens the heart of unbelief. We commit ourselves to Him and trust ourselves to Him for that salvation of which he is the Author. In the act of thus entrusting ourselves to Him for his salvation, we receive the benefit and are saved immediately and forever.

The salvation we receive is based entirely upon His righteousness and none other. It is not salvation based upon our worth and merit. Romans 10 and Romans 1:16,17 show this to be so. Salvation is a completed action, being passed from death unto life, and then is followed by a continuing action. A person is sanctified upon his conversion (all that is needed to be saved) and then continues to be sanctified in his walk or conduct (bringing forth Spiritual maturity). Verse 10 defines this ongoing work as *His workmanship*.

9 *Not of works, lest any man should boast.* The nature and the origin of such grace take away any opportunity for boasting. Paul is not suggesting that a person could work and, by his works, receive pardon or forgiveness for his sins and thus be accepted on the merits of his working for salvation. It is impossible; if it were possible, however, man would have a boastful spirit. Paul, in these few words, destroys such an argument. He is explaining why religious works do not merit one's salvation. The pattern of human works was initially set by Cain when he offered an unholy, unacceptable offering to God. Just as God would not accept an offering by Cain in place of the offering meant to foreshadow His Son's perfect and complete offering of Himself, which it did not, neither would He accept an inferior offering to replace His Son having been offered, in the form of dead works. If he had, Paul says the glory would be transferred from God to man, which cannot happen.

10 *For we are his workmanship, created in Christ Jesus unto good works, which God hath before ordained that we should walk in them.* He chose to reveal the magnitude of His grace by His own design. That said, we can be called "His trophies of grace." Just like the hunk of clay on the potter's wheel is to be skillfully molded by the trained potter, even so, the Master Potter carefully molds us. The potter has a vessel built in his mind before on his wheel. His intention is for us to be conformed to His image, as Romans 8:28-30 teaches. He knows where and how much pressure to put on the clay.

CHAPTER FIVE
Ephesians 2:11-22

Remember Your Past Relationship

Paul lets the Church at Ephesus know that they should not forget how they once were *Gentiles in the flesh*. As such, they were aliens from the common-wealth of Israel, were spoken of in derogatory manners by the Jews, and did not have national or spiritual benefits that the Jews had enjoyed. Paul wanted them to know that they should never forget those benefits that came from Christ alone.

VERSE SUMMARIES 2:11-22

11 *Wherefore remember, that ye being in time past Gentiles in the flesh, who are called Uncircumcision by that which is called the Circumcision in the flesh made by hands;* The term circumcision was such an identifying aspect of being a Jew. It was also one of the most apparent markers identifying the male Jew beginning shortly after birth. The Jews took great pride in their identifying with Abraham this way. They often alluded to Abraham as "Father Abraham," further indicating their ties to the total concept of Judaism and their separation from the Gentiles.

12 *That at that time ye were without Christ, being aliens from the commonwealth of Israel, and strangers from the covenants of promise, having no hope, and without God in the world:* The word alien describes them being viewed and considered as foreigners to the family of Israel, also as Strangers, having no apparent hope, and above all else being without God. Paul was reminding them of how desperate their plight was before their new birth.

13 *But now in Christ Jesus ye who sometimes were far off are made nigh by the blood of Christ.* The Jews and the Gentiles, who were separated from each other in almost every way, were made near by the blood of Christ having been shed. Their present relationship and the privileges they enjoy were made possible by His shed blood. Some corrupt theologians want to diminish the value of Christ's shed blood. When they do so, they are taking issue with and attacking cardinal Truth, which cannot be compromised. Without the shedding of blood, there is no remission of sin.

14 *For he is our peace, who hath made both one, and hath broken down the middle wall of partition between us.* There was a physical barrier that separated the Jews and the Gentiles from each other. In addition to that, there was a spiritual divide. Thus, the saying "The ground is level at the cross, communicates what this verse teaches.

15 *Having abolished in his flesh the enmity, even the law of commandments contained in ordinances; for to make in himself of twain one new man, so making peace;* Paul is saying that it took a work involving His flesh, which refers to Jesus becoming a man while remaining God when He came to the earth to die the death, even the death of the cross. That work was required to bring about unity or make one out of what had previously been divided as two who were separate in every way. Such reconciliation was accomplished as verse 16 teaches only by the cross.

16 *And that he might reconcile both unto God in one body by the cross, having slain the enmity thereby:* Paul is telling the Church at Ephesus that the cross made the difference, including their difference. The mystery of the cross destroys hatred or enmity that separates or divides. Jesus is the true Peace Giver.

17 *And came and preached peace to you which were afar off, and to them that were nigh.* He was on a mission to bring together unbelievers who were estranged from God and each other. He accomplished this by the work of the cross, which was available to all who would believe. Paul gives the Jews and the Gentiles as being a classic example of such people who were separated and enemies towards each other.

18 *For through him we both have access by one Spirit unto the Father.* The work of Christ is what brings us to the Father upon our believing in the Lord Jesus Christ.

19 *Now therefore ye are no more strangers and foreigners, but fellowcitizens with the saints, and of the household of God.* This was such wonderful news to tell the Church at Ephesus that Christ alone made them become fellow heirs together as the church. With that blessing, they made us "His house."

20 *And are built upon the foundation of the apostles and prophets, Jesus Christ himself being the chief corner stone;* This building Paul is speaking of is indeed special because the building's strength and design depend upon Him being the Cornerstone. This graphic metaphor illustrates how the church is likened to a building.

21 *In whom all the building fitly framed together groweth unto an holy temple in the Lord:* It is interesting how Paul uses the word that is used similarly when describing when a husband and wife come together in holy matrimony as being *fitted together*. The two become as one. Christ also likens Himself as being in relationship to the church, with the church being His bride.

22 *In whom ye also are builded together for an habitation of God through the Spirit.* The Ideal here is that the building (church) is inhabited by a perfect Christ. Paul told the Ephesian church that Christ in you is the "Hope of glory."

The Beginning of the Commentary (Vv. 11-22)

11 *Wherefore remember, that ye being in time past Gentiles in the flesh, who are called Uncircumcision by that which is called the Circumcision in the flesh made by hands;* The term circumcision was such an identifying aspect of being a Jew. It was also one of the most apparent markers identifying the male Jew beginning shortly after birth. The Jews took great pride in their identifying with Abraham this way. They often alluded to Abraham as "Father Abraham," further indicating their ties to the total concept of Judaism and their separation from the Gentiles.

Paul continues to reveal to Ephesus and remind the Ephesians that they were not connected racially or Spiritually with the Hebrews and had no privileges that were theirs to enjoy initially by the Abrahamic Covenant that the Jews could enjoy. They had to wait for the promise of the Seed that allowed both Jews and Gentile's special privileges, as shown in Galatians 3:16-19: **16** *Now to Abraham and his seed were the promises made. He saith not, And to seeds, as of many; but as of one, And to thy seed, which is Christ.* **17** *And this I say, that the covenant, that was confirmed before of God in Christ, the law, which was four hundred and thirty years after, cannot disannul, that it should make the promise of none effect.* **18** *For if the inheritance be of the law, it is no more of promise: but God gave it to Abraham by promise.* **19** *Wherefore then serveth the law? It was added because of transgressions, till the seed should come to whom the promise was made; and it was ordained by angels in the hand of a mediator.*

The problem of transgressions in the Old Covenant was resolved when the promised Seed, Christ, came. He lived perfectly, qualifying to be the payment for sin, and at the same time, He confirmed the promises made unto Abraham—and they were made absolutely and eternally binding. God then proposed the New Covenant previously shown in prophecy (Jeremiah 31). God has presented it to all of mankind—not just to Abraham's physical descendants. Then, the identity of the Jews and the Gentiles was further differentiated by the Jew being referred to as the Circumcision and the Gentile as the Uncircumcision. The Old Testament Law prescribed this according to Moses the Law Giver and ultimately from God Himself. Colossians speaks of the circumcision in this manner. **11** *In whom also ye are circumcised with the circumcision made without hands, in putting off the body of the sins of the flesh by the circumcision of Christ:* The circumcision spoken of here being done with hands is referring to the natural or fleshly circumcision. At the same time, circumcision without hands is a Spiritual circumcision that, when used as a metaphor, refers to the cutting away of the sins of the flesh, which takes place at the time of one's conversion. It seems Paul is dealing with many issues that can bring distortion and affect one's belief, causing that person to succumb to heresy, and in the case of Colossi, it has been called the *Colossian Heresy*. With this concern, Paul brings up a term we know as the rite of circumcision, which means cutting away the flesh. Circumcision is the surgical removal of the prepuce, or foreskin, of a male. The word circumcise means "to cut around." As a religious rite, circumcision was required of all of Abraham's descendants as a sign of the covenant God made with him (Genesis 17:9–14; Acts 7:8). The Mosaic Law repeated the requirement (Leviticus 12:2–3), and Jews throughout the centuries have continued to practice circumcision (Joshua 5:2–3; Luke 1:59; Acts 16:3; Philippians 3:5). (Alderman)

Things The Gentiles Were Without

12 *That at that time ye were without Christ, being aliens from the commonwealth of Israel, and strangers from the covenants of promise, having no hope, and without God in the world:* The word alien describes them being viewed and considered as foreigners to the family of Israel, also as Strangers, having no apparent hope, and above all else being without God. Paul was reminding them of how desperate their plight was before their new birth. The idea that Gentiles were not circumcised indicated to Jews that they did not have the five privileges that were given to the nation Israel.

Having described in verses one to 10 what the Ephesians were before salvation, Paul now developed what they were as Gentiles. "ye were without Christ [Messiah],"

First, as Gentiles, they did not know the Christ, the Messiah. They did not possess the salvation He provided. They were "without" or separated from the Messiah, being aliens from the Commonwealth of Israel.

Second, Gentiles did not belong to the theocratic nation of Israel. They were "aliens" or *estranged* from Israel's kind of people. Sometimes, we forget that Israel was more than a spiritual entity; it was a state or national entity as well and strangers from the covenants [contracts] of promise,

Third, Gentiles were "strangers" to God's promises. They could not claim the Abrahamic covenant (Ge 12:1-3; 15:18-21; 17:1-8), the Palestinian covenant (Dt 28-30), the Davidic covenant (2 Sa 7:16; Ps 89:1-4), or the New covenant (Jer 31:31-34). These covenants promised the coming Messiah and the blessings that flow from Him—not having the covenants meant not belonging to the theocratic nation of Israel.

An unconditional covenant is a contract that God makes with His people. It is a promise that God makes for those who are His own, without any strings attached. God gave covenants about a coming King, a kingdom, and a land having no hope,

Fourth, Gentiles did not have hope. They had no anticipation of a coming Messiah who would offer them salvation. The nation Israel had hope because God had given them promises; they could count on Him keeping His word. However, Gentiles had no basis for objective hope; they had nothing to hope for. Hope is based on promises from God. It is confidence in the person of God and what He says. The Jews had hope in the promises of God; the Gentiles had none and were without God. Hope is directed toward the future. Once we have received what we have hoped for, hope ceases (Rom 8:24). Thus, the ultimate focus of Christian hope, according to the NT, is the return of Jesus Christ (Tit 2:13), the resurrection from the dead (Acts 23:6), God's ultimate salvation of his people, and the resultant eternal life in a restored creation (Rom 8:20–21; Gal 5:5; Eph 1:18; Tit 1:2; 3:7). At that point, we will live in eternal glory, centered in Jesus Christ himself, "the hope of glory" (Col 1:27; 1 Tim. 1:1).

Christian hope is strengthened by the Scriptures (Rom 15:4), by the work of Jesus (1 Pet. 1:3, 21), and by God's present gift of the Spirit to believers (Rom 5:5). God wants us to wear hope around our heads as a helmet (1 Thess. 5:8) and to be ready at all times to share our hope with others (1 Pet. 3:15). By contrast, those who do not have God in their lives are without hope (Eph 2:12). (Mounce)

Hope and faith walk closely together, as Hebrews 10:22, 23, 35, and 11:1-6 teach us. In Hebrews, the writer instructs the believer not to cast away his confidence (hope) that has great recompense of reward. Yet, before their conversion,

Christ being raised from the dead, and the veil of the temple was rent from top to bottom, the Gentiles had no access or hope in approaching God.

Fifth, Gentiles were in the desperate situation of being "without God." The words "without God" form the Greek word for atheists. Although the Ephesians, as Gentiles, had many gods of polytheism, they had no true God. Gentiles in Paul's day were polytheists but did not have a true and living God. Notwithstanding their plurality of gods, they still had no genuine hope or confidence in the true God. They did not have God because they did not want Him. (Grant)

The Gentiles were "in the world" instead of being in the commonwealth of Israel, having no relationship. Still, upon their conversion, they could enjoy the relationship found in the church. This will be like saying, "Oh, what a difference Christ Jesus makes!"

13 *But now in Christ Jesus ye who sometimes were far off are made nigh by the blood of Christ*. The Jews and the Gentiles, who were separated from each other in almost every way, were made near by the blood of Christ having been shed. Their present relationship and the privileges they enjoy were made possible by His shed blood. Some corrupt theologians want to diminish the value of Christ's shed blood. When they do so, they are taking issue with and attacking cardinal Truth, which cannot be compromised. Without the shedding of blood, there is no remission of sin.

This verse with the words "But now" speaks of or signals Divine intervention when Christ Jesus shed His blood and provided a payment necessary for their redemption. When this took place, not only was righteousness imputed, but Spiritual life was imparted. This is Paul's way of describing the separation that the Gentiles felt towards both the Jews and God before they were made nigh by the blood of Christ. The previous verse tells such, and then Paul said all had been changed upon their conversion. The blood of Christ was the perfect sacrifice to precisely accomplish what Paul described while writing to the Church at Colossi. The blood of Christ is not just some symbolic gesture by God to symbolize the sufferings of the cross. The blood was Jesus' actual blood that God required, which was the offering necessary to redeem man from the awful sin curse. Many old songwriters were correct when wording their songs: "What Can Wash Away My Sins…Nothing but the blood." "There is Power in the Blood"; The words, "There is a fountain drawn from Emanuels Veins," which speaks of His blood. Paul emphasizes the great price of redemption as he writes to the Colossians.

The Wall Broken Down

14 *For he is our peace, who hath made both one, and hath broken down the middle wall of partition between us.* There was a physical barrier that separated the Jews and the Gentiles from each other. In addition to that, there was a spiritual divide. Thus, the saying "The ground is level at the cross, communicates what this verse teaches. Paul continues by saying there is one who has brought peace and has done so by doing away with the Old Covenant and replacing it with the New Covenant of Grace, which allows complete access into the most Holy of Holies, with Christ being our propitiation for our sins. The Father was completely satisfied by His Son's offering Himself as a ransom for all. The evidence of this was when the wall was broken, and the veil was rent in twain, granting men access to a better way by the blood of Jesus. When Jesus offered Himself, there was no further need for having a day of atonement to put off the wrath of God. This allowed both Jews and Greeks to have access into the church through conversion. This was so because whether the wall was figurative or literal, the middle wall meant that the Greeks were separated from the Jews. Once it was broken, it granted them equal access. Paul had to deal with them in their new state to help remove any animosity between them. The church was Christ's way of bringing them together in belief. Upon their entrance into the Church, there is neither Jew nor Gentile, bond or free legally, as Galatians 3:28,29 teach us. 28 There is neither Jew nor Greek, there is neither bond nor free, there is neither male nor female: for ye are all one in Christ Jesus. 29 And if ye be Christ's, then are ye Abraham's seed, and heirs according to the promise.

Paul likely has a literal wall in mind that served as a fence to separate the Gentiles from the Jews in the one place where God mediated his presence to the people—the temple of Jerusalem. The temple complex was extensive, covering an area slightly smaller than one-quarter of a mile square (or nearly forty acres). The perimeter of this area was enclosed by a double colonnade of pillars standing thirty-seven feet high. Within this paved area was a series of courts that included the court of the Gentiles and then the interior courts of the temple, which led to the sanctuary. Surrounding the inner courts was a four-and-one-half-foot-high wall, called the song, that separated the court of the Gentiles from the court of the Israelites and the court of the women and kept Gentiles from ever coming near the sanctuary. Josephus says that thirteen stone inscriptions were erected at various points on this balustrade or fence that warned Gentiles not to enter under penalty of death.23 Two of these inscriptions have been discovered. The text of the inscription reads: "No foreigner is to enter within the forecourt and the balustrade around the sanctuary. Whoever is caught will have himself to blame for his subsequent death."24 This "dividing wall" or "fence" surrounding the temple's inner courts symbolized the extraordinary division between Jew and Gentile. (Ephesians, Zondervan). Also, when Paul says, "hath broken down the middle wall of partition between us," he recognizes himself as having been a Jew, and they were Gentiles. By Paul saying the wall has been removed, he is speaking in agreement with the Scriptures that says they are neither Jew nor Gentile, bond or free, but *church!* (Galatians 3:27,28)

15 *Having abolished in his flesh the enmity, even the law of commandments contained in ordinances; for to make in himself of twain one new man, so making peace;* Paul is saying that it took a work involving His flesh, which refers to Jesus becoming a man while still also being God when He came to the earth to die the death, even the death of the cross. That work was required to bring about unity or make one out of what had previously been divided as two who were separate in every way. Such reconciliation was accomplished as verse 16 teaches only by the cross.

The Lord removed the hostility that existed between the Jews and Gentiles and made them united in peace, and that peace let them both be reconciled unto God. It was accomplished by the work on the cross and the resurrection of Jesus, who was put to death for our sins. To the Jews and according to the Torah, the law of commandments contained in their ordinances is where their primary focus lies. The Pharisees were known for adding to the law and making it of no effect when they did so. In the New Testament, the Jews would also broaden their phylacteries to impress for outward show. Phylacteries, sometimes called tefillin, are small, square leather boxes containing portions of Scripture worn by Conservative and Orthodox Jews during prayer services. Phylacteries are worn in pairs—one phylactery is strapped on the left arm, and one is strapped to the forehead of Jewish men during weekday morning prayers. Phylactery comes from a Greek word meaning "safeguard, protection, or amulet."

The phylactery strapped to the arm is called the *shel yad* and has only one compartment; the one on the forehead, containing four compartments, is called the *shel rosh*. The letter shin (ש) is printed on either side of the head phylactery. Various rules govern the length and width of the connecting straps, the tying of the knots to secure the phylacteries, and the color of the boxes (black). Inside each phylactery are four passages from the Old Testament: Exodus 13:1–10, 11–16; Deuteronomy 6:4–9; 11:13–21. The verses must be written in black ink on parchment specially prepared for this purpose, using the skin of a clean animal. Other rules specify the type of writing instrument to be used, the number of printed lines devoted to each verse, the arrangement of the pieces of parchment within each compartment, etc. (Got Questions) Observing this aspect of how they were keeping the law, moving away from God's intended purpose for the Law to make it a ceremonial means of boasting on how they kept the law. Around the third century, they even took pride in recognizing all 613 laws while bragging about how many they could keep. Such thinking gives reason for why Paul stressed that our focus and emphasis should not be on the law but on Him, who abolished the handwriting of ordinances against us. Hebrews 12 tells us to look unto Jesus, the Author and Finisher of the Faith.

What the Law could not do in that it was weak (because it could not provide our justification), Christ did do.

16 *And that he might reconcile both unto God in one body by the cross, having slain the enmity thereby:* Paul is telling the Church at Ephesus that the cross made the difference, including their difference. The mystery of the cross destroys hatred or enmity that separates or divides. Jesus is the true Peace Giver. Just as had been spoken in verse 15, the hatred or enmity was abolished or destroyed, and in this verse, the word slain is used, which parallels how Jesus was also slain on the cross. The crucifixion (slaying of Jesus) involved a personal slaying to affect the *slaying of the enmity* between the Jew and the Gentile alike. Those who were separately identified are now seen as agreeing, being reconciled unto God in one body by the cross. This strong word shows the intense enmity or hatred between them that only Christ could resolve. As stated, the purpose was to bring about a total reconciliation *between all parties.*

17 *And came and preached peace to you which were afar off, and to them that were nigh.* When Jesus came to the earth, He was on a mission to bring together unbelievers who were estranged from God and each other. He accomplished this by the work of the cross, which was available to all who would believe. Paul gives the Jews and the Gentiles as being a classic example of such people who were separated and enemies to each other. Jesus, before His crucifixion and His resurrection, preached this about the origin of peace in John 14:26,27: *"But the Comforter, which is the Holy Ghost, whom the Father will send in my name, he shall teach you all things, and bring all things to your remembrance, whatsoever I have said unto you.* **27** *Peace I leave with you, my peace I give unto you: not as the world giveth, give I unto you. Let not your heart be troubled, neither let it be afraid."* There can be no real peace that comes only from God, except through reconciliation. One can only expect misery when there is no reconciliation taking place. Paul is showing the Church at Ephesus how great grace is in God, showing His favor when we were so unworthy. Paul mentioned those being preached to as being near and far, including those who think of themselves in any manner as in a relationship to each other and God. Paul was probably referring to the Jews as being nigh and the Gentiles as being at a "guilty distance," but in the case of both, their only hope was in Christ by having a personal conversion being born again from above. It seems to be a statement that suggests an all exclusiveness about it as though to say, "For whosoever will let him come."

18 *For through him we both have access by one Spirit unto the Father.* The work of Christ is what brings us to the Father upon our believing in the Lord Jesus Christ. The Jews and the Gentiles alike have equal and complete access by one Spirit unto the Father. This verse indicates that all that takes place is after the death, burial, resurrection, and Christ's ascension back to God's right hand and after the Spirit had been sent to minister to the saints. Christ intercedes by one Spirit unto the Father, which also gives us an advocate and comforter, as John 14 mentions.

The Hostility Removed

19 *Now therefore ye are no more strangers and foreigners, but fellowcitizens with the saints, and of the household of God;* This was such wonderful news to tell the Church at Ephesus that Christ alone made them become fellow heirs together as the church. With that blessing, they made us "His house." Paul is laying out the formula for the Gentiles to be included as fellowcitizens and as family, which is also indicated in the Scriptures. Before conversion and Calvary, they were granted no rights that the Gentiles or Greeks could claim by their natural birth and lineage. To many of the Jews, they were previously only known as Gentile dogs, having no national or even religious rites that the devout Jews could freely enjoy. In almost every way, they were strangers and foreigners and could not fit in. "But God!"

20 *And are built upon the foundation of the apostles and prophets, Jesus Christ himself being the chief corner stone.*

This building Paul is speaking of is indeed special because the building's strength and design depend upon Him being the Cornerstone. This graphic metaphor illustrates how the church is likened to a building. Some like to think that the foundation is built on those of the Old Testament who were prophets and those who served as Apostles. They determine this mainly by the use of the word prophets by Paul. However, after carefully studying the church and how it is in the economy of Grace, as emphasized in this chapter, one must understand that the church had no preexistence before Christ, and He did not reach back into the Old Testament economy to build the Church. I also want to suggest, as a student, a reason why Christ, the apostles, and the prophets make up the foundation. Remember that much of what is going on in the Book of Acts is transitional. The Foundational work of the Church as it is being built falls in this transitional period as well. Before the Canon of Scriptures was completed, the foundational part of the Church was still taking place.

Let me explain it this way. I grew up in a builder's home and know the value of the foundation and that the foundation is the very first part of the building before the edifice is built on top of it. If there is a weak foundation, there will be a weak structure on the foundation, as described by Jesus when he spoke of the man building his house on the sand. Paul describes the foundation as being comprised of three parts, as mentioned. In a prophetic sense, John the Apostle was writing the prophetic book of Revelation; he served as both an apostle and a prophet along with the other Apostles in the foundation.

Consequently, he, as an example, was a part of the foundation. The holy temple in verse 21 is built on Christ, the Apostles, and the Prophets. Upon this foundation, the building is fitly framed together, and verse 21 tells us it continues to grow as a holy temple. This temple is still being built, and the foundation is complete and not to be added unto. We recognize this temple as a metaphor describing the church and practically also recognize it as a local church. Paul explains that every time a soul is saved and added to the church, the *holy temple is added unto*. Christ is referred to in our immediate text as Chief Corner Stone, which means that everything about the church has its reference back to Him. The chief cornerstone in construction was necessary for a well-built building. Three dominant qualities should be in every building. There should be plumb, square, and level. In ancient buildings, the Chief cornerstone would always reference these qualities.

Years ago, I had the privilege of going to Ramses Tutankhamun, also known as Ramses II's exhibit, who was thought to be the Pharaoh Moses stood before. Many artifacts were at the show. Among those was his mummy. I saw his mummy, and it was imposing. The thing that was even more impressive to me was the chief cornerstone that was a significant part of the exhibit. Having grown up in a builder's home, I learned there had to be a dependable point of reference to establish the needed qualities throughout the building. On the Chief Cornerstone, two sides were smoothed like glass at a 90-degree angle. This was to develop the squareness of the building. Two lines were inscribed in the smooth facets to guarantee the level needed in a well-built structure. Then, for those two qualities to be present, the cornerstone had to be placed in the ground straight up and down to guarantee the plumb required throughout the edifice. The cornerstone serves as a metaphor to communicate how Christ Jesus is the One to whom the Church has its reference. The Bible is the way it is established and known. He is the Living Word, and the Bible is the written Word. It is like the Bible is the blueprint and the operation manual.

21 *In whom all the building fitly framed together groweth unto an holy temple in the Lord:* It is interesting how Paul uses the word that is used similarly when describing when a husband and wife come together in holy matrimony as being *fitted together*. The two become as one. Christ also likens Himself as being in relationship to the church, with the church being His bride. Each precious soul saved continues to add to or grow unto the holy temple of the Lord. The unusual aspect of this new temple is that it has never been finished. It is a structure that continues to increase in size. Paul's temple imagery is derived from the Jerusalem temple, not the Artemis temple of Ephesus or any other pagan temple. This is consistent with using temple imagery in his other letters to characterize the church. The term he uses for temple (ναός) refers to the sanctuary in Jerusalem and not to the entire temple complex, which would include the various courts surrounding the sanctuary. (Zondervan Exegetical Commentary on the New Testament series Book 10)

The use of the word temple was a way to describe in Jewish terms the ways that the church functioned. The church was relatively new to Christianity, and Paul descriptively used the word temple to show additional ways the church operated or was viewed. The temple was a place to be respected and reverenced. The expression "fitly framed together" shows God's intent for the church to function in a way that would be done decently and in order, with Him being *the perfect Builder*. This also speaks of how Christ is the ideal craftsman, knowing how to fit everything and everyone together to serve His noble purpose. Paul is letting the Ephesian church know they are a vital part of God's economy, and He does everything well as He is also the Head. The church members are not perfect members with no weaknesses, for that will be taken care of at the final glorification. This is why we have the Bible to instruct us on how to live as members of the church and society until that final glorification.

22 *In whom ye also are builded together for an habitation of God through the Spirit.* The Ideal here is that the building (church) is inhabited by a perfect Christ. Paul told the Ephesian church that Christ in you is the "Hope of glory." Paul says that the Holy Spirit inhabits the Church and grants man an intimacy with the Lord that most could not enjoy before the New Covenant came into effect. A man had to stand at a guilty distance from God and depend upon the High Priest on the day of atonement to put off the wrath of God for another year…and now we can come boldly to the throne of Grace in the time of need!

"God dwells with his people 'by the Spirit.' The Spirit is how God inhabits this corporate body of believers (see also 1 Cor 3:16–17; 2 Cor 6:16).87 Fee rightly notes that 'by the indwelling of the Spirit, both in the individual and in the community, God (or Christ) indwells his people.' Because the Spirit is the Spirit of power, 'this lends a dynamic aspect to God's presence in the temple' and thus lays the foundation for the lifestyle admonitions of the second half of this letter." (Arnold)

CHAPTER SIX
Ephesians 3:1-9

The Mysteries Revealed to the Church (1-9)

Paul has some explaining to do...that is how it seems. The Gentiles never knew until now, after their conversion and becoming a part of the dispensation of Grace, what it meant to have the shared benefits of Christ. Paul is telling them everything that he tells them from a Roman prison. No Gentiles, nor Jews either, in the ages before them could have the privileges they now enjoy. When Paul speaks to them as a converted Jew, he does not boast and brag about his worth from that vantage point. He did not indicate that he enjoyed the grace of God applied in his own life as being attributed to his race or nationality, but instead, he let them know he was the least of the saints. At least, that is the way he describes himself. He also insists that they understand that the Ephesians could only enjoy what they enjoy by Christ's indescribable love for them. Paul begins this chapter by referring back transitionally using the word *For*.

VERSE SUMMARIES 3:1-9

1 *For this cause I Paul, the prisoner of Jesus Christ for you Gentiles.* Paul, who was a Jew, was ministering to the Gentiles. We refer to him as a missionary and like studying his missionary journeys. He is an example of the true missionary willing to remove himself from his familiars and go to the "whosoever" wherever they might be. We may call him an exemplar in more technical language, for he indeed serves as a model of what the Bible says should describe the witness of souls.

2 *If ye have heard of the dispensation of the grace of God which is given me to you-ward:* If one cared to listen to Paul speak or read what Paul had written, he would have heard of the grace of God. Paul is introducing the dispensation of grace to the Gentile people who previously had been removed from any benefits that the Jews enjoyed.

3 *How that by revelation he made known unto me the mystery; (as I wrote afore in few words.* Revelation is formed from the root word reveal, and Paul is saying that which had been hidden and contained in the mind of God only is now being made known even as he told the Church at Colossi.

4 *Whereby, when ye read, ye may understand my knowledge in the mystery of Christ).* Paul was speaking with much clarity and wrote likewise, so there was and is no excuse for learning the truth about what was previously a mystery.

5 *Which in other ages was not made known unto the sons of men, as it is now revealed unto his holy apostles and prophets by the Spirit;* God reserved to disclose to a most unworthy lot of people the great riches where people would understand and recognize by that virtue to whom he offered (the Gentiles) and when He provided the magnitude of such a gift.

6 *That the Gentiles should be fellowheirs, and of the same body, and partakers of his promise in Christ by the gospel:* This section of the third chapter develops and explains the truth as it pertains to the Gentiles. If you told the Gentile person that they would enjoy the same benefit as the Jews, they would have laughed you to scorn. But it was so!

7 *Whereof I was made a minister, according to the gift of the grace of God given unto me by the effectual working of his power.* Paul attributed his ministry and calling to God, ensuring that the Church at Colossi knew it was so and was according to the gift of the grace of God. He also let them know the source of his power and authority came from God.

8 *Unto me, who am less than the least of all saints, is this grace given, that I should preach among the Gentiles the unsearchable riches of Christ;* He knew that he had nothing in which to boast and marveled that he was able to enjoy the grace of God when he had been such an enemy of Christ before his conversion.

9 *And to make all men see what is the fellowship of the mystery, which from the beginning of the world hath been hid in God, who created all things by Jesus Christ:* Understanding that the converted, or those born again receive the things of God, the expression "all men see" is reserved only for the redeemed. However, I am sure that Paul would like to have seen all men saved and, thus, be able to see the *fellowship of the mystery, also*.

The Beginning of the Commentary (3:1-9)

1 *For this cause I Paul, the prisoner of Jesus Christ for you Gentiles.* We refer to him as a missionary and like studying his missionary journeys. He is an example of the true missionary willing to remove himself from his familiars and go to the "whosoever" wherever they might be. We may call him an exemplar in more technical language, for he serves as a model of what the Bible says should describe the witness to souls. Paul, when using the phrase "For this cause," seems to be letting the Ephesians know that he is praying for them but immediately digresses when he says even though he is writing from Prison to the Church at Ephesus, he still has credibility to tell them about and explain to them how they now as saved members of the Church can stand before God with the same status as the converted Jew. Paul also lets the Church at Ephesus know that even though he is a prisoner of Nero and Rome, he is not referring to himself that way. He lets them know first that he is willingly a prisoner of Jesus Christ and ministering as a prisoner of Jesus Christ for them (you Gentiles). The prison in Rome just happened to be the place God wanted Paul to serve Him as a bound slave. (Theologians and students of this Epistle believe that Paul began to pray and digress from his praying, only to pick it back up in verse 14.)

2 *If ye have heard of the dispensation of the grace of God which is given me to you-ward:* If one cared to listen to Paul speak or read what Paul had written, he would have heard of *the grace of God.* Paul is introducing the dispensation of grace to the Gentile people who previously had been removed from any benefits that the Jews enjoyed. Paul undoubtedly is referring back to Colossians 1:26,27, which speaks of the mystery that Paul is referring to or to teachings that occurred during the three years he had been in Ephesus with them. 26 Even the mystery which hath been hidden from ages and from generations, but now is made manifest to his saints: Paul was entrusted with the previously unknown truths that apply to the dispensation of grace. Among these mysteries are the previously unknown truths about Christ's incarnation. He was the one who was given the truth about the church by revelation. Neither the Gentiles nor the Jews could at all comprehend their being together in one singular body of belief. Even after it became so, Paul had to explain it to them as in his letter to the Ephesians. Paul did not assume they all had heard. Thus, he used "if" to qualify his statement without assuming everyone had heard; there could have been new converts who were still ignorant, having not heard yet. Paul also tells them he is not hoarding this truth unto himself but was sharing it with the Church at Ephesus so they might, too, understand the revealed mysteries about the church.

With Paul speaking of grace here, there is an added sense now in which Paul uses the term "grace" to refer not only to the gift of salvation but also to his call to apostleship and God's empowerment to carry it out. This is similar to the way Paul speaks of grace in Gal 1:15–16, when he says that God "set me apart from birth and called me by his grace, as taught here, **15** *But when it pleased God, who separated me from my mother's womb, and called me by his grace,* **16** *To reveal his Son in me, that I might preach him among the heathen; immediately I conferred not with flesh and blood:* Paul frequently associates his experience of God's grace with his apostleship (see Rom 1:5; 12:3; 15:15; 1 Cor 3:10; 15:10; Gal 2:9). (Ephesians, Zondervan Exegetical Commentary on The New Testament series Book 10)

THE MYSTERY REVEALED TO THE CHURCH

3 *How that by revelation he made known unto me the mystery; (as I wrote afore in few words.* Revelation is formed from the root word reveal, and Paul is saying that which had been hidden and contained in the mind of God only is now being made known even as he told the Church at Colossi. Paul is using the same word (revelation) that was used in Galatians 1:12 to describe his experience on the road to Damascus to let the Church at Ephesus know that this was not something that Paul conceived in his mind but that it was divinely revealed unto him by the Lord. There is so much cardinal truth revealed to Paul; perhaps some of the Truth related to the mystery came at the moment of his conversion on the road to Damascus. Paul does not give the time of his being revealed any additional truth; it could also be a continual revelation as he served. There also could have been a revealing of Truth as he spent three years in what is known as modern-day Turkey preparing. The Lord Jesus Christ taught Paul. After his conversion and fleeing Damascus due to persecution (Acts 9:20-25), Paul spent three years in Nabataean Arabia (modern-day Turkey). Some biblical scholars believe God gave him three years there because the original 12 had three years with Jesus. Paul was given three years to learn directly from the Lord Jesus (Galatians 1:11-12, 15-18). This could be where he received the mysteries about the church that no one had previously received.

4 *Whereby, when ye read, ye may understand my knowledge in the mystery of Christ).* Paul was speaking with much clarity and wrote likewise, so there was and is no excuse for learning the truth about what was previously a mystery. Paul is telling them that as they read what he is writing about, which was previously a mystery, they could accept it credibly, for he was speaking and writing the truth. "In English, a 'mystery' is dark, obscure, secret, puzzling. What is 'mysterious' is inexplicable, even incomprehensible. The Greek word mysterion is different, however. Although still a 'secret,' it is no longer closely guarded but open... More simply, mysterion is a truth hitherto hidden from human knowledge or understanding but now disclosed by the revelation of God." (Stott) Paul's saying you may understand him as knowing the mystery of Christ could be attributed to his testimony and reputation as an apostle. Also, the Holy Spirit gives spiritual discernment to the spiritually born. In contrast, the natural man, or the unregenerate, receiveth not the things of the Spirit of God, for they are foolishness to them. I Corinthians 2. Paul was granted special insight that came from God by the Spirit and the teachings of Christ in whatever manner he taught Paul. When we notice any mention of reading, realizing how expensive it was to produce a parchment or scroll, we must also think about public readings, where someone would open the Letter or parchment in an open assembly and read it in a public hearing or setting. They could not just conveniently open the Book and start reading as we are privileged to do today. In addition to that being so, the entire Canon of Truth was not available in the 66 books of the Bible, as we now have them included as one. This was an exciting time as the Truth was revealed in their time on the earth. Many would sometimes hear the Truth that we may even take for granted by having it within our constant reach. For them to hear, they were doing so maybe for the very first time and did not have the luxury of opening up the Scriptures at will as we are able.

5 *Which in other ages was not made known unto the sons of men, as it is now revealed unto his holy apostles and prophets by the Spirit;* God reserved to disclose to a most unworthy lot of people the great riches where people would understand and recognize by that virtue to whom he offered (the Gentiles) and when He provided the magnitude of such a gift. God used the different ones mentioned to write the Scriptures using their personalities and backgrounds, etc., without compromise. He said the holy apostles and prophets who made up the church's foundation and were used by God to pen the words of Truth, which included the apostle Paul, whose sacred words became part of the Canon of Truth or the Bible. Paul clearly says those previously unknown mysteries were revealed to him and the others mentioned, including the dispensation of grace. The Bible mentioned seven, with five dispensations recorded in the Old Testament and two in the New Testament. They are as follows:

Each of the five dispensations of the Old Testament began with God's grace and ended *with man's failure*. The first dispensation began with the creation of Adam and Eve.

It is called *innocence* and lasted until the fall. The second dispensation is called *conscience*, which ended with the flood in Noah's time. The third dispensation is *human government*, which ended with building the Towel of Babel. The fourth dispensation began with Abraham and is called *promise*, and this period lasted until the Egyptian captivity when God raised a deliverer for Israel named Moses. This marked the beginning of the final dispensation of the Old Testament called law. (Yandin) The sixth dispensation is the dispensation that begins with the resurrection. It is the grace dispensation and is referred to as the church age. The final dispensation will be the Millennium, after which we will enter eternal bliss! The mysteries Paul speaks of were unknown in other ages and did not apply to them. The mysteries Paul speaks of only take place and are described as associated with the church age. The tribulation and the millennium are not considered mysteries because they occurred not during but after the church age. This further proves that the church will not be a part of, nor go through the tribulation, but will be caught up in the air, as we commonly refer to it as *the rapture* or the *catching away*. Paul shows this benefit as belonging to the Gentiles, who will be included as *fellowheirs* with the Jewish believers, as explained in verse 6. With this being so, we too can enjoy this wonderful blessing and benefit through the New Birth.

6 *That the Gentiles should be fellowheirs, and of the same body, and partakers of his promise in Christ by the gospel:* This section of the third chapter develops and explains the truth as it pertains to the Gentiles. If you told the Gentile person that they would enjoy the same benefit as the Jews, they would have laughed you to scorn. But it was so! The Gentiles are fellow heirs. They have the same right to the inheritance as the Jews. The inheritance is all the benefits of the covenant of grace; the knowledge of the truth, all church privileges, justification, adoption, and sanctification; the indwelling of the Spirit, and life everlasting; an inheritance so great that to comprehend it requires divine assistance, and elevates the soul to the confines of heaven. Hence, Paul prays (1, 17.18) that God would give the Ephesians the Spirit of revelation that they might know the riches of the glory of the inheritance to which they had been called. (Hodge)

It is such a fantastic truth that someone so despised can enjoy the full benefits of the grace of God found in Christ by the gospel. The only thing that made this possible is what Christ did on the cross when he shed His blood and became a Ransom for all. This was a national example of what Christ can do for such a despised people as was the Gentile nation (especially by the Jews) and then on a personal level as it involves the most wicked and heinous person that one could be who comes to Christ with true repentance and is gloriously saved. John Newton described the work of grace well in this regard when he said, "And saved a wretch like me." Paul tells the Church at Ephesus that they could enjoy warm fellowship as fellow heirs while walking together as one. The reference to them being of the same body pertains to the church, and they are *partakers of his promise in Christ by the gospel*, meaning it was all made possible by the death, burial, and resurrection of the Lord Jesus Christ.

Gentiles participate in these blessings when they hear and respond to the gospel and enter a dynamic union with Christ, who is alive. By entering a relationship with Jesus Christ, the Gentiles become children of Abraham and heirs to the promised blessings made to him (Gal 3:7, 26–29). Union with Christ reverses the curse of exclusion that Paul spoke of in Eph 2:12. (Arnold)

7 *Whereof I was made a minister, according to the gift of the grace of God given unto me by the effectual working of his power.* Paul attributed his ministry and calling to God, ensuring that the Church at Colossi knew it was so and was according to the gift of the grace of God. He also let them know the source of his power and authority came from God. Paul says he is a minister, but that is a title of service, not exaltation. In the classical literature of ancient Greece, the minister (diakonos) "is a table waiter who is always at the bidding of his customers." (Wood) Paul uses a personal example of how he was made a minister by the effectual working of Christ's power. Paul told the church that having been made a minister could only be possible by the gift of grace. Salvation is a gift of grace; likewise, the ability to minister effectually is also a gift of the grace of God. Paul wanted them to know that even though he had been an arch-enemy of the church and persecuted it night and day while killing those who had a testimony of embracing Christ, he was now zealous in his service to Christ. He once loathed Christ, and now he loves Christ. The word minister is used for a "waiter" at a wedding feast (John 2:5, 9), a servant of a king (Matt 22:13), a disciple who is a servant of Christ (Matt 20:26 = Mark 10:43–44 = Luke 22:26), a minister (2 Cor 3:6; Col 1:23), and a "deacon" of a church (1 Tim 3:8, 12). (Hoehner)

In this verse, Paul transitions and concludes his discussion on the mysteries. He explains how he was made a steward to serve God's will faithfully. In Acts 26:16, Paul was commissioned as a steward of the grace of God. A marvelous change occurred that projected Paul into his work as a servant of Christ with the unique privilege of ministering the grace of God. No one else had that privileged responsibility that Paul then had. He recognizes when God makes you a minister; He gives you the grace necessary to minister. His grace is more than adequate; it is sufficient. Years ago, I recall hearing of the Rolls Royce salesman being asked how much horsepower the Rolls had. He answered: "It is adequate." That is certainly true in all regards in our salvation and our service to the Lord.

PAUL WAS USED TO REVEAL THE MYSTERY

8 *Unto me, who am less than the least of all saints, is this grace given, that I should preach among the Gentiles the unsearchable riches of Christ.* He knew that he had nothing to boast and marveled that he could enjoy the grace of God when he had been such an enemy of Christ before his conversion. Paul said that before his conversion, he was "the chiefest of sinners." This is such a notable contrast that he pictures all conversions in both a relative and actual sense (for all conversions are a contrast to before their conversion), as shown when he now says that he is less than the least of all saints. Each conversion dynamically reveals a new creature (2 Corinthians 5:17). Paul almost exclaims how unworthy he is and simultaneously shouts how wonderful God is in providing the needed grace. At least contextually, that is the energy in which it is being conveyed. It is a sudden outburst of amazement that God would use him this way. He uses that to challenge those to whom he speaks. When I think of how much Paul was used in the Lord's work and with such zeal, I wonder how he could think of himself as less than the least of all saints. When feeling like this, I would be tempted to believe it was false humility on his part. Yet, with additional thinking and observing what he had written, it seems that Paul could never escape the reality of how he worked against Christ and put to death believers while blaspheming anything about God. By reading such passages, he always seems to marvel that Christ would forgive him, much less use him for what he once so much hated.

"But while Paul was thus thankful for his office, his success greatly humbled him. The fuller a vessel becomes, the deeper it sinks in the water. A plenitude of grace is a cure for pride. Preachers ought to grow in grace, for their very calling places them at a great advantage since they are bound to search the Scriptures and to be much in prayer. It is a choice mercy to be permitted to preach the gospel. I wish some of you would be ambitious, for earnest preachers are wanted." (Spurgeon)

To one thus guilty, it was a great favor to be allowed to preach Christ. The expression unsearchable riches of Christ, riches which cannot be traced, past finding out, may mean either the riches or blessings that Christ bestows or the riches he possesses. Both ideas may be included, though the latter is doubtless the more prominent. The unsearchable riches of Christ are the fulness of the Godhead, the plenitude of all divine glories and perfections which dwell in him; the fulness of grace to pardon, to sanctify and save; everything in short, which renders him the satisfying portion of the soul. (Hodge) Value usually can be appraised and counted, but not so when describing the unsearchable riches of Christ. Those riches are unfathomable; also, His riches are incomprehensible. Paul said he could not measure the totality of Christ's greatness according to His riches; it was more than he could compress. It was as though Paul was saying I cannot explain or describe how great Christ's grace is, including all His virtues.

9 *And to make all men see what is the fellowship of the mystery, which from the beginning of the world hath been hid in God, who created all things by Jesus Christ:* Understanding that the converted, or those born again receive the things of God, the expression "all men see" is reserved only for the redeemed. However, I am sure that Paul would like to have seen all men saved and, thus, be able to know the fellowship of the mystery, also. Once people are saved, there is the additional responsibility of ensuring all who were saved understand what being saved means. Paul is, in some ways, the prototype of the Pastor today as he studies and prepares his own heart to deliver truth so that the believers will continue to understand the fellowship of the mystery, which includes the plan of the mystery to make it practically and spiritually available. Everything about the church was hidden in God until he revealed it to Paul and the others entrusted with the stewardship, including the plan of the mysteries being exercised. When Paul speaks of the fellowship of the mystery, which from the beginning of the world hath been hidden in God, he is letting the Ephesians know that all that was mysterious and was not revealed until Paul and some of the other Apostles were before that in the mind of God hidden until He saw fit for it to be shown along with the plans to implement them. For God to reveal Himself to humanity, there had to be one who would receive it and further reveal it without making changes to accommodate his thinking. Paul was such a man. He had been skillfully trained in the Old Testament Law and was very devout to it, so much so that he was unwilling to accept Jesus as the Messiah. That was due to his natural ignorance of such truth. But after his Damascus Road experience, things changed because he was changed. Paul had such gravity and seriousness about the things of God and, at the same time, marveled that God would use him. With that mental and Spiritual state and being a chosen vessel, God revealed the mystery to him. Therefore, the hidden things were finally revealed. The mysteries were in Christ's mind and always were, as they were revealed, and the created design of those mysteries was made by the same who created all things.

CHAPTER SEVEN
Ephesians 3:10-21

THE CHURCHES SPECIAL ROLE

VERSE SUMMARIES 3:10-21

We can understand so much about the church that the Church at Ephesus could not before Paul taught them. We are blessed to have the Canon of Truth, the Word of God, complete. Just the same where the Church at Ephesus was blessed to have Paul speaking to them of the mysteries about the Church directly through this ancient Letter. We both can recognize the church's unique role. It is through the church that the wisdom of God is known.

10 *To the intent that now unto the principalities and powers in heavenly places might be known by the church the manifold wisdom of God.* This is a remarkable statement and very weighty in that it seems to be saying that the church is modeling the work of God for those in heavenly places, such as the angels, both the fallen and otherwise, to witness.

11 *According to the eternal purpose which he purposed in Christ Jesus our Lord.* God has a purpose and intent for all that goes on. Paul was letting the Church at Colossi know that this purpose was defined by *Christ Jesus our Lord*.

12 *In whom we have boldness and access with confidence by the faith of him.* Here, Paul is letting the Church, which included the Gentiles, know that they can approach the Throne of Grace with much confidence and boldness, which previously was unapproachable.

13 *Wherefore I desire that ye faint not at my tribulations for you, which is your glory.* Paul lets the Church at Ephesus know there was no need for them to be overwrought, for he was effectively serving with great purpose while accomplishing all that God required of him.

14 *For this cause I bow my knees unto the Father of our Lord Jesus Christ.* After Paul had expounded upon the greatness of God as it pertained to both the Greeks and the Hebrews, he continued to pray where he left off and from what he said in between it made his prayer more understandable.

15 *Of whom the whole family in heaven and earth is named.* Paul refers to praying to the Father of the Lord Jesus Christ, and the word Father is notable as indicated in this verse. This is how Paul shows the origin of all blessings in the Christian Family belongs to Him and Him alone when using this title.

16 *That he would grant you, according to the riches of his glory, to be strengthened with might by his Spirit in the inner man.* This is a rich verse when speaking of the riches of His glory as identified as the Person with omnipotence, omniscience, and omnipresence.

17 *That Christ may dwell in your hearts by faith; that ye, being rooted and grounded in love.* Faith Comes from the Word of God. The more that the Word of God has taken root and the Spirit fills the believer; the more evident the dwelling of Christ in our hearts will be.

18 *May be able to comprehend with all saints what is the breadth, and length, and depth, and height;* The old students of Scripture indicate this statement is a mathematical term used in describing more than "range and domain." It is an incomprehensible statement that does not allow Christ's goodness to be boxed in.

19 *And to know the love of Christ, which passeth knowledge, that ye might be filled with all the fulness of God.* The infinite love of Christ is to be known but not comprehended to the extent that it can be measured. When the adverb "so" is used in John 3:16, it implies the great sacrifice on the cross by Jesus!

20 *Now unto him that is able to do exceeding abundantly above all that we ask or think, according to the power that worketh in us,* power of Christ Jesus works in us who are believers on a plane that we are incapable of understanding.

21 *Unto him be glory in the church by Christ Jesus throughout all ages, world without end. Amen.* Paul ends the prayer to the Ephesians in a way that ensures that all the glory goes to Him.

The Beginning of the Commentary (3:10-21)

10 *To the intent that now unto the principalities and powers in heavenly places might be known by the church the manifold wisdom of God.* This is a remarkable statement and very weighty in that it seems to be saying that the church is modeling the work of God for those in heavenly places, such as the angels, both the fallen and otherwise, to witness. This verse comes across as written most simply but is profound in its theology. It is saying something about how, through the church, God reveals His triumph. E. F. Scott has provided a helpful and eloquent explanation of the drama of God's unfolding plan of salvation as a display of his wisdom:

"The hostile powers had sought to frustrate the work of God and believed they had succeeded when they conspired against Christ and brought about his Crucifixion. But unwittingly, they had been mere instruments in God's hands. The death of Christ had been the very means He had devised to accomplish His plan. So it is here declared that after their brief apparent triumph, the hostile powers had become aware of a divine wisdom they had never dreamed of. They saw the Church arising as the result of Christ's death and giving effect to what they could now perceive to have been the hidden purpose of God." (Scott)

It is through the church God designed especially to manifest His intelligence's highest order, infinite power, grace, and wisdom; in her consummation, the church must be the most glorious of his works. It should be recognized that only God could be the reason for all the church accomplishes. Thus, the church should realize that "where the Spirit of the Lord is, there is liberty." 2 Corinthians 3:17. The church should be glorious without "spot or wrinkle" because that is God's intent. Paul believed that *preaching the Gospel* was how God ordained this to be accomplished. Paul regarded it as such a great joy and high honor, and so should it be with every preacher ordained by God to preach. To me, Paul said less than the least was this grace given. And to imagine that the angelic beings, principalities, and the powers in heaven have the church as a teaching model. Just grasping this thought causes me to shudder. I cannot comprehend what is being said, but slightly. I am not sure, but it could be possible that the fallen angels, including Satan himself, are gleaning from or observing what Christ does through His church. If so, they must acknowledge that God showed His strength in man's weakness. If we genuinely regard this, it should cause us to be more responsible in what we do regarding our fellow human beings, but in addition to that, God had chosen His church to reveal His greatness in a way beyond just that.

His wisdom is revealed to principalities and powers in heavenly places. See Ephesians 1:21; 6:12; Colossians 1:16: 2:10,15; 1 Peter 1:9-12. Principalities and powers are rulers, authorities, or possessors of power of various kinds. Since these are in heavenly places, they must be spiritual. Chapter 1 revealed that, due to Jesus 'role in our salvation, God highly exalted Him above all these principalities and powers. The references show that these terms can be used for either good or bad spirit beings. I am unsure what is meant here, but both are probably included. 1 Peter 1:12 says that angels learn from this revelation as it is known. In the past, it had been hidden from them and men. In any case, it surely is true that, as God's will was revealed through the church, spirit beings, good and bad, were enabled for the first time to understand the mystery God had previously hidden. (Pratte)

11 *According to the eternal purpose which he purposed in Christ Jesus our Lord.* God has a purpose and intent for all that goes on. Paul was letting the Church at Ephesus know that this purpose was defined by Christ Jesus our Lord. Paul lets the Church at Ephesus know it is God's Plan, reason, and purpose for all that takes place. He is the Sovereign One who ordained everything done decently and in order. When Paul mentioned "according to the eternal purpose," he was saying this was not an afterthought he came up with as a stop-gap to take care of what was happening, but that it was foreordained based upon His foreknowledge. When words like eternal are applied, they refer to God and God alone, for He is the only One with eternality. This verse shows how carefully God protects Truth. Then Christ Jesus, the Holder of this Truth, revealed it through Paul to the Church. (And others under Confluent Inspiration without compromise who are a part of the Canon in their sacred writings that pertain to those mysteries). This also means that the government of God is under His control. His control is also ordained, and that is so because He has perfect knowledge and awareness, as shown in Romans 13:1-3, 1. Let every soul be subject unto the higher powers. For there is no power but of God: the powers that be are ordained of God. 2 Whosoever therefore resisteth the power, resisteth the ordinance of God: and they that resist shall receive to themselves damnation. 3 For rulers are not a terror to good works, but to the evil. Wilt thou then not be afraid of the power? do that which is good, and thou shalt have praise of the same:

Everything in God's creation is under His control. Just as He rules the governments on earth, so does he govern the creation in the Heavenlies.

12 *In whom we have boldness and access with confidence by the faith of him.* Here, Paul is letting the Church, which included the Gentiles, know that they can approach the Throne of Grace with much confidence and boldness, which previously was unapproachable. Paul does not suggest that his boldness and ability to access different situations come from himself alone but from God. This is the meaning of Philippians 4:13. When Paul said he could "do all things through Christ, which strengthens me," it was with the same belief as when he said, "We have boldness and access with confidence by faith in him." To properly understand the *access and the boldness* that Paul speaks of requires understanding in contrast to the old economy of Law, including its priests and the priestly requirements, where there was no boldness whatsoever during the Priestly exercise. The entire concept of the Old Testament priesthood was based upon a Holy dread. The priest had to meet over 140 external requirements to approach the most holy place where the offering was made on the day of atonement. The dread was based on whether or not God would accept His offering. The priest would likely think of the two sons of Aaron who were struck down with the fire of God for offering *strange fire* when they were presenting their offerings lest they make a similar mistake. *Boldness and access* were not descriptive words to describe those ancient offerings.

Yet, in the new economy, Christ has once and for all put off the wrath of God by sacrificing Himself as indicated here in Hebrews 10:9-13: **9** *Then said he, Lo, I come to do thy will, O God. He taketh away the first, that he may establish the second.* **10** *By the which will we are sanctified through the offering of the body of Jesus Christ once for all.* **11** *And every priest standeth daily ministering and offering oftentimes the same sacrifices, which can never take away sins:* **12** *But this man, after he had offered one sacrifice for sins for ever, sat down on the right hand of God;* **13** *From henceforth expecting till his enemies be made his footstool.*

With this being so, it does not mean that we should carelessly or casually enter into the presence of God. There should be no arrogance but great respect when entering by faith into His holy presence, as indicated in Hebrews 4:16, "*Let us therefore come boldly unto the throne of grace, that we may obtain mercy, and find grace to help in time of need.*"

13 *Wherefore I desire that ye faint not at my tribulations for you, which is your glory*. Paul lets the Church at Ephesus know there was no need for them to be overwrought, for he was effectively serving with great purpose while accomplishing all that God required of him. He wants the church at Ephesus to know they need not be overwhelmed by what Paul was going through because he was not. He genuinely felt that the prison was where God wanted him to be to serve God's purpose, showing how God can achieve so much with seemingly so little from the standpoint of him being in prison yet getting so much accomplished. God used him extensively as he wrote the other Prison Epistles, including Philemon, Colossians, and Philippians. Paul does not want them to lose heart and perhaps even be mindful of how God had richly blessed the church. Here are some examples of what has already been mentioned:

1. Blessed us with every spiritual blessing in Christ (Ephesians 1:3-14). **2.** Seated us in Christ, at God's right hand (Ephesians 1:20-22). **3.** Loved us with great love and made us alive, regardless of our past (Ephesians 2:1-5). **4.** Promised to show us kindness in future ages (Ephesians 2:6-7). **5.** Gave us the gift of salvation (Ephesians 2:8-10). **6.** Brought Gentiles near to Him after ages of alienation (Ephesians 2:1-19). **7.** Fitted believers together for His habitation (Ephesians 2:20-22). **8.** Revealed the mystery of including the Gentiles in His eternal purpose (Ephesians 3:1-11). (Crews)

As the song says, we often need to count our blessings, "naming them one by one." By doing so, it will uplift our spirits. It was like Paul here was saying, "Look what we have in Christ," and with it being so, "Don't worry about me." Paul felt that as long as they were being helped by any suffering he experienced, he was willing to suffer on their behalf, knowing it would redound to God's glory.

THE PRAYER RESUMES

As he began offering prayer to the Church at Ephesus, as noted in verse number one, Paul digressed and then said some essential things about the *mysteries being revealed* that we may not have known about had there not been such a digression. In verse fourteen, he picks up where he left off in prayer for the church and, in a very humble way, "bows his knees before the Lord" in humble adoration and prayer on behalf of the Church at Ephesus.

14 *For this cause, I bow my knees unto the Father of our Lord Jesus Christ*; After Paul had expounded upon the greatness of God as it pertained to both the Greeks and the Hebrews, he continued to pray where he left off and from what he said in between made his prayer even more understandable. Paul paused until now and perhaps picked it up with even greater zeal. Paul had great reason to pray a prayer with a heart of thanksgiving. After he paused his prayer and explained the ramifications of the mystery, there was so very much that was revealed about how the blessings of God befell the Church at Ephesus. In this state, Paul bows his knees unto the Father to show respect and adoration to the Lord for the ones he prays for. This manner of prayer is not an absolute pattern for body posture but mainly an indication of Paul's heart and how his heart attitude moved him to pray in such a manner. He was not just bowing before an earthly king but before God the Father of our Lord Jesus Christ, who is "King of Kings and Lord of Lords." Paul expresses much love as he communicates with the Church at Ephesus, a church he had not preached to or visited, yet he prays fervently for them. Christ's love was also his love. Christ loved the church and gave Himself for it.

The peculiar Christian designation of God expresses the covenant relation in which he stands to believers. Because he is the Father of our Lord Jesus Christ, our incarnate God and Saviour, he is our Father and accessible to us in prayer. We can approach him acceptably in no other character than as the God who sent the Lord Jesus to be our propitiation and mediator. Therefore, by faith in him as reconciled, we address him as the Father of our Lord Jesus Christ. (Hodge)

15 *Of whom the whole family in heaven and earth is named.* Paul refers to praying to the Father of the Lord Jesus Christ, and the word Father is notable, as indicated in this verse. This is how Paul shows the origin of all blessings in the Christian Family belongs to Him and Him alone when using this title. When Paul, in the previous verse, spoke of the Father of the Lord Jesus, there is a paternal sense being expressed just as the earthly father is spoken of as the head of the family. This designation says our relationship connects to the heavenly Father, as seen in the Christian family. Paul is not referring to a relationship with Him being our Creator but with Him being our Spiritual Father. But as Creator God and the One who sustains all, He is the Father (Originator) of all groups. The expression *Father of* is used in many ways, as one would say that Sigmoid Freud is the father of modern psychology, or Galileo has been called the Father of Modern Science. Hippocrates has been called the Father of Medicine. But there is One who supersedes them all, and that is God. Specifically, however, Paul seems to be referring to God as the Father of the redeemed.

God the Father is the one who creates (3:9) and thus names every family in heaven and on earth. He is a God alive and acting now, rather than a god who has died and is no longer active in history. God's ability to create and name every family in heaven and on earth stresses his sovereignty and fatherhood. He is the one who can perform more than we ask or think, as expressed in the doxology in verses 20–21. It should be noted that the early disciples of Jesus extolled God as the sovereign Lord who created heaven, earth, and sea (Acts 4:24). It is to this sovereign God that Paul prays the following prayer. (Hoehner)

16 *That he would grant you, according to the riches of his glory, to be strengthened with might by his Spirit in the inner man;* This is indeed a rich verse when speaking of the riches of His glory as identified as the Person with omnipotence, omniscience, and His quality of omnipresence. **17** *That Christ may dwell in your hearts by faith; that ye, being rooted and grounded in love.* The more that the Word of God has taken root and the Spirit fills the believer; the more evident the dwelling of Christ in our hearts will be. These are additional things Paul is praying for. He wanted the Church at Ephesus to know that all the mentioned blessings were to bring strength to the Ephesians so they might experience His strength with might by His Spirit in the Inner man. All was by *the riches of His glory* that Paul speaks of, which cannot be measured. Paul is saying the strengthening takes place within the inner man. This is a way that Paul describes our feelings, emotions, relationships (how we feel in those relationships), and all the things that make us who we are. He is saying that is where Jesus is living within us, and as Colossians reminds us, "*Christ in you the hope of glory.*" Paul spoke of what this means as it pertains to the riches of His glory, "*To whom God was pleased to make known what is the riches of the glory of this mystery among the Gentiles, which is Christ in you, the hope of glory.*"—Colossians 1:27. His Spirit is strengthening our spirit and is to be enjoyed by the church continually. Christ will be eternally revealing Himself to us so that we may continually have His strength to accomplish those things necessary before we go into eternity according to the great riches He has for us. Our abundance is based entirely upon His abundance, and we can do nothing without Him but all things "through Christ which strengthens us." (Philippians 4:13).

The Holy Spirit strengthens this very center of a person, resulting in the deep indwelling of Christ in one's heart by faith. Hence, in Ephesians, the indwelling involves the individual believer instead of the corporate indwelling mentioned in 2:21–22. Interestingly, once again, as elsewhere in Ephesians (cf. 1:4–14, 17; 2:18, 22; 3:4–5, 14–17; 4:4–6; 5:18–20), Paul includes the Trinity: the Father (v. 14), the Spirit (v. 16), and the Son (v. 17). All three persons of the Trinity are very involved in the redemption and growth of believers. Here, Paul prays to the Father that the Spirit strengthens them with the result that Christ be deeply rooted in the lives of the believers through faith. (Hoehner)

When Paul prayed that his readers might be strengthened in the inner man, he prayed that Christ might dwell in them.

The omnipresent and infinite God is said to dwell wherever he specifically and permanently manifests his presence. Thus he is said to dwell in heaven, Ps. 123, 1; to dwell among the children of Israel, Numb. 35, 34; in Zion, Ps. 9, 11; with him, that is of a humble and contrite spirit, Is. 57, 11; and in his people, 2 Cor. 6, 16. Sometimes it is God who is said to dwell in the hearts of his people, sometimes the Spirit of God; sometimes, as in Rom. 8, 9, it is the Spirit of Christ; and sometimes, as Rom. 8, 10, and in the passage before us, it is Christ himself. (Hodge)

The result of this taking place is that the love of God may be the result and the continuing result of what happens when the Spirit takes up residence with us, which will affect all we do. Later in this Epistle, the Lord shows the effect of the Spirit living within us and how His love can impact our relationships by having a Spirit-filled life (Ephesians 5:18-33). Paul is letting the Ephesians know they are incredibly blessed to have the capacity to think and act according to the Spirit and know when the Word of God is constantly planted in the believer's hearts. With this being so, we have the means and the knowledge to act accordingly. In addition to the working of the Spirit, we must let the Word of Christ dwell in us richly, as Paul told the Church at Colossi.

18 *May be able to comprehend with all saints what is the breadth, and length, and depth, and height;* The old students of Scripture indicate this statement is a mathematical term used in describing more than "range and domain." It is an incomprehensible statement that does not allow Christ's goodness to be boxed in. **19** *And to know the love of Christ, which passeth knowledge, that ye might be filled with all the fulness of God.* The infinite love of Christ is to be known but not comprehended to the extent that it can be measured. When the adverb "so" is used in John 3:16, it implies the great sacrifice on the cross by Jesus! The terms breadth, length, depth, and height are also ways of expressing an infinite love and the potential of being filled with all the fullness of God. Wow! And that is what Paul must have been saying. It was like he was standing on the top of Mount Everest, viewing as far as the eye could see in every direction, and saying, "Wow, this does not begin to describe who and what God is." Or could it be like gazing into the skies knowing that there are billions of stars in its many galaxies, but we can only adequately see a very small few, which are just a tiny part of our solar system? Though we cannot see them all, we have learned to believe there is much more than what we see with our naked eyes. So is the love of God; we can only recognize a small portion of his total love for us. Paul is speaking of the magnitude of these things. Still, with all these resources, Paul was letting the Ephesians and all believers know that we have all that we need and can be filled with all the fullness of God, which comes from saturating oneself with the Word of God and the work of the Spirit. He wants them to see what he is seeing and feel what he is feeling.

20 *Now unto him that is able to do exceeding abundantly above all that we ask or think, according to the power that worketh in us*, power of Christ Jesus works in us who are believers on a plane that we are incapable of understanding. **21** *Unto him be glory in the church by Christ Jesus throughout all ages, world without end. Amen.* Paul ends the prayer to the Ephesians in a way that ensures that all the glory goes to Him. Paul is writing a doxology of praise while closing out his prayer, and with it so clearly said and with such feeling as Paul used when closing out this chapter, there is not much more that can be said to add to the words he had spoken. They are so clearly said and exclaim themselves. "Praise God from whom all blessings flow!"

In these three chapters, we have seen the wealth believers

can enjoy that agrees with the overall theme of Ephesians. But by way of application, and very importantly, he wanted the kind of glory he speaks of to resonate throughout the church. Every song sung, every testimony given, and every sermon preached ought to reveal Christ's glory. Then, as the church moves about collectively and individually, it should be showing forth and impacting its homes, its businesses, its government, and its schools. Let the world see the glory of Christ, knowing that Christ in you is the hope of glory! As the Scriptures teach us: **16** *Let your light so shine before men, that they may see your good works, and glorify your Father which is in heaven.*

CHAPTER EIGHT

Ephesians 4:1-6

The Conditions for the Believer's Walk

VERSE SUMMARIES 4:1-6

1 *I therefore, the prisoner of the Lord, beseech you that ye walk worthy of the vocation wherewith ye are called.* After Paul shows the Church at Colossi its profound riches that are found in Jesus Christ, he challenges them to a responsible walk being found worthy of the vocation, (ministry) that they have been called.

2 *With all lowliness and meekness, with longsuffering, forbearing one another in love.* Paul, in a kind way, insists that their motives and ministry be according to their love for each other. Humbleness of heart should character the true church.

3 *Endeavouring to keep the unity of the Spirit in the bond of peace.* Loving each other as they should requires much discipline, as indicated by the word endeavoring. Paul will further address the unity aspect of their relationship in the verses, showing that their walk ought to be unified.

4 *There is one body, and one Spirit, even as ye are called in one hope of your calling*; Paul is letting the church know that they are not a many-bodied church but just one, monitored and led by one Spirit, for them to attend to their specific calling.

5 *One Lord, one faith, one baptism;* Paul wanted the Church in Ephesians to know for them to ensure unity in faith and *knowledge*; they had to know that one Lord was representing one faith. Just as there was one circumcision in the Old Testament for the Jews, there was one baptism for the believer.

6 *One God and Father of all, who is above all, and through all, and in you all.* God's triune work is shown in this verse: above, through, and in you all. This is about the church and its government, including His power.

The Beginning of the Commentary (4:1-6)

Walking With Gratitude

Unity is the theme of this section, where Paul shows how important it is for faith and truth to agree. Knowing that faith cometh by hearing and hearing by the Word of God, there must be the ministering of Truth to accomplish that. Otherwise, there would be no Spiritual growth or absolute unity. Paul also wants them to know the tremendous value they have come from Christ, and their walk ought to be in appreciation.

1 *I, therefore, the prisoner of the Lord, beseech you that ye walk worthy of the vocation wherewith ye are called; therefore, the prisoner of the Lord.* "His imprisonment, which might have been supposed more likely to render him despised, is appealed to, as we have already seen, to confirm his authority. It was the seal of that embassy with which he had been honored. Whatever belongs to Christ, though in the eyes of men, it may be attended by ignominy, ought to be viewed by us with the highest regard. The apostle's prison is more venerable than the splendid retinue or triumphal chariot of kings." (Adam Clarke)

After Paul shows the Church at Colossi the profound riches found in Jesus Christ, he challenges them to a responsible walk, being found worthy of the vocation (ministry) they have been called. In the first three chapters, Paul has laid his foundation of truth regarding the exceeding great riches that the Ephesians and, for that matter, all believers have in Christ. As chapters one through three show the believer's wealth, we will examine the believer's walk in chapters four through five and the believer's warfare in chapter six. The transitional word "Therefore" hinging what he speaks now on everything that has been said about Christ's greatness, His love, His relationship with the Father, and the Children in the family of God as known by the church. Paul speaks much more but wants the mainly Gentile Church to know that they are equal heirs to the blessings that come through Christ that would have been previously directed toward the Jews. They are now in Christ as the church as one body. Paul begins by reminding them that he is a prisoner, emphasizing being the Lord's prisoner and saying it is a "badge of honor" to be his prisoner. In the best and the worst of conditions, Paul leads by example. What an example he was. Yet, he does not challenge them in a haughty manner but instead in a humble manner. He calls for their humility by saying, "Walk worthy of the vocation wherewith ye are called." There is a call for unity, as shown by the multiple use of the word "one" in Ephesians. This unity is possible because the believers share a common belief that, socially and Spiritually, they can work out their differences and cooperate for the glory of Christ in the church. He expounded on that with the church doing so that the powers in the heavenlies could observe it as being not a mere work of man but a true work of God. This work through the Church was how the mystery was revealed. The vocation to which they were called was both a Spiritual work on God's part and human work on their part, with Christ working through them to further expound the work of Christ in and through the Church. This is why Paul instructs them after showing them all God has done so they may live their lives and be fulfilled in the faith. For that to occur, they must obey God so they may not be unworthy of such distinguished grace. In the next two verses, there are five graces mentioned on the part of the believer, with the first being mentioned as lowliness followed by meekness, which should be revealed in the following manner as written by *Wilhelmus à Brakel* (1635-1711)

2 *With all lowliness and meekness, with longsuffering, forbearing one another in love*; Paul, in a kind way, insists that their motives and ministry be according to their love for each other. Humbleness of heart should character the true church...Meekness is the believer's even-tempered disposition of heart, which originates from union with God in Christ, consisting of self-denial and love for his neighbor. This results in having fellowship with his neighbor in an agreeable, congenial, and loving manner in relinquishing his rights, enduring the violation of his rights without becoming angry, being forgiving, and rewarding it with good. The essence of this virtue is having an even-tempered disposition of heart, resulting in there being strength under control. (Brakel) Meekness cannot take place unless there first is *lowliness of heart*. Lowliness of heart is humility. Humility is the opposite of pride, from which comes rudeness of speech, quarreling, contempt for others, contentions, boasting, arrogance, and a hot temper, among many more sins of passion.

Longsuffering also fits neatly in Paul's description of what will constitute a good Godly walk that helps let others see Christ in you. Notice what William Barclay says of longsuffering: "Makrothumia is the spirit which bears insult and injury without bitterness and complaint. The spirit can suffer unpleasant people with graciousness and fools without irritation. The most illuminating thing about it is that it is commonly used in the New Testament as the attitude of God towards men (Romans 2:4; 9:22; I Timothy 1:16; I Peter 3:20) If God had been a man, he would have wiped out this world long ago, but he has that patience which bears with all our sinning and will not cast us on our dealing with our fellow men; we must reproduce this loving, forbearing, forgiving, patient attitude of God towards ourselves. Paul asks the impenitent sinner if he despises the patience of God (Romans 2:4). Paul speaks of the perfect patience of Jesus to him. Peter speaks of the patient waiting in the days of Noah." (Barclay) Had God been man, he would not be forbearing or patient, wiping us all out.

A favorite way of describing longsuffering of mine is what I heard years ago when a speaker said that longsuffering means "slow to thunder." When lightning strikes and is a great way off, it is perceived immediately, but the thunder takes a while, depending on its distance. That is the kind of longsuffering Paul thought of when he wrote to the Ephesians (being slow to thunder). How much better would it be not to react suddenly without thinking about what you are saying or will do in a given situation? Someone said when you speak, use a rule of carpentry, "measure twice and saw once." That could help one to be more longsuffering or slow to thunder. The next word Paul used was forbearing, which goes along with longsuffering. It is being patient and letting the love of God help you tolerate certain things one normally would not tolerate. Your tolerance has an endpoint to minister further to the one doing wrong. This does not also mean that you condone that which is wrong. Not at all. If you did, you would be a partaker of one's evil deeds. Sometimes, we are upset by the sins of others. Some people think longsuffering means you overlook it, say little or nothing, and continue fellowshipping them. Many Scriptures teach that love requires us to speak out, oppose sin, and refuse to in any way encourage it (Ephesians 5:11; 2 Timothy 4:2-4; Revelation 3:19). But still love suffers long – we do not seek to harm them but help them to repent and try to keep others from being influenced by them. If they repent, we must be willing to forgive. (Pratte) Forbearing one another in love. This agrees with what is elsewhere taught, that "love suffereth long and is kind." (1 Corinthians 13:4.) Where love is strong and prevalent, we shall perform many acts of mutual forbearance. (Clarke)

3 *Endeavouring to keep the unity of the Spirit in the bond of peace.* Loving each other as they should requires much discipline, as indicated by the word endeavoring. Paul will further address the unity aspect of their relationship with each other in the following verses, showing that their walk ought to be unified. It should be more than normal for the believer to strive for unity in the church where the Spirit of the Lord brings liberty. The love of God directs one's heart in agreement with the Word of God and then is safely led by His Spirit. The Spirit is a special gift to the church to help it maintain unity, and that unity can be easily destroyed even by one disgruntled person who is not filled with and led by the Spirit. Paul is warning the Church at Ephesus and all believers to give all diligence, as Peter said in his Epistle, maintaining unity and devotion to Him, thereby ensuring peace. This indicates that the Lord brought them together, and there was peace when the Lord did so and is writing to encourage them to maintain their peace. Peace and unity are wonderful commodities for the church to enjoy together when the Spirit leads. The Jews and the Gentiles in the church, because of this, are already enjoying a bond between them that before would have otherwise seemed impossible.

Because of the work of the Spirit who incorporates us into this new body (1 Corinthians 12:13), believers experience the reality of a new community where there are no racial divisions or schisms of any kind. It is incumbent on believers to preserve this unity that has been attained at a great cost. Christ's peace is like a rope that ties believers from diverse backgrounds together into a unified whole. The word Paul uses here for "bond" (σύνδεσμος) is related to the term at the beginning of the passage that describes his imprisonment: Paul is a prisoner (δέσμιος [4:1 and 3:1], a cognate of δεσμά ["chains"] and of δέω, which means "to bind"). Just as Paul is bound to his guard by his chain, he wants these believers in Asia Minor to be bound together in peace and love. (Arnold) In these three verses, Paul encourages the church to walk in a manner that would reveal a Christ-like Spirit before those they walk, showing forth a testimony of Grace as they do and with them being bonded by peace.

Notice the One's in This Section

Notice how "one" is the theme or what this section emphasizes as Paul wrote to the Ephesians in verses four through thirteen. One body, one Spirit, one hope, one Lord, one faith, one baptism, One God and Father, and the unity of faith (as one). We will examine this section as Paul emphasizes the parallels related to unity. There are 7 "ones" mentioned in verses 4,5 and 6.

4 *There is one body, and one Spirit, even as ye are called in one hope of your calling;* Paul is letting the church know that they are not a many-bodied church but just one, monitored and led by one Spirit, for them to attend to their specific calling. Paul begins by mentioning one body in reference to the church, which also speaks of the unity that should describe the church without schisms and divisions. In a practical sense, Paul speaks to the Ephesians as one church body, representing all true churches in their function and mode of operation, including their empowerment. In the ultimate and universal sense, the completed church will not be recognized as such until the Church of the Firstborn, as Hebrews 12:27 speaks of. "To the general assembly and church of the firstborn, which are written in heaven, and to God the Judge of all, and to the spirits of just men made perfect." This will be the final gathering of all the redeemed, including the Jews and the Gentiles. Meanwhile, everything now is geared around the local church, and to be practically understood requires us to think that way. As described by Paul, the unity spoken of involves the work of the Holy Spirit to achieve such. Christ, in you the hope of glory. The calling is to salvation and service. The hope is the grandest expectation of what is described in the Bible that will occur with certainty.

5 *One Lord, one faith, one baptism*; Paul wanted the Church in Ephesians to know for them to ensure unity in faith and knowledge; they had to know that one Lord represented one faith. Just as there was one circumcision in the Old Testament for the Jews, there was one baptism for the believer. When describing the church, Paul did not boast about or explain the plurality of gods to choose whom you would but declares there is only One true and living God who is Lord over all. Thus, he says One Lord. In this verse, the word Lord refers to Christ, the Head of the Church. In the previous verse, he spoke of the Holy Spirit, who empowers the church. In the next verse, he says of the Heavenly Father over everything. He shows the work of the Trinity in the church. Just as the Trinity is seen in the church's work and its founding, so was the Trinity at work at creation. The "one baptism" most likely refers to the internal reality of having been baptized into (identified with) the "one Lord" using the "one faith" mentioned in this verse. The one baptism is so because it happens at conversion, a one-time event. One faith. This is the fifth bond of union enumerated by the apostle. Many commentators deny that the word πίστις is ever used for the object of faith or the things believed; they, therefore, deny that one faith here means one creed. But as this interpretation is by the general usage of language, and as there are so many cases in which the objective sense of the word is best suited to the context, there seems to be no sufficient reason for refusing to admit it. In Gal. 1:23, Paul says, "He preached the faith;" in Acts 6, 7, men, it is said, "were obedient to the faith." The apostle Jude speaks of "the faith once delivered to the saints." In these and many other instances, the objective sense is natural. In many cases, both senses of the word may be united. (Hodge). Water baptism pictures an aspect of this baptism and also identifies the believer with Christ's crucifixion, including His death, burial, and resurrection. Another picture baptism includes is circumcision, which identifies the Jew with the Old Covenant; baptism identifies the church member with the New Covenant and, of course, the church.

6 *One God and Father of all, who is above all, and through all, and in you all.* God's triune work is shown here in reference to the church. Above, through, and in you all is about the church and its government, including His power. When Paul is saying, One God it is such a comforting statement. If there were two or more gods, there would be disharmony if they were both gods; by definition, who God is would make multiple gods an impossibility. Yet, there were and are those who operate as though there is no God to be accountable or responsible to. In a practical-spiritual sense, God is to be reckoned as the God of creation and all that there is, as well as God over the church. Here, Paul is not speaking of God as the ruler and sustainer of all things as in the universal, but in the government that belongs to the church Spiritually. This identity is accurate, not God being God from a remote or distant location. It is Him being a part of the church's breath, life, and function, preferably from a position of unity. The term Father denotes this in a family way. When people begin to feel harmony and closeness to each other, they refer to themselves as a family. I listened to an interview of a star Georgia football player describing him and his fellow players as a family. You could sense their camaraderie toward each other, which showed their unity. That should characterize the church as a family of believers, with God being the Father of all, as the football coach would be over his players.

CHAPTER NINE
Ephesians 4:7-16

The Way the Church Operates

The humility of Christ resulted in His exaltation and serves as a pattern of how we, when becoming servants of Christ, should do so with Him being our example and what an Example is He. When He was seated on the right hand of God and given authority over all creation, He also chose to give to those who minister to Him and are called to do so gifts to serve His purpose. Paul tells the Church at Ephesus to recognize what wealth was there and how important it is to serve with gratitude.

VERSE SUMMARIES 4:7-16

7 *But unto every one of us is given grace according to the measure of the gift of Christ.* This is a statement by Paul saying that all church members will have stewardship responsibilities given by God to whom He pleases, as much or as little as He pleases—remembering that God owns everything as the Creator. He has endowed us with something for a lifetime, which makes us stewards, and we are accountable to God at the Judgment Seat.

8 *Wherefore he saith, When he ascended up on high, he led captivity captive, and gave gifts unto men.* Paul seems to be referring to or at least thinking about an event that took place in the Old Testament described in the Psalms and making a similar statement recalling ancient warfare, representing a victorious warrior parading his captures.

9 *(Now that he ascended, what is it but that he also*

descended first into the lower parts of the earth? This is where Paul is describing in a somewhat parallel fashion to the Psalms 68 description of the described war, and the Psalm has Messianic qualities about it.

10 *He that descended is the same also that ascended up far above all heavens, that he might fill all things.)* This seems to be Paul's description of the completed work of Christ as he is exalted back to the Father's right hand.

11 *And he gave some, apostles; and some, prophets; and some, evangelists; and some, pastors and teachers.* This list given by Paul shows how the church was inaugurated and, in some ways, continues. The purpose is shown in verse 12.

12 *For the perfecting of the saints, for the work of the ministry, for the edifying of the body of Christ:* To bring about the perfecting or the maturing of the saints, the work of the ministry, and the edifying of the church these ministers mentioned are so given.

13 *Till we all come in the unity of the faith, and of the knowledge of the Son of God, unto a perfect man, unto the measure of the stature of the fulness of Christ:* Paul was saying the purpose of ministers is to aid in the development of unity. The two aspects Paul emphasizes are faith and knowledge (doctrine) to agree to the purpose of growing continuously in the fullness of Christ.

14 *That we henceforth be no more children, tossed to and fro, and carried about with every wind of doctrine, by the sleight of men, and cunning craftiness, whereby they lie in wait to deceive;* Paul in 1 Corinthians speaks of babes, and here as children meaning the Church is to mature beyond the baby or child stage and perform as being adults. He knew this would protect against instability and deception by them not knowing the Truth.

15 *But speaking the truth in love, may grow up into him in all things, which is the head, even Christ*: Love is the dominating theme coming from Christ, and Paul understands that to be so. Therefore, he shows the importance of the church in exhibiting love in all they do. The ministry workers were to speak the Truth, knowing that as they did, they should temper it by having God's love when they spoke. They were to do this knowing they were to answer to Christ, the head of the church.

16 *From whom the whole body fitly joined together and compacted by that which every joint supplieth, according to the effectual working in the measure of every part, maketh increase of the body unto the edifying of itself in love.* Paul is simply using the metaphor of the body as representing or picturing the church that there should be the effective working of the ministry to build up the church in love. Satan is not only an enemy of Truth and faith but also promotes hatred instead of love.

The Beginning of the Commentary (4:7-16)

The unity of believers stems from a common calling by God. Unity is also based on a relationship with the one true God, who has called us into a bond with himself. Four different times in this passage, Paul uses the word "call" as part of the basis of his appeal. This calling is God's invitation to each of us to respond in faith to his offer of salvation and to become part of the people he is gathering to be his very own. Based on his choosing us, this calling is our opportunity to experience God's grace, mercy, and love because he has redeemed us, forgiven our sins, and united us with Christ in his resurrection and exaltation. Our privilege is to experience peace with God, closeness, and intimacy with him by virtue of our identification with Christ

(Ephesians Commentary, Zondervan). With proper respect, God the Father is above all, and through all, and in us all, as Paul said in this verse. Our calling represents God's initiative and his unmerited grace upon us. As Peter O'Brien has noted, we are "a society of pardoned rebels" on whom God has showered his favor.

To Everyone Given

7 *But unto every one of us is given grace according to the measure of the gift of Christ.* This is a statement by Paul saying that all church members will have stewardship responsibilities given by God to whom He pleases, as much or as little as He pleases—remembering that God owns everything as the Creator. He has endowed us with something for a lifetime, which makes us stewards, and we are accountable to God at the Judgment Seat. Paul explains to the Church of Ephesus the work of the Lord as determined by Christ in giving each member's gifts as a grace to complement and accomplish the church's work. Each person should strive to make sure they are discerning what God's grace or gift is for them. The gifts given are to be proportionately given for the benefit and the purpose of mutually helping each other, even as bearing one another's burdens if that should be the dominant need of the church or working together as a unit or as one for the edifying of the church. Paul tells the Church at Corinth the same thing in 1 Corinthians 14:4 and 1 Corinthians 12: 27-31: "Now there are diversities of gifts, but the same Spirit." "Us" in our Text verse means we are not to work apart from the main church as an isolated appendage.

As believers and thus members serve in the church, each person should covet the best gift, not selfishly, to the glory of Christ and the Father. **27** *Now ye are the body of Christ, and* *members in particular. 28 And God hath set some in the church, first apostles, secondarily prophets, thirdly teachers, after that miracles, then gifts of healings, helps, governments, diversities of tongues. 29 Are all apostles? are all prophets? are all teachers? are all workers of miracles? 30 Have all the gifts of healing? do all speak with tongues? do all interpret?31 But covet earnestly the best gifts: and yet shew I unto you a more excellent way.* Paul describes the foundational ministries and ministers as the church being formed in its early beginnings before the Scriptures were compiled and completed as the Canon, which contained 66 Books, with 39 in the Old Testament and 27 in the New Testament, which we refer to as the Bible. Paul uses the rhetorical method to distinguish among the members and to let them know that each member does not carry the same office or responsibility. Paul asks seven questions to accomplish this distinction. When he says, "Yet shew I unto you a more excellent way," he refers to Christ and the seeking after Him to make their ministry viable and very much alive with His power. These thoughts in Corinthians complement what is being said in Ephesians using the principle of hermeneutics that involves comparing Scripture with Scripture.

8 *Wherefore he saith, When he ascended up on high, he led captivity captive and gave gifts unto men.* Paul seems to be referring to or at least thinking about an event that took place in the Old Testament described in the Psalms and making a similar statement recalling ancient warfare, representing a victorious warrior parading his captures.

9 *(Now that he ascended, what is it but that he also descended first into the lower parts of the earth?* This is where Paul is describing in a somewhat parallel fashion to the Psalms 68 description of the described war and that Psalm has Messianic qualities about it.

10 *He that descended is the same also that ascended up far above all heavens, that he might fill all things.)* This seems to be Paul's description of the completed work of Christ as he is exalted back to the Father's right hand. There are several interpretations of these three verses, with seemingly very little strong agreement. I am unsure of its complete meaning to write as such. Still, I believe that Paul may have been thinking about Psalm 68, describing ancient warfare and the ensuing victory that comes from God as shown here, similar to what Paul is saying and maybe what is prompting him to say what is said in verses 18 and 19. *Thou hast ascended on high, thou hast led captivity captive: thou hast received gifts for men; yea, for the rebellious also, that the Lord God might dwell among them.***19** *Blessed be the Lord, who daily loadeth us with benefits, even the God of our salvation. Selah.* Instead of investing much time in explaining what all of this means, I would prefer to give a general understanding based on what is more obvious and how it relates when comparing scripture to scripture. He begins with a general statement: "When he ascended upon on high, he led captivity captive and gave gifts unto men." Then, he parenthetically makes an explanatory statement that includes verses nine and Ten. I remember that in math, one of the first rules for solving an equation was to clear up the parenthesis and proceed. That may be an excellent rule to follow in this instance.

Within the parenthesis, there is a brief explanation of the opening statement. The first word in the opening statement is "Wherefore," which refers to at least verse seven, which speaks of the gift of Christ from which is given grace in measured proportions as the Giver so desires. Then He ascended up high, but within the parentheses, it says He ascended *first* into the lower parts of the earth. Some interpret this as Christ, while in His Spirit before His resurrection, going into the heart of the earth (hell). I do not know… but I do know that there is very little that suggests that, so along with some of the ancient students of the Scriptures, I prefer to look at this as a description of Him humbling Himself and coming to the earth, even the grave. The God-Man's body is placed in the grave. That is as low as you can get for Jesus' body to be placed in the tomb because the tomb is associated with death and death with the curse. Yet He became a sin curse for us. Galatians 3:13 : "Christ hath redeemed us from the curse of the law, being made a curse for us: for it is written, Cursed is every one that hangeth on a tree:"

Then He ascended far above the heavens, which I believe refers to the visible or second heaven, and then is seated at God's, His Father's, right hand, which would be the third heaven and would be a triumphant victory over sin and death. This interpretation seems to agree with the total context, and Philippians and Colossians are also written from the same prison. As the Scriptures tell us, every word is to be established by two or three witnesses. The witness here seems to be these three prison epistles with the same theme regarding Jesus' crucifixion that began with His incarnation and concluded with His ascension. This is hermeneutically a way of interpreting Scripture by comparing Scripture with Scripture. Paul does not mention going to Hell (if it is the lowest part of the earth, as discussed here) in any other of his writings. If it were of such importance to be mentioned here, it would have been further explained elsewhere. I am not trying to sidestep the problematic manner of interpreting this section. Still, rather than developing all the possibilities, I discovered they each have problems. This interpretation, as it deals with the incarnation, crucifixion, and resurrection, would be consistent with the parallel Scriptures found in the other two prison Epistles.

The Different Ministries of the Church

11 *And he gave some, apostles; and some, prophets; and some, evangelists; and some, pastors and teachers;* This list given by Paul shows the way the church was inaugurated and in some of the ways continues. The purpose is shown in verse 12. When Paul said "he gave," that is the same as saying He Himself gave, speaking of Christ. Every good and perfect gift comes from above, and Christ is the One who does the giving. Paul lists the gifts for the benefit of the church (perfecting of the saints), beginning with the apostles.

And he gave some apostles. That is, he gave them gifts by which they were qualified to be apostles; who were such as were immediately called by Christ, and had their doctrine from him, and their commission to preach it; and were peculiarly and infallibly guided by the Spirit of God, and had the power to work miracles for the confirmation of their doctrine; and had the authority to go everywhere and preach the Gospel, and plant churches, and were not confined to any one particular place or church; this was the first and chief office in the church and of an extraordinary kind, and is now ceased; and though the apostles were before Christ's ascension, yet they had not received till then the fulness of the Spirit, and his extraordinary gifts to fit them for their office; nor did they enter upon the discharge of it in its large extent till that time; for they were not only to bear witness of Christ in Jerusalem, in Judea and Samaria but in the uttermost parts of the earth. (Gill) They were the original apostles specially chosen and commissioned by Jesus Christ. There were also other apostles during the church's beginning. Paul met two primary qualifications for an apostle: "He had seen the risen Christ, and Christ specially commissioned him for the work of the ministry. He also claims that he was an apostle in Acts 9:13: Am I not an apostle? am I not free? have I not seen Jesus Christ our Lord? are not ye my work in the Lord?" Rhetorically, Paul offered his argument as to why he was an apostle. There were several others mentioned but not with the same pedigree. Barnabas is mentioned but not with the same ministry authority as the twelve, with consideration to Judas, who betrayed Christ and killed himself, and Matthias was selected by the other apostles with the casting of lots. The status of Matthias has been questioned, but it was never denied anywhere in the Scriptures that he was an apostle, and he later died as a martyr, as did all of the apostles except John, according to church history. Barnabas, and perhaps several others, were apostles, with Barnabas mentioned in this verse. 14 "Which when the apostles, Barnabas and Paul, heard of, they rent their clothes, and ran in among the people, crying out…"

"and some, prophets" And some he gave to be prophets — Whose office it was to explain infallibly the true meaning of the ancient prophecies, and also to predict future events, by the extraordinary revelations made to them. (Benson) *In the New Testament,* John the Baptist *foretold the Messiah* (Matthew 3:1). *Jesus Himself came as prophet, priest, king, and Messiah, fulfilling many of the messianic prophecies of the Old Testament.*

The early church also included prophets. For example, Ananias was given a prophecy about the apostle Paul's future (Acts 9:10–18). Acts 21:9 mentions four daughters of Philip who could prophesy. Prophecy is listed as a spiritual gift in 1 Corinthians 12 and 14. In the end times, two "witnesses" will prophesy from Jerusalem (Revelation 11). Usually, the prophets God sends are despised, and their message is unheeded. Isaiah described his nation as a "rebellious people, deceitful children, children unwilling to listen to the Lord's instruction. They say to the seers, 'See no more visions!' and to the prophets, 'Give us no more visions of what is right! Tell us pleasant things, prophecy illusions" (Isaiah 30:9–10). Jesus lamented that Jerusalem had killed the prophets God sent to them (Luke 13:34).

Of course, not everyone who "speaks forth" a message is God's prophet. The Bible warns against false prophets who claim to speak for God but who deceive the people they purport to inform. King Ahab kept 400 such false prophets in his employ to tell him what he wanted to hear (2 Chronicles 18:4; cf. 2 Timothy 4:3). In the New Testament, we have many warnings against false prophets. Jesus taught, "Watch out for false prophets. They come to you in sheep's clothing, but inwardly they are ferocious wolves" (Matthew 7:15). He later noted that, in the end times, "false messiahs and false prophets will appear and perform great signs and wonders to deceive, if possible, even the elect" (Matthew 24:24). Revelation speaks of a false prophet who will arise in the Tribulation and deceive people around the world (Revelation 16:13; 19:20; 20:10). To avoid being led astray, we must always "test the spirits to see whether they are from God" (1 John 4:1). A true prophet of God will be committed to speaking God's truth. They will never contradict God's revealed Word. A true prophet will say, with the prophet Micaiah just before his fateful confrontation with Ahab, (2 Chronicles 18:13), "And Micaiah said, As the Lord liveth, even what my God saith, that will I speak." (2 Chronicles 18:13). (Got Questions)

and some evangelists. In Acts 21:8, Philip is named as an evangelist, and in 2 Timothy 4:5, Paul encourages Timothy to *do the work of an evangelist*. These are the only three uses of the word *evangelist* in the entire Bible. Other people could be considered "evangelists" in that they preached the good news (Gospel), including Jesus Himself (Luke 20:1) and

Paul (Romans 1:15). Still, Philip is the one person specifically called an evangelist in Scripture. Today, evangelists and missionaries are sometimes used interchangeably. The basic meaning of evangelist is simply those who *preach the Gospel.*

pastors and teachers. The word pastor in Latin means shepherd. The words Preacher, pastor, Bishop, and elder are used interchangeably when describing the office of a pastor. The preacher is the one who heralds glad tidings and expounds the word of God in his preaching-teaching. The pastor is the one who is called to a church to preach and to pastor or minister to the sheep (his congregation). The Bishop is the title that describes his responsibility as the overseer while taking heed to the flock (Acts 20:28) 28 "Take heed therefore unto yourselves, and to all the flock, over the which the Holy Ghost hath made you overseers, to feed the church of God, which he hath purchased with his own blood." Some separate the pastor and the teacher from each other. Yet, the church pastor should also teach his people while pastoring. I am over-whelmed when I hear of pastors of churches who do not invest in their flock and care for them. This is so foreign to the overall teachings of the Scriptures. Especially when there is several members that could be easily managed by the pastor of the church, when the size of the church is beyond the capability of the pastor to visit and tend to their needs, they should have in their church the structure and the ministers who can pastor the people, but not ignore them. Things certainly have changed; people are more private and do not open their homes to pastoral visits and ministry as they once did. Even so, there should be a way to connect more closely when someone requests prayer while in the hospital, there should be those to minister to their need. (I am sure an entire book could be written on this aspect of ministry).

Paul uses prepositions frequently to introduce different aspects of ministry. Here are the ways they appear in these two verses, verses 12 and 13. **1.** For the perfecting of the saints **2.** For the work of the ministry, **3.** For the edifying of the body of Christ **4.** Till we all come in the unity of the faith **5.** For the perfecting of the saints **6.** For the work of the ministry, **7.** For the edifying of the body of Christ. These are seven prepositional phrases Paul uses to show how the ministers minister to their churches.

12 *For the perfecting of the saints, for the work of the ministry, for the edifying of the body of Christ:* To bring about the perfecting or the maturing of the saints, the work of the ministry, and the edifying of the church these ministers mentioned are so given. Having mentioned the officers Christ gave his church, the apostle states the purpose for which this gift was conferred —it was for the perfecting of the saints, the work of the ministry, and the edifying of Christ's body.

The perfecting of the saints speaks of how the members should be guarded and grown to reach maturity safely. Additionally, the work of the ministry should not be relegated to the pastors or the deacons only but the work of the church should involve every one and not just a few. The ministry operating as it ought should result in edifying the body of Christ. Bible programs and the preaching of the Word should be geared that way. The people individually and the church as an entire body should be lifted in strength to perform the intended work of the church as outlined by the Apostle Paul and shared with the Church at Ephesus.

The Unity of Faith and Knowledge

13 *Till we all come in the unity of the faith, and of the knowledge of the Son of God, unto a perfect man, unto the* *measure of the stature of the fulness of Christ:* Paul was saying the purpose of ministers is to aid in the development of unity. The two aspects Paul is emphasizing is for faith and knowledge (doctrine) to be in agreement to the purpose of growing continuously in the fulness of Christ. A strong church is a unified church, and that unity is hindered by evil and sin, which causes divisions, as Paul taught the Corinthians and explained it as seen here in chapter 3:1-4 **1** *And I, brethren, could not speak unto you as unto spiritual, but as unto carnal, even as unto babes in Christ.* **2** *I have fed you with milk, and not with meat: for hitherto ye were not able to bear it, neither yet now are ye able.* **3** *For ye are yet carnal: for whereas there is among you envying, and strife, and divisions, are ye not carnal, and walk as men?* **4** *For while one saith, I am of Paul; and another, I am of Apollos; are ye not carnal?* Paul's rebuke described some of the things that caused divisions in a church then and now. This verse also states that faith and knowledge should be identical, not contradicting each other. If faith does not agree with knowledge, then the knowledge is inferior. The knowledge should be safely derived from the Word of God only. Hodge said that "knowledge ought to be lost in faith."

The purpose of the ministry leaders is to perfect holiness in each person so that they may be more Christ-like. Their Criteria or Example is Christ. Becoming a perfect man means being no longer children but spiritually mature unto all good works. Paul told them to measure themselves (not to each other) but let Christ be their measuring rod. To the fullness of Christ when describing the body of believers as filled with the presence, power, agency, and riches of God and Christ. To pattern themselves after Christ the Living Word, one must rely upon Christ the Written Word to instruct and fill them, letting the Word of Christ dwell within them richly, as Paul told the Church of Colossi. Colossians

3:16: *"Let the word of Christ dwell in you richly in all wisdom; teaching and admonishing one another in psalms and hymns and spiritual songs, singing with grace in your hearts to the Lord."*

14 *That we henceforth be no more children, tossed to and fro, and carried about with every wind of doctrine, by the sleight of men, and cunning craftiness, whereby they lie in wait to deceive;* Paul in 1 Corinthians speaks of babes, and here as children meaning the Church is to mature beyond the baby or child stage and perform as being adults. He knew this would protect against instability and deception by them not knowing the Truth.

The word children speaks of Spiritual immaturity, as babes in Christ when he addressed the Corinthians. Paul told the Church at Ephesus how to guard against disunity. The division is not the only concern that Paul addresses here. It is also the collapse of Doctrine or the unbiblical and improper interpretation and practice of Truth, so much so that the church members were victims of deceivers and false teachers. Paul was stressing that proper ministry and correct teaching should keep such instability from taking place. tradition. In this passage, the apostle attributes departure from the truth to cunning craftiness and deceit, characteristic of error or false teachers. In Rom. 16,17.18; 2 Cor. 2,17; 11, 13; Gal. 2, 4; Col. 2, 8.18, the same character is given to those who seduce men from the faith. Error can never be harmless, nor false teachers innocent—any departure from Truth results in error.

15 *But speaking the truth in love, may grow into him in all things, which is the head, even Christ*: *This is a great verse... speaking the truth in love,* for love is the principle thing just as wisdom is spoken of in Proverbs. Therefore, he shows the importance of the church in exhibiting love in all they do. The ministry workers were to speak the Truth, knowing that as they did, they should temper it by having God's love when they spoke. They were to do this knowing they were to answer to Christ, the head of the church. There are so many ways of delivering truth and orthodoxy. But it loses its intended value if it is not attended with love. I know even with my child-raising, I often spoke not with love but harshness. The Lord had to teach me the difference. By not doing it in God's way and provoking your children to wrath, you will likely raise a rebel. The same can be done in church as preachers preach. "A word fitly spoken is like apples of gold in pictures of silver." (Proverbs 25:11). If they preach the truth in love, they can preach strong messages if the love is there. But speaking harshly, even though it is Truth, can quickly turn the listening ear away. Paul tells the Church in Ephesus that the most incredible connection is that one "may grow into him in all things which is the head, even Christ." Paul is again using the body as a metaphor for the church. He wants each limb, appendage, foot, finger, ear, eye, etc., to grow into Him with such a close connection that the church reveals Him above all else.

16 *From whom the whole body fitly joined together and compacted by that which every joint supplieth, according to the effectual working in the measure of every part, maketh increase of the body unto the edifying of itself in love.* Paul is simply using the metaphor of the body to represent or picture the church, stating that there should be the effective work of the ministry to build up the church in love. Satan is not only an enemy of Truth and faith but also promotes hatred instead of love. The body metaphor continues in this verse, showing that the church is not just growing into but increasing, with love dominating. The measuring rod of a strong church is having faith, truth, and love. For them to love others, they must also love each other. If one shuts up his bows of compassion how dwelleth the love of God in him. (1

Corinthians 3:17).

CHAPTER TEN
Ephesians 4:17-5:6

VERSE SUMMARIES 4:17-5:6

17 *This I say therefore, and testify in the Lord, that ye henceforth walk not as other Gentiles walk, in the vanity of their mind.* Paul says to them they are different as a new creature in Christ and your walk should show it. What you once loved should now be an abhorrence therefore walk differently from other unconverted Gentiles.

18 *Having the understanding darkened, being alienated from the life of God through the ignorance that is in them, because of the blindness of their heart:* He reminds them that the unconverted Gentiles in their state of separation from God with no understanding is in a condition of having Spiritual blindness. They can neither comprehend nor understand the things of God. Such understanding can only come through the New Birth.

19 *Who being past feeling have given themselves over unto lasciviousness, to work all uncleanness with greediness.* Paul clearly states that these Gentiles mentioned have no sensitivity to the things of God and, for that reason, follow after the flesh rather than after God with a greedy heart.

20 *But ye have not so learned Christ;* Paul commends them by saying they were not students of Christ in a way that yielded no change. Their lives were remarkably changed to learn and continue being taught by Him.

21 *If so be that ye have heard him, and have been taught by him, as the truth is in Jesus:* Paul speaks to the Ephesians in a pastoral way, saying if they had a relationship with Christ based upon Truth as Christ being that Truth, they were to continue in the faith as verse 22 teaches diligently.

22 *That ye put off concerning the former conversation the old man, which is corrupt according to the deceitful lusts*; They were to live differently in their conduct from what once described them. Their previous conduct was corrupt and against Christ.

23 *And be renewed in the spirit of your mind.* This renewal was first that which only Christ could do, and then it involved the mind, which required a diligent effort to let the Word of God work in the transformation.

24 *And that ye put on the new man, which after God is created in righteousness and true holiness.* In this section, some taking off and putting on are likened to what you would do with an outfit such as a cloak. The unrighteous garment is to be replaced with righteousness and true holiness.

25 *Wherefore putting away lying, speak every man truth with his neighbour: for we are members one of another.* Telling a lie says much about a person and his level of Spirituality. As I think about this, I will elaborate on what I am suggesting as the thoughts come to mind to support the statement that "telling a lie says much about a person."

26 *Be ye angry, and sin not: let not the sun go down upon your wrath*: There is a kind of anger that does not cross the threshold of becoming a sin. It should be expected of the believer to be angry about some things. Christ was angry about some things, and it was sinless and very much justified for Him to be so.

27 *Neither give place to the devil.* Do not set a place for the devil, and certainly not let him be invited company. He is to be resisted, and we are to flee from him, for he walketh about like a roaring lion.

28 *Let him that stole steal no more: but rather let him* *labour, working with his hands the thing which is good, that he may have to give to him that needeth.* Work is good for a person in so many ways. When a person gives an honest day's work for an honest day's pay, that is a great combination. One thing that should help deter is the temptation to steal.

29 *Let no corrupt communication proceed out of your mouth, but that which is good to the use of edifying, that it may minister grace unto the hearers.* "Watch your mouth!" Or "Watch your tongue?" I heard when my mother corrected my speech, and I am grateful I had that kind of mama. She once washed my mouth with "devil lye" soap because of something I said. At that time in her life, she was a very young Christian but still knew the importance of speaking correctly. Most of our society was like that back in the 1950's. Sadly, there has been much change from then until now. Christians certainly should follow Paul's admonition even today.

30 *And grieve not the holy Spirit of God, whereby ye are sealed unto the day of redemption.* Paul is telling us that even though God the Holy Spirit has Omnipotence, yet He can be grieved by the sins of mere mortals which shows how sensitive He is to us and who we are. That should challenge us likewise to be grieved at doing any wrong.

31 *Let all bitterness, and wrath, and anger, and clamour, and evil speaking, be put away from you, with all malice*: Paul begins with a list of evil which comes from the wicked heart and can be spoken by believers and nonbelievers. When Spoken by the Christian, Paul reminds the Ephesians to be put away.

32 *And be ye kind one to another, tenderhearted, forgiving one another, even as God for Christ's sake hath forgiven you.* Why not be kind, tenderhearted, and forgiving one another? The reason is that to do these things spoken of by

Paul contradicts one's sinful nature. We, by nature, do not want to be kind when we feel wronged by someone; we want to get even. We are not by nature tenderhearted, but again, especially if someone has hurt us and they are suffering for some reason, we would probably say, "Why not? He deserved it." To forgive is not natural for a person who is not spirit-led; such a person would prefer to retaliate. Yet He should be the believers' exemplar.

Chapter 5:1 *Be ye therefore followers of God, as dear children.* In this fifth Chapter of Ephesians, Paul continues the theme of the Believers' walk. He said with all that God has and is still doing, we ought to follow Him with the same love and respect that we would have for a wonderful earthly Father.

2 *And walk in love, as Christ also hath loved us, and hath given himself for us an offering and a sacrifice to God for a sweetsmelling savour.* The epitome or perfect example for us to follow is Jesus as He offered Himself as a sacrifice, which was a *sweetsmelling savour in the nostrils of God*.

3 *But fornication, and all uncleanness, or covetousness, let it not be once named among you, as becometh saints*; Not "one named among you." Certainly, we should strive for the sanctification that our Holy God expects of His own. This level of Holy commitment will certainly be satisfying when standing at the Bema Seat and hearing the words, "Well done."

4 *Neither filthiness, nor foolish talking, nor jesting, which are not convenient: but rather giving of thanks.* Paul continues to reiterate the theme of purity and holiness, conveying the truth that true believers ought to abstain from and not participate in wicked deeds and those that come from a defiled or carnal heart. The giving of thanks rather than an unthankful heart should mark the believer.

5 *For this ye know, that no whoremonger, nor unclean*

person, nor covetous man, who is an idolater, hath any inheritance in the kingdom of Christ and of God. The penalty of unbelief is not only not having any inheritance in the kingdom of Christ and of God but eternal retribution in the Lake of Fire with no possibility of escape. Paul could have a twofold purpose in what he is saying. First, to warn the wicked of the consequences of unbelief, which contributes to wicked living as an ongoing practice. Second, to warn the Ephesians and the Christians of all ages.

6 *Let no man deceive you with vain words: for because of these things cometh the wrath of God upon the children of disobedience.* Deception is a crippler because it takes you away from the Truth. So often, that is accomplished with words. The kind of words is referred to as vain words. Anything spoken that is foreign to truth is worthless, having no value. The result of such is God's wrath and God's chastening.

The Beginning of the Commentary Ephesians 4:17-32; 5:1-6

In these last verses in this chapter discussing the "Believers Walk," Paul will be stressing that the believers and members of the Church at Ephesus no longer walk as they did before their conversion. He will specify how different the walk should be—his instructions model how all Christians should walk and should take heed. His instructions call for unity, holiness, and love, each patterned exclusively by the Word of God. May it now be so as well. God's children are to walk in unity, as we see in chapters 4:1–16, holiness (4:17–32), and love (5:1–6). This particular section is divided into two parts: (1) the positive, walk in love (vv. 1–2); and (2) the negative, abstain from evil (vv. 3–

6) (Hoehner).

The challenge to a different walk

17 *This I say therefore, and testify in the Lord, that ye henceforth walk not as other Gentiles walk, in the vanity of their mind.* Paul says to them they are different as new creatures in Christ, and your walk should show it. What you once loved should now be an abhorrence. Walk differently from other unconverted Gentiles. With respect to what has been previously spoken, and as he continues to give testimony in the Lord, Paul now writes. His holy plea is that they not walk as other Gentiles in the vanity of the mind. The word *vanity* speaks of walking with no respect for the Truth, with perversity, depravity, being frail, and inattentive to the holy things of God. Paul warns them strongly against such. He lets them know that such activity begins in the mind. The Greek and the Roman world were known for their vain philosophies. Paul went to the Agora, which was the marketplace where people, including their orators, would go to the public meeting area to talk and to listen to themselves talk and test their theories about what they thought about things and try to impress others after the tradition of Aristotle, Plato, and other renown philosophers. Paul was not there to debate; he was there to preach. He there told them that it was the true and the living God instead of the many icons or idols they would worship. For it was in Him that we are able to live, move, and have our being, telling them this as he preached to them and they received him not Paul determined not to know anything, but Jesus and Him crucified in his preaching, and they refused to hear. Paul understood how the Gentiles were influenced by the Greek world, having the Greek mindset as a result of constantly absorbing the teachings of their surroundings. This is similar to how humanism now affects our world.

The mind, therefore, in the passage before us, does not refer to the intellect to the exclusion of the feelings nor the feelings to the exclusion of the intellect. It includes both; the term comprehends the reason, the understanding, the conscience, and the affections. Sometimes, one and sometimes another of these modes of spiritual activity is specially referred to, but in the present case, the whole soul is intended. According to the scriptural usage, the word vanity includes moral and intellectual worthlessness or fatuity. It is of all that is comprehended under understanding and the heart that this vanity is predicated. Everything included in the following verses respecting the blindness and depravity of the heathen is therefore understood in the word vanity. (Hodge, Charles. Commentary on Ephesians).

18 *Having the understanding darkened, being alienated from the life of God through the ignorance that is in them, because of the blindness of their heart*: He reminds them that the unconverted Gentiles in their state of separation from God with no understanding is in a condition of having Spiritual blindness. They can neither comprehend nor understand the things of God. Such understanding can only come through the New Birth.

19 *Who being past feeling have given themselves over unto lasciviousness, to work all uncleanness with greediness.* Paul speaks of the unconverted Gentiles and how their understanding is affected just as he spoke of the Corinthians who were unconverted, whom he described as natural men who could not receive the things of the Spirit of God for they were foolishness unto them and they had no discernment. (cf. I Corinthians 2-14). The ignorance Paul was speaking of was because they were incapable of understanding things of God being removed from and alienated from God's Word and the Holy Spirit. Their foolish heart was darkened. This is only compounded when they continue to reject God, and God turns them over to a reprobate mind because they do not like to retain God in their knowledge. A believer can become cold and calloused when they become casual and careless to the Word of God, and as Hebrews warns, they forsake the assembling of themselves together. God will use different measure to bring them back into His will for whom the Lord loveth He chastens, as Hebrews 12 teaches. But for the unbeliever, they can become past feelings with no hope for conversion. Paul warned strongly against reaching that state of mind and condition. Charles Hodge stated, "The practical proof of their being in the state described is to be found in the fact that being without feeling they give themselves to the sins mentioned. Conscience ceases to upbraid or to restrain them. The heathen give themselves up to uncleanness and covetousness. These two vices are elsewhere thus associated, as in ch. 5, 3. 5, "Let not uncleanness or covetousness be named among you." "No unclean person, nor covetous man, &c." See also Col. 3, 5. Rom. 1, 29. 1 Corinthians 5, 10. As in Romans 1 24, immorality is connected with impiety as its inevitable consequence." (Hodge) This is such a horrible state to be in... Yet, sadly, they seem not to care. *Who being past feeling*. The account that had been given of natural depravity is followed by a description of the worst of all evils brought upon men by their sinful conduct. Having destroyed the sensibilities of the heart and allayed the stings of remorse, they abandon themselves to all manner of iniquity. We are by nature corrupt and prone to evil; nay, we are wholly inclined to evil. Those destitute of the Spirit of Christ give loose reins to self-indulgence till fresh offenses, producing others in constant succession, bringing down upon them God's wrath. The voice of God, proclaimed by an accusing conscience, still continues to be heard; instead of producing its proper effects, it appears to harden them against all admonition. Because of such obstinacy, they deserve to be altogether forsaken by God. (Calvin)

20 *But ye have not so learned Christ*; Paul commends them by saying they were not students of Christ in a way that yielded no change. Their lives were remarkably changed to learn and continue being taught by Him. Paul again distinguishes the regenerated person who has so graciously been birthed into the family of God and is a new creature with no appetite for the things of this world but abhors that which is evil except at which times he may be tempted or tried and drifts only to be corrected by guilt, conscience, and above all the Word of God with the Spirit of God, from the unbeliever. The ungodly are going contrary to the things of God and learning more about the ways of the heathen, whereas the believer is admonished not to learn the ways of the heathen but to embrace God only. The spirit-filled believers have no appetite for the things of the world because the Word of Christ is *dwelling in them richly*, and when that happens, their actions will show it.

Deists argue that God created the earth and allowed it self-determination. The God of the Bible reveals that he not only created the earth but also continually sustains it. It is the same for those who have been redeemed. God not only redeems but also demands and enables a new lifestyle. Christ uses Paul to teach and develop the lifestyle that He intends. Paul has presented both the nature and practice of the old person and will now discuss the position and practice of the new person. (Hoehner) Rather than operating with self-determination, believers chose to be taught by and learn Christ by His Word, as mentioned.

21 *If so be that ye have heard him, and have been taught by him, as the truth is in Jesus*: Paul speaks to the Ephesians in a pastoral way, saying if they had a relationship with Christ based upon Truth as Christ being that Truth, they were to continue in the faith as verse 22 teaches diligently. The "if" shows that the results mentioned that describe one as being Spiritual require their hearing Him and being taught by Him; at the same time, the Scriptures are revealing Him, and the Spirit allows Christ to teach the believer by Himself through the aid of the Holy Spirit. Jesus declared Himself to be the Way, the Truth, and the Life. (John 14:6) When Jesus is mentioned, and His name Christ is mentioned, the first mention of the name Jesus refers to His work on Earth. Christ is the New Testament name for Messiah and is used when describing His work as our High Priest, beginning with the crucifixion. When it says the Truth is in Jesus, it is the same as saying Christ because Christ and Jesus are One and the Same.

Paul was saying that believers should not only believe in Christ but also acknowledge him in Jesus. However, this makes a dichotomy between Christ and Jesus, which was not a problem in Paul's day. It is unlikely that Paul is combating either the Gnostic tendency to divorce the saving Christ from the historical Jesus who was crucified or the dichotomy of the Bultmannians (an ancient group that was in error regarding the Theology of Jesus) between the Christ of faith and the Jesus of history. Both of these debates occurred long after Paul's time. The assumption that the Christ of faith and the Jesus of history are one and the same person is implicit in Paul's writings. (Hoehner, Harold)

22 *That ye put off concerning the former conversation the old man, which is corrupt according to the deceitful lusts*; They were to live differently in their conduct from what once described them. Their previous conduct was corrupt and against Christ. Paul is using an expression that could be likened to one changing outfits or taking off a coat. The instructions to the Church of Ephesus and all believers is that once one is converted, one should no longer be satisfied with how things were. There is a radical change; one's appetite changes, the places one frequents change, one's attitude changes, and so much more regarding the converted person changes. As an illustration of that, Paul uses the removal of those things, likening it to removing a coat, and once it is removed, it is no longer being worn. When he says, *ye put off*, it has nothing to do with what only Christ can do in one's conversion. Instead, Paul indicates that beyond a person's conversion, he has a requirement in his own humanity. Paul is letting the Ephesians know, as Peter would say in his epistles, that there is diligence involved on the part of the Christian to go on to perfection or Spiritual maturity. The word conversation used here refers not just to one's speech but to his entire conduct or manner of living. He describes it as being corrupt (ties in with the word depravity, or being defiled) and being deceived by things that plague one's appetite when one craves what is forbidden by Christ's laws and teachings. Though any converted person is also capable of such, it should not describe that one, nor be a pattern of how one lives. When one does sin, he is chastened as a son.

Hodge describes this as sanctification, which includes dying to sin, mortifying the flesh, and living to righteousness, or, as expressed here, putting off the old man and putting on the new man. The obvious allusion is to a change of clothing. To put off is to renounce, to remove from us, as garments which are laid aside. To put on is to adopt, to make our own. We are called upon to put off the works of darkness, Rom. 13, 12, to put away lying, Eph. 4, 25; to put off anger, wrath, malice, &c., Col. 3, 8; to lay aside all filthiness, James 1, 21. On the other hand, we are called upon to put on the Lord Jesus Christ, Rom. 13, 14, Gal. 3, 27; the armor of light, Rom. 13, 12; bowels of mercy, Col. 3, 12; and men are said to be clothed with power from on high,

Luke 24, 49; with immortality or incorruption, &c., 1 Cor. 15, 53. (Hodge)

23 *And be renewed in the spirit of your mind.* This renewal was first that which only Christ could do, and then it involved the mind, which required a diligent effort to let the Word of God work in the transformation. When Paul also wrote to the Church in Rome, he spoke in a similar manner as here. Notice the similarities of how the mind had been, as we would say today, "Completely programmed by the world." Because of this, "It needs to be reprogrammed., or as Romans 12:2 "transformed by the renewing of your mind." What better way than by God's Word?

In Romans 12:1,2 notice:

1 *"I beseech you therefore, brethren, by the mercies of God, that ye present your bodies a living sacrifice, holy, acceptable unto God, which is your reasonable service.* **2** *And be not conformed to this world: but be ye transformed by the renewing of your mind, that ye may prove what is that good, and acceptable, and perfect, will of God."* To be renewed in the spirit of your mind would be for comparison purposes, like having a bucket full of mud. Instead of emptying the bucket, you begin pouring water into it, and as you do, the mud will eventually wash out, and there will be only pure water. This example may be crude, but it pictures how the thoughts that are impure thoughts that fill our minds can be removed or replaced by filling our minds with the Word of God. This takes place when God's Word dwells in one richly. Another similar thought in Paul's writing is in Philippians 2:5. *"Let this mind be in you, which was also in Christ Jesus:"* Having the mind of Christ will protect one from evil thinking which results in evil activities.

Put on the New Man

24 *And that ye put on the new man, which after God is created in righteousness and true holiness.* In this section, some taking off and putting on are likened to what you would do with an outfit such as a cloak. The unrighteous garment is to be replaced with righteousness and true holiness. This refers to the human effort involved in relationship to what God has done or is doing as one matures in the faith. As we are called to put off our corrupt nature as a ragged and filthy garment, we must put on our new nature as a garment of light. And as the former was personified as an old man, decrepit, deformed, and tending to corruption, so the latter is personified as a new man, fresh, beautiful, and vigorous, like God, for it is after God created in righteousness and holiness of the truth. The parallel passage is said to be renewed "after the image of God" (Hodge). Paul uses metaphors to communicate truth as one would use object lessons. Here, there is the use of personification, as righteousness is likened to a man to be put on or taken off. True holiness is acquired from the Spirit in agreement with the Word of Truth.

The Holy Ghost is called the Spirit of truth as the author of this divine illumination, which irradiates the whole soul. This truth came from Jesus Christ, John 1, 17. He is the truth and the life, John 14, 6. We are made free by the truth and sanctified by the truth. The Gospel is called the word of truth, as the objective revelation of that divine knowledge which subjectively is the principle of spiritual life. Taking the word in this sense, the passage coincides with the parallel passage in Col. 3, 10. Here, the image of God is said to consist in righteousness and holiness of the truth; there, it is said to consist in knowledge. "the new man is renewed unto knowledge after the image of him that created him." (Hodge)

Therefore, true holiness cannot come from anyone but Christ, who is Truth. Paul will now specify some of the things to be put off or put away that require diligence on the believer's part in the following verses until the end of the chapter.

25 *Wherefore putting away lying, speak every man truth with his neighbour: for we are members one of another.* Telling a lie says much about a person and his level of Spirituality. As I think about this, I will elaborate on what I am suggesting as the thoughts come to mind to support the statement that "telling a lie says much about a person." **1.** To tell a lie indicates your fear of telling the truth seems greater than answering to God for telling the lie. **2.** To tell a lie, you are not considering the Biblical consequences for having done so, even eternity in hell (the lie is not what sends you to hell; the wicked heart of unbelief does.) **3.** To tell a lie usually involves betraying someone and, upon discovery, will they not have the same respect they may once had for the one lying. **4.** To tell a lie brings hurt to the one you lie to and means you do not love them as you should, or else you would tell the truth. **5.** To tell a lie hurts the one telling it, so much so that the basis for a Polygraph Test is how the body reacts to telling a lie. Even hardened criminals react to the telling of a lie. Yet it is also true the more you tell lies, the easier it becomes, and this goes along with how the Bible describes the heart becoming harder as it continues in sin. Research was done on what to look for as a person lies:

Experts recommend looking for clusters of signals when trying to spot a liar. The signals include:
- Avoiding eye contact or shifting eyes
- Stuttering, pausing, or clearing the throat
- Changing voice tone or volume
- Offering multiple excuses for a situation instead of just one

- Standing in a defensive posture with arms crossed over the chest
- Reddening slightly on the face or neck
- Rubbing, stroking, or pulling on the nose
- Making a slip of the tongue while denying something
- Deflecting attention from the issue
- Appearing uncomfortable (Holloway)

6. To tell a lie never fixes the problem, even if it seems to. (There are people who have lied to me that I have later learned that their lying compounded their own problem for having lied.) **7.** Lying affects your reputation and especially your testimony. (Case in point, though there may be very honest car salesmen, for example, who are portrayed as not being honest, not for their lying, because of other car salesmen who lied, and they get a "bum rap." That is sad, and can be said about many different people groups. One thing that is the same as stealing is for someone to give a cost estimate on things not broken or needed as though they were and add to the total cost; this is a wicked form of lying). **8.** Lying takes a very heavy toll on marriage when the couple is not honest with each other; this can contribute to jealousy and other sins. Proverbs say that the husband can safely trust in his wife if she is a virtuous woman. Likewise, the wife can safely trust her husband if he tells the truth. **9.** Telling a lie is often a form of imagination where the imagined thing is told as real; by telling it long enough, it begins to seem real.

The theme of this verse is speaking the truth. Lying is a grievous sin characterizing those who will be forever in the Lake of Fire. (Revelation 21:8) "But the fearful, and unbelieving, and the abominable, and murderers, and whoremongers, and sorcerers, and idolaters, and all liars, shall have their part in the lake which burneth with fire and brimstone: which is the second death." This shows the seriousness of the Lie. For one to lie, he is a liar. When he spoke these words to the Ephesians about putting away lying, Paul was not excluding the importance of truth being communicated to all but emphasizing the importance of not deceiving the very elect, for such would be anathema. It is a wicked betrayal regarding the church family to lie to them.

26 *Be ye angry, and sin not: let not the sun go down upon your wrath*: There are many different ways and reasons for a person to be angry. Some are proper, and others are not. It should be expected of the believer to be angry about some things. Christ was angry about some things, and He was sinless, and, in those instances, it was very much justified for Him to be so. One may say, "How can one be angry without sinning?" The verse is initiated in this manner, "Be ye angry…without sinning." There is a kind of anger that could be righteous indignation coming from the word angry here, which, as its Greek root word, is a very passionate word. There are things we certainly ought to be passionately angry about, to the point even of abhorrence. If you were bothering or hurting one of my grandchildren, I would be very disturbed, and having that kind of passionate anger would respond accordingly, causing me to rise and defend that precious one.

There are things that we ought to be angry about, especially those things that have their origin in the world, the flesh and the devil, which are our arch-enemies. A malicious kind of anger that is sinful should be corrected, making sure that the sun does not go down with that kind of anger before it is corrected, or in a positive, non-sinful sense, we should never let the sun set on our anger as it involves the devil, etc. In other words, keep being angry with the devil and his devices.

27 *Neither give place to the devil.* Do not set a place for the devil, and certainly not let him be invited company. He is to be resisted, and we are to flee from him, for he walketh about like a roaring lion. This means that in addition to resisting the devil, we should not entertain him nor be entertained by him, giving him a place of authority, allegiance, or control in our lives.

28 *Let him that stole steal no more: but rather let him labour, working with his hands the thing which is good, that he may have to give to him that needeth.* Work is good for a person in so many ways. When a person gives an honest day's work for an honest day's pay, that is a great combination. One thing that work should help deter is the temptation to steal. Paul contrasts those further radically changed by conversion and saying if you were a thief, stop it and do it no more. Instead, earn what you get by hard work, as "labour" implies. Perhaps the same hands that were thieving hands are now working hands. There is also a kind of thievery that is not as easily recognizable as it involves overcharging for labor or products, merchandise, food, etc. It is easy to let greed cause one to keep increasing his prices, and that can become a kind of thievery, perhaps more so than we recognize. To illustrate this, I recall someone telling me about my daddy, who built houses. He told me that as hard as my dad worked, he could have been one of the wealthiest men in our hometown. He asked my dad, "Why don't you charge more?" He answered, "I just hate to beat anybody out of anything." I honor his memory because that is the kind of man he was. Christ made all the difference in his life as it should be.

29 *Let no corrupt communication proceed out of your mouth, but that which is good to the use of edifying, that it may minister grace unto the hearers.* "Watch your mouth!" Or "Watch your tongue?" I often heard my mother saying that when she corrected my speech, and I am grateful I had that kind of mama. She once washed my mouth out with "devil lye" soap because of something I said. At that time in her life, she was a very young Christian but still knew the importance of speaking correctly. Most of our society was like that back in the 1950's. Sadly, there has been much change from then until now. Christians certainly should follow Paul's admonition even today.

Once again, Paul gives a contrast involving speech and how one should be careful to speak about what would be more edifying and conducive to walking as a Christian. The result of speaking rightly regarding one's words is that it should have a positive or ministering effect. It will show love, not malice or anger towards others, which is sadly missing today. The word "Corrupt" means literally "rotten or putrid." It seems on social media, as an example, that there are those out there who, when they see something they disagree with, will attack the one posting with such malice and anger and even use vulgar speech as they do it. The language in such communication is *rotten* or *putrid*. Especially, the believer should not speak words contrary to the Scripture's teachings but let them be pleasant and precious words.

30 *And grieve not the holy Spirit of God, whereby ye are sealed unto the day of redemption.* Paul is telling us that even though God the Holy Spirit has Omnipotence, yet He can be grieved by the sins of mere mortals which shows how sensitive He is to us and who we are. That should challenge us likewise to be grieved at doing any wrong. These things spoken of and mentioned by Paul when committed by the believer, can grieve the holy Spirit of God. "And grieve not the Holy Spirit of God," i.e., by such corrupt language, the apostle includes, as appears from Col. 3, 8, all irreligious, malicious, and impure language, which injures others and grieves the Holy Spirit. As a temple is sacred, and everything that profanes it is an offense to God, so the indwelling of the Holy Ghost in the people of God is made the reason why we should treat them with reverence, as this apostle teaches when he says, "Know ye not that ye are the temple of God, and that the Spirit of God dwelleth in you? If any man defile the temple of God, him will God destroy; for the temple of God is holy, which temple ye are." 1 Cor. 3, 16. 17. To pollute, therefore, the souls of believers by suggesting irreligious or impure thoughts to them is a profanation of the temple of God and an offense to the Holy Ghost. (Hodge)

We are sealed by the holy spirit as an *earnest payment* or guarantee until the day of redemption, which is a guarantee that should insist upon us to live accordingly, especially as stated in this passage for us to guard our speech, among other things.

Put Away Some Things

31 *Let all bitterness, and wrath, and anger, and clamour, and evil speaking, be put away from you, with all malice*: Paul begins with a list of evil activities that originate in the wicked heart and can be spoken by believers and nonbelievers. When Spoken by the Christian, Paul reminds the Ephesians to let such speech be put away. Five words related to speech in this verse are word descriptions of what the tongue can reveal about the disposition of the heart. "A good man out of the good treasure of his heart bringeth forth that which is good; and an evil man out of the evil treasure of his heart bringeth forth that which is evil: for of the abundance of the heart his mouth speaketh." So, one may readily see the correlation between speech and actions. Paul showed this by mentioning these descriptions of what the unconverted was like before his conversion. It will serve a good purpose for us to examine these words carefully.

The first word is *bitterness*, and I immediately think of the 12th Chapter of Hebrews, which speaks of a *root of bitterness* that has devastating effects when one becomes bitter by taking one's eyes off of Jesus. (Hebrews 12:15) "Looking diligently lest any man fail of the grace of God; lest any root of bitterness springing up trouble you, and thereby many be defiled;" This word comes from the word acridity (especially poison) and is a way of describing as a metaphor a kind of bitter hatred void of Christian love. According to Hebrews 12, this happens when one takes their eyes off of Jesus. A Christian should strive to keep his eyes on Jesus through the Word of God. When they take their eyes off of the Word, they are taking their eyes off of Him. The next word mentioned in Paul's list is the word *wrath*. As used here, Wrath is a passionate, boiling-up kind of anger, passion (as if breathing hard). The word *anger* is a synonym of wrath. Paul is saying it in two different ways to emphasize how much it should be avoided and perhaps how easy it is to become that way if not kept in check.

The word *clamor* is an old English word that seems to describe an outcry that would be attributed to losing one's control, which could be like crying "fire" in a crowded theater when there is no fire, thus causing others to panic or causing a state of pandemonium. The words *evil speaking* also tie into the context of Paul's writing. This kind of speaking is speech that is injurious even as it could be speaking evil of God in some way, or as is common where people take God's Name in vain. One should guard their words. As described in Luke 6:45, "A good man out of the good treasure of his heart bringeth forth that which is good; and an evil man out of the evil treasure of his heart bringeth forth that which is evil: for of the abundance of the heart his mouth speaketh." Paul said all of these were to be put away, including *malice* as having ill will. As you might note, all of these words describe a mean-spirited person who does wickedly, which should be non-characteristic of a Christian.

32 *And be ye kind one to another, tenderhearted, forgiving one another, even as God for Christ's sake hath forgiven you.* Why not be kind, tenderhearted, and forgiving one another? To do these things spoken of by Paul is a contradiction to one's sinful nature. We, by nature, do not want to be kind when we feel wronged by someone; we want to get even. We are not by nature tenderhearted, but again, especially if someone has hurt us and they are suffering for some reason, we would probably say, "Why not? He deserved it." To forgive is not natural for a person who is not spirit-led; such a person would prefer to retaliate. Yet He should be an exemplar in his being kind, tenderhearted, and forgiving.

Instead of being like those whom Paul warned against, he gives instructions that should be characteristic of those who are changed by conversion and who should use Christ as their example. Forgiving one another means not carrying a grudge because of how you were offended or wronged by someone. Many relationships have been destroyed because there was no forgiving spirit, even though it was sought after in an attempt to make restitution and reconciliation. Having a compassionate spirit will mean being kind and tenderhearted one to another. This chapter closes, showing that God's children are to walk in unity (4:1–16) and holiness (4:17–32). Then, looking to the next chapter of Colossians, the emphasis is walking in love (5:1–6). This particular section is divided into two parts: (1) the positive, walk in love (vv. 1–2); and (2) the negative, abstain from evil (vv. 3–6).

The Charity in the Believers 'Walk

5:1 *Be ye therefore followers of God, as dear children.* This section will mainly look at the family, the church, and the relationship that the slave has with the master and, in an updated sense, the employee to the employer. The admonition is to have a tender relationship likened to a wonderful Christian home operating as it should while following God according to His Word. In this fifth Chapter of Ephesians, Paul continues the theme of the Believers' walk. He said with all that God has and is still doing, we ought to follow Him with the same love and respect that we would have for a wonderful earthly Father. The walk in love is strongly emphasized in verses 1-6; verses 1 and 2 highlight the positive, and verses 3-6 emphasize the negative. The relationship that should be enjoyed is a tender and loving relationship, as you would discover in a Christian home where there is much respect between and among the parents and their children. The parents in such a wholesome setting could refer to their children as "dear children." Paul called the Ephesians' *children* and challenged them to follow God as *dear children*, with God being their Heavenly Father. It begins with the children being followers or imitators of God. What more excellent example and challenge for us than to let Christ be our perfect Example? The expression *dear children* carry two recognizable meanings. It speaks of our value to Him as being dear and the spirit and love we should have for Him where we would live in such a manner as to be referred to as "dear children."

2 *And walk in love, as Christ also hath loved us, and hath given himself for us an offering and a sacrifice to God for a sweetsmelling savour.* The epitome or perfect example for us to follow is Jesus as He offered Himself as a sacrifice, which was a *sweetsmelling savour in the nostrils of God*. Paul tells them that the imitating involved walking in love, as Christ "also hath loved us and given himself for us." If you want to see a strong and correct pattern or example of love, keep your eyes upon Him...always. That kind of love is a sacrificial love that is *a giving love* that shows up in their practical living. When Jesus offered Himself back up to God, it was a perfect, sinless sacrifice described rightly as a "sweetsmelling savor."

The two words, an *offering*, and *sacrifice*, convey that Christ handed himself over as the offering and sacrifice that would fulfill all the offerings and sacrifices in the OT. When one looks at the calendar of feasts (Lev 23) and all of the offerings and sacrifices for which each Israelite was responsible. All the offerings and sacrifices that the priests had to offer for all the people (both the daily offerings and the annual celebrations), it is astounding that the one supreme offering and sacrifice of Christ met all their requirements. The Book of Hebrews (9:26; 10:10–12) carries a parallel idea when it speaks of Christ's "one" offering and sacrifice when He offered up Himself. (Hoehner)

3 *But fornication, and all uncleanness, or covetousness, let it not be once named among you, as becometh saints.* Not "once named among you." Certainly, we should strive for the sanctification that our Holy God expects of His own. This level of Holy commitment will certainly be satisfying when standing at the Bema Seat and hearing the words, "Well done." Once again, Paul shows an example of things that should not mark the believer. These are the negative things that should not characterize the believer. As it was true then in this regard, so is it now. *Fornication* is a sexual sin or impurity that could be descriptive of almost any form of sexual impurity. Anything that is defiling as to the way God intended for sexuality to be conducted between the marriage partners is to be avoided. Sex outside of marriage is not God's intention or design. Vine further defines fornication this way: "Fornication" "is used (a) of 'illicit sexual intercourse, 'in John 8:41; Acts 15:20,29; 21:25; 1

Corinthians 5:1; 6:13,18; 2 Corinthians 12:21; Galatians 5:19; Ephesians 5:3; Colossians 3:5; 1 Thessalonians 4:3; Revelation 2:21; 9:21; in the plural in 1 Corinthians 7:2; in Matthew 5:32; 19:9 it stands for, or includes adultery; it is distinguished from it in 15:19; Mark 7:21..."(Vine.)

Uncleanness can speak of letting yourself go and not caring for your body or just being "plain nasty," as my mother would say. Still, she also would use that word to describe not only filthiness in a physical sense but also the moral filth that Paul is speaking of in verse 4, the impurity of lustful, luxurious, profligate living. Within the context of Paul's Letter, it could be mostly, in this instance, referring to sexual impurity. *Covetousness* could very easily tie back to the word uncleanness as used here. As used here, it primarily speaks of greed as described in 1 Timothy 6:10, *"For the love of money is the root of all evil: which while some coveted after, they have erred from the faith, and pierced themselves through with many sorrows."* This verse is self-explanatory even as rich men howl in their miseries. Solomon wisely spoke of the vanity of putting one's trust in money. Such greed takes its toll on people, causing them to step on others to get what they want, and it is not always money, even as one would covet another man's wife (Exodus 20:17; Deuteronomy 5:21). The seriousness of these being mentioned caused Paul to say that they should not once be mentioned as something a Christian is involved in, not even once. "Greediness" ("covetousness") "...lit., a desire to have more'... always in a bad sense, is used in a general way in Mark 7:22...; Romans 1:29; Ephesians 5:3; 1 Thessalonians 2:5. Elsewhere it is used, (a) of material possessions, Luke 12:15; 2 Peter 2:3; 2 Corinthians 9:5..." – Vine.

4 *Neither filthiness, nor foolish talking, nor jesting, which are not convenient: but rather giving of thanks.* Paul continues reiterating the theme of purity and holiness, conveying that true believers should abstain from and not participate in wicked deeds and those that come from a defiled or carnal heart. The giving of thanks rather than an unthankful heart should mark the believer. The word filthiness is synonymic with uncleanness. The old commentators saw this word as describing what is shameful, disgraceful, and debased as describing the general conduct. This term is related to the word for lasciviousness or licentiousness (see 4:19). Mark 7:20-23 – Lasciviousness, like murder or fornication, etc., is a sin that proceeds from the heart and defiles the man. Galatians 5:19-21 – Those who practice it will not inherit the kingdom of God. Romans 13:13,14 – We also, as believers, should avoid making provision to fulfill this lust of the flesh. (Pratte)

It also refers to the wrong kind of talking, which would include foolish talking, which is not principled and lacks integrity of speech, even with proud boasting involved. It would be any manner of speaking that does, despite to the Word of God, not take its precepts and instructions seriously. Jesting would be lighthearted, not taking things that ought to be serious seriously. It also can be a kind of condescending speech and joking that is condescending or belittling the person you are speaking to.

One's speech reveals what is going on in the person's heart. Luke 6:45: "A good man out of the good treasure of his heart bringeth forth that which is good; and an evil man out of the evil treasure of his heart bringeth forth that which is evil: for of the abundance of the heart his mouth speaketh." Paul saying "not convenient" means as we would say appropriate with purpose. Our speech ought to be respectful, and always, as a Spirit-filled person, there should be speech filled with thanksgiving coming from a thankful heart.

Also, this jesting referred to within the context before us could be grossly sinning and making light of sexual impurity as though it is not even that serious. This shows that any impurity that originates in a wicked heart is a gross sin that Paul and Christ condemn.

5 *For this ye know, that no whoremonger, nor unclean person, nor covetous man, who is an idolater, hath any inheritance in the kingdom of Christ and of God.* The penalty of unbelief is not only not having any inheritance in the kingdom of Christ and of God but eternal retribution in the Lake of Fire with no possibility of escape. Paul could have a twofold purpose in what he is saying. First, to warn the wicked of the consequences of unbelief, which contributes to wicked living as an ongoing practice. Second, to warn the Ephesians and the Christians of all ages. With Paul mentioning the sins in this chapter and warning against them, he now summarizes the seriousness of his speech. This verse summarizes things Paul had been speaking about that do not characterize a true believer. He lists them again and shows how this kind of wickedness can result in the practice of idolatry, which removes our affection for God. Such people were described in our Text as were the Gentiles around Ephesus before their conversion. Those kinds are not converted and have no right to the "inheritance in the kingdom of Christ and of God." In their unconverted state, they will spend their eternity in the Lake of Fire instead. Such is the penalty for unbelief.

6 *Let no man deceive you with vain words: for because of these things cometh the wrath of God upon the children of disobedience.* Deception is a crippler because it takes you away from the Truth. So often, that is accomplished with words. The kind of words is referred to as vain words. Anything spoken that is foreign to truth is worthless, having no value. The result of such is God's wrath and God's chastening. Deception was commonplace in Paul's day. The same is true even today. He especially warned against the worthless words having no meaning being spoken and listened to by the Ephesians and all believers. To guard against such deceptions requires a steady diet in the Word of God. The wrath of God is His Holy outpouring of judgment against all ungodliness. There were Greek and Roman philosophers who were revered by the heathen as they tried to explain God in ways different from the Word of God or attempted to remove Him altogether with their denials. They would also influence the common people with their vain, swelling words. Therefore, Paul was warning them lest they fall victim to their lies and then face the wrath of God.

CHAPTER ELEVEN

Ephesians 5:7-19

Beware! Watch Who You Hang Out With.

VERSE SUMMARIES 5:7-19

7 *Be not ye therefore partakers with them.* One should neither partner nor fellowship with the children of disobedience. The word means there should be no participation that will link you to their evil doings, which would further impact you by partaking in the evil they partake of.

8 *For ye were sometimes darkness, but now are ye light in the Lord: walk as children of light:* This verse says, as the course of the song, "Things are different now, something happened to me!" A radical difference occurs, which may be more noticeable in some than others depending on the degree of their sinning. Paul said those who were characterized by their walking in darkness are now characterized as children of the light no longer walking in darkness.

9 *(For the fruit of the Spirit is in all goodness and righteousness and truth;)* The fruit of the Spirit for the believer who is Spirit-filled will have the fruit of the Spirit accompanying his doing good, which will make it even better. The fruit of the Spirit will also be present in the works of righteousness. «Righteousness" lies in living in obedience to the law of God, in attending the worship and service of him, and in discharging our duty to our fellow creatures; and this, as goodness, is very imperfect and not to be boasted of, or trusted to, nor is salvation to be expected from it: "truth" is opposed to lying, to hypocrisy, to error and falsehood; and where the Spirit of God, and the work of grace are, there will be more or less an appearance of these fruits. (Gill)

10 *Proving what is acceptable unto the Lord. Proving* is a metallurgical term that means to be put to the test, determining that the standard is met. The standard for the believer is the Lord. All comparisons should be made to him with respect to the Word of God.

11 *And have no fellowship with the unfruitful works of darkness, but rather reprove them.* Paul is saying that the children of Light and, in this instance, the Ephesian believers were to have no fellowship or not to partner with the children of darkness.

12 *For it is a shame even to speak of those things which are done of them in secret.* Paul tells them their sinning was so gross that even speaking of it was shameful.

13 *But all things that are reproved are made manifest by the light: for whatsoever doth make manifest is light.* The light is opposed to darkness, and the darkness does not have that ability because it is the light that reveals and reproves. In the darkness, things are hidden.

14 *Wherefore he saith, Awake thou that sleepest, and arise from the dead, and Christ shall give thee light.* Paul offers hope to those who are asleep or dead in their sins. He is communicating that there is salvation if you would put your faith and trust in Christ, for He truly is the light Giver, for He is Light.

15 *See then that ye walk circumspectly, not as fools, but as wise.* The use of the word circumspectly means to be vigilant and watchful, not being ensnared by Satan's devices and as a fool who is not wise fall in one of Satan's snares or traps. Be on guard!

16 *Redeeming the time, because the days are evil.* Paul is speaking while challenging them to not only be on guard but to have a great sense of urgency that causes them to be on guard and pursue the enemy. This is because of the perilous evil days that they were experiencing.

17 *Wherefore be ye not unwise, but understanding what the will of the Lord is.* It is totally unwise to forsake the Word of God and, when doing so, forfeit knowing the Word of God. By not knowing the Word of God, one becomes incapable of doing the will of God.

18 *And be not drunk with wine, wherein is excess; but be filled with the Spirit*; The intoxication of the worst kind is to be intoxicated with that which is fleshly as the example of drunkenness implies instead of being filled with the Spirit.

19 *Speaking to yourselves in psalms and hymns and spiritual songs, singing and making melody in your heart to the Lord*; This should be the inward language of the Spirit-filled person who cannot contain what lies inside of oneself when such is so but must be expressed verbally and publicly as though to say, "One cannot contain himself."

Beginning of Commentary Vv. 7-19

Light and Darkness

This section is divided into three parts: (1) do not become involved with evildoers (vv. 7–10); (2) do not become involved with their works (vv. 11–13); rather (3) have the approval of Christ's light (v. 14). (Hoehner) Paul very orderly structures his letter to the Ephesians in Spiritual and practical terms. He wants them to know from whence they were delivered to where they had come in their radical change from Children of Wrath or the flesh to Children of Light. There is the prohibitive aspect of their being different and not reverting to a lifestyle that mimics how they were and instead living like Christ, with Him being their Example and trying to keep them safe. Paul constantly helped them by continually exposing them to the Truth as he prayed for and challenged them. This Letter is also used as a way to protect them as he stands on guard for them.

7 *Be not ye therefore partakers with them*. Paul tells the Ephesian believers, and all believers for that matter, that there should be no participation that will link you to their evil doings, which would further impact you by partaking in the evil they partake of. "Partakers" means participants or having fellowship. Don't participate in the deeds of their sin or with those who live apart from God. As we learn from 1 Corinthians 3:3, "For ye are yet carnal: for whereas there is among you envying, and strife, and divisions, are ye not carnal, and walk as men?" Verse 7 also lets us know that believers can and do act like unbelievers. God does not warn of things that do not exist. "Do not become participants with sinners. Participate with God." Let God fill your speech and actions. (Yandian) The inferential conjunction "therefore" (οὖν) reaches back into the two preceding verses that speak of "the children of disobedience" and their sinful practices. Paul said do not characterize or pattern yourself after the evil workers of unbelief, nor have their manner of speaking. Paul insists on the Church at Ephesus to ensure their lives contrast those of the Gentiles who were still in unbelief. Paul is not saying to ostracize or totally separate themselves from the unbelievers, but to not join in with their unholy deeds, but be a witness and example to them. Because they are fellow participants with Christ, they are not to be fellow partakers *with them*. Likewise, we have a great opportunity to bring the Light to unbelievers so they may come to the Light.

8 *For ye were sometimes darkness, but now are ye light in the Lord: walk as children of light:* A radical difference occurs, which may be more noticeable in some than others depending on the degree of their sinning. Paul said those who were characterized by their walking in darkness are now characterized as children of the light no longer walking in darkness. Darkness and light were images commonly used in all ancient religions. The image is especially prominent in an entire document of the Dead Sea Scrolls that speaks of an impending end-time battle between "the sons of light" (the faithful covenant people of Godly) and "the sons of darkness" (the devil, his angels, and all of God's human enemies). Some Jewish documents even use this image with reference to conversion to Judaism (Joshua 8:10; 15:13). With darkness expressed that way, it is important to note Paul's exact language when he said, "Ye were sometimes darkness," not in darkness but were darkness. Again, in contrast, it says, "Now are ye light." This indicated that they were a part of what they are now against. The darkness is a morbid, gloomy state to be in, described as a *preview of things to come,* yet without the extreme pain of outer darkness where there will be "weeping and gnashing of teeth and where the worm dieth not." A person in this life has to grope along without the revealing Light of God, nor His Word, which is so dismal and without conversion, will be in an eternal state that will intensify once being cast at the Great White Throne Judgment into the Lake of Fire.

When Paul contrasts the darkness with the light, He says walk as such. Mostly, the word light is used metaphorically. In the transfiguration, Jesus' garments are said to have become white as light (Matt 17:2). John particularly liked to use light imagery. In John's Gospel, Jesus claims that he is the light of the world (John 8:12; 9:5; 12:46) and God is described as light, in whom there is no darkness (1 John 1:5).

Also, John states that the natural person loves darkness rather than light (John 3:19). Since Jesus identified himself as the light, John promises that those who believe in the light become sons of light (John 12:35–36) and cannot remain in darkness (12:46). Here, too, in Ephesians Paul states that believers were once darkness but now they are light. Light and darkness oppose each other (e.g., Isa 5:20; 9:2; 50:10; Amos 5:18; Mic 7:8; Matt 6:23 = Luke 11:34; John 3:19; 8:12; 3:19–20, 24–25). Light and darkness cannot coexist. However, darkness has no qualifier as there is with light. People in darkness are on their own or are there by their own doing, but not so with light. The prepositional phrase ἐν κυρίῳ indicates that the believer is light in the Lord. The source of light is God and Christ. Christ is identified as the source (vv. 8, 14). (Yandin)

The Spirit-Filled Life

9 *(For the fruit of the Spirit is in all goodness and righteousness and truth;)* The fruit of the Spirit for the believer who is Spirit-filled will have the fruit of the Spirit accompanying his doing good, which will make it even better. The fruit of the Spirit will also be present in the works of righteousness. "Righteousness" lies in living in obedience to the law of God, in attending the worship and service of him, and in discharging our duty to our fellow creatures; and this, as goodness, is very imperfect and not to be boasted of, or trusted to, nor is salvation to be expected from it: "truth" is opposed to lying, to hypocrisy, to error and falsehood; and where the Spirit of God, and the work of grace are, there will be more or less an appearance of these fruits. (Gill)

Paul gives a trilogy here that further describes how the fruit of the Spirit is administered in the church's work. Paul's saying indicates how the Spirit works among the Children of Light to assist them in their walk, whereas those of the flesh walk in darkness with that associated fruit. Paul has already stated goodness as a marked characteristic of the converted, born-again Children of Light. Marking this trilogy of truth with parenthesis seems to be an orderly way to define the dominant characteristics of the Children of Light. Certainly, righteousness is a word that Paul understands, as He indicated, especially in Romans 10:1-13. It is worthy of our present consideration as it considers especially the righteousness of God in one's salvation.

1 *Brethren, my heart's desire and prayer to God for Israel is, that they might be saved.* **2** *For I bear them record that they have a zeal of God, but not according to knowledge.* **3** *For they being ignorant of God's righteousness, and going about to establish their own righteousness, have not submitted themselves unto the righteousness of God.* **4** *For Christ is the end of the law for righteousness to every one that believeth.* **5** *For Moses describeth the righteousness which is of the law, That the man which doeth those things shall live by them.*

10 *Proving what is acceptable unto the Lord.* Proving is a metallurgical term that means to be put to the test, determining that the standard is met. The standard for the believer is the Lord. All comparisons should be made to him with respect to the Word of God. The word of God is the absolute standard of Truth and is not to be compromised or compared to any other, for it stands alone. Everything that is done should be modeled after the Word of God and also for the purpose of protecting one, as using the word of God to "test" your steps as David did when he said: Psalms 119:105 *"Thy word is a lamp unto my feet, and a light unto my path."* And also, Psalm 119:11 *"Thy word have I hid in mine heart, that I might not sin against thee."* David wisely knew the value of the Word for his own safety and well-being and also to instruct himself in the ways of the Lord. There were times that he did not and it had devastating effects upon him and could have been avoided by "proving what was God's will." **11** *And have no fellowship with the unfruitful works of darkness, but rather reprove them.* Paul is saying that the children of Light and, in this instance, the Ephesian believers were to have no fellowship or not to partner with the children of darkness. Instead of fellowshipping with them, their lifestyle was to be radically different from theirs and, by it being so, were to serve as a reproving agent.

12 *For it is a shame even to speak of those things which are done of them in secret.* Paul tells them their sinning was so gross that even speaking of it was shameful. The culture during Paul's day was greatly influenced by the wicked lifestyle of the Romans, who were very degraded, heading to their own fall, which could be attributed to the way they had become in their wickedness and could serve as a warning to those of us who are living today. Such wicked and defiling sins are shameful to do and talk about. **13** *But all things that are reproved are made manifest by the light: for whatsoever doth make manifest is light.* The light is opposed to darkness, and the darkness does not have that ability because it is the light that reveals and reproves. In the darkness, things are hidden. Romans 1:16,17 Tells us that the righteousness of God is revealed from faith to faith and comes from God and characterizes those whom the Gospel of the Grace of God has converted. Then, in addition to being a righteousness necessary for one's salvation, there also needs to be a "rightness" regarding a Christian witness and testimony before others. The last word mentioned in this trilogy is "truth." The word truth summarizes all that he said about the evils of lying. Anything that violates truthfulness is a lie and foreign to Christ, who is Truth. Children of Light walk in truth.

14 *Wherefore he saith, Awake thou that sleepest, and arise from the dead, and Christ shall give thee light.* Paul offers hope to those who are asleep or dead in their sins. He is communicating that there is salvation if you would put your faith and trust in Christ, for He truly is the light Giver, for He is Light. Paul was a strong student of the Old Testament, and just as students and preachers will quote from the Scriptures they are acquainted with and familiar with, so did Paul. It is not a direct quote from the Old Testament Book of Isaiah, but what he says relates to what he tells the Church in Ephesus. It also includes those still asleep Spiritually and has never been quickened or made alive by the new birth to awake upon hearing the Voice of conviction that comes from the Word of God by the Holy Spirit. Also, notice in particular how he quotes from Isaiah how it predicts the conversion of the Gentiles as they come to the Light. Notice this passage in Isaiah 60:1-3 noticing the similarities.

1 *"Arise, shine; for thy light is come, and the glory of the Lord is risen upon thee.* **2** *For, behold, the darkness shall cover the earth, and gross darkness the people: but the Lord shall arise upon thee, and his glory shall be seen upon thee.* **3** *And the Gentiles shall come to thy light, and kings to the brightness of thy rising."* Just as the Lord speaketh conviction through the Spirit, He also gives Light because He is the Light, and there is no darkness in Him. Then, in this passage found in John, Jesus prophesied that His Voice would be heard when Christ calls the dead forth from their graves. John 5:25: "Verily, verily, I say unto you, The hour is coming, and now is, when the dead shall hear the voice of the Son of God: and they that hear shall live." All these passages show the Lord working in different economies, and now He speaks to the Gentiles.

The Results of Spirit-Filled Life

In Paul's Letter to the Church at Ephesus, he refers to the ministry of the Holy Spirit in their lives (1:3, 13, 14, 17; 2:18, 22; 3:16; 4:30; 6:17–18). In chapter four, Paul spoke of how the Spirit is involved in renewing each believer's mind (4:23). Paul now shows how believers can fully receive the Spirit's work to engage in all their relationships practically with Spiritual results and on a Spiritual basis. These chapters address the word walk several times, with verse 15 being the 6th time.

15 *See then that ye walk circumspectly, not as fools, but as wise.* The use of the word circumspectly means to be vigilant and watchful, not being ensnared by Satan's devices, and, as a fool who is not wise, fall in one of Satan's snares or traps. Be on guard! This is now the sixth occurrence of the verb "walk" (περιπατεῖτε) in the second half of the letter—his favorite term for expressing moral exhortation in Ephesians (see 4:1, 17 [2x]; 5:2, 8) (Zondervan Ephesians). We labeled this entire second part of Ephesians as the "Walk of the Believer" because of the emphasis given. Paul uses the metaphor "Walk" and says the believer's walk should be done circumspectly, accurately, or ideally with much diligence and not as a fool, emphasizing not walking *unwise*. He goes on to say, instead of being unwise, "Understand the will of the Lord." The spirit of what Paul is saying involves the diligence of not sleeping but being vigilant while chasing away sleep. By doing so, one must be very careful; otherwise, he will not be walking in the will of the Lord. Believers should seize every opportunity to walk wisely, doing good as Children of Light.

In Christ in chapters 1–3, believers are called to walk in unity; (2) in 4:17, where believers are commanded to walk in *holiness* and not as the Gentiles; (3) in 5:1–2, where believers are told to walk in love; and (4) in 5:7–8 where believers are told to walk in *light* by not becoming involved with the evildoers and their works. Now, for the last time, in 5:15, his next challenge to believers is to walk in *wisdom*. (Hoehner) It benefits the student and the believer by studying the wise sayings found in the Proverbs. A careful study can foster prudence in walking the correct walk. Then James 1:5 teaches us: *"If any of you lack wisdom, let him ask of God, that giveth to all men liberally, and upbraideth not; and it shall be given him."* Wisdom is needed in all of our undertakings and responsibilities.

16 *Redeeming the time because the days are evil.* Paul is speaking while challenging them to not only be on guard but to have a great sense of urgency that causes them to be on guard and pursue the enemy. This is because of the perilous evil days that they were experiencing. While sitting under the preaching of the late Harold Sightler, while a student at Tabernacle Baptist College, I recall when he read this verse as it involved the words "Redeeming the time," I remember him saying that it meant to seize up the time that you have and make best use of that time while you are able. That explanation has stuck with me for over four decades. I certainly try to do so just as I am involving myself in writing these commentaries. His definition is also very appropriate; as Paul told the Ephesians, an excellent reason for doing so is that the days are evil, and in 2 Timothy, these days are called perilous days. As we serve God, we should do so with a driving sense of urgency. Paul said, *"I press toward the mark for the prize of the high calling of God in Christ Jesus."* (Philippians 3:14)

17 *Wherefore be ye not unwise, but understanding what the will of the Lord is.* It is totally unwise to forsake the Word of God and, when doing so, forfeit knowing the Word of God. By not knowing the Word of God, one becomes incapable of doing the will of God. To wisely appropriate and use the time you have been given, one should know that everything is a byproduct of time. Services rendered require giving one's time; giving a gift requires the use of time by many before the gift is given. There is the work involved in making the purchase, and depending on the gift, there are those involved in every facet of making the gift available. Slothfulness is a killer of time, thus the expression, "He is just killing time." To make wrong use of time as a believer means working out of the will of God, for which reason the believer must understand what the will of God is. There is a lot of just "busy work" found among Christian workers, with not much being accomplished because they do not know God's will as they work. Paul's warning is to use wisdom wisely to achieve God's intended purpose.

The following verses show the command to be filled with the Spirit and how being filled is recognized. The imperative is not to be "drunk with wine." The wine is not only something one is not to be intoxicated with, but the principle is not to let anything intoxicate you. Some can be drunk on pleasure, and others drunk on materialism. Anything that cools your affection for God can become a god to you or be something that intoxicates or controls you. Such is to beware of.

18 *And be not drunk with wine, wherein is excess; but be filled with the Spirit.* The intoxication of the worst kind is to be intoxicated with that which is fleshly, as the example of drunkenness implies, instead of being filled with the Spirit. One of the main reasons that the Lord has condemned the use of drinking and drugs is that their very first effect is to weaken inhibitions and moral judgment. Even before speech or motor skills are noticeably impaired, moral judgment and self-control are diminished. What concerns God about the use of alcoholic beverages, including the use of recreational drugs, is the effect it has on the brain. To avoid temptation and control oneself to practice what is right, one needs the full mental capacity to recognize right from wrong and the strength of willpower to do right. Alcoholic beverages hinder all of this, and that problem begins long before any outwardly noticeable evidence of physical effects. See 1 Peter 5:8; 1:13-17; 1 Corinthians 9:25-27; 1 Thessalonians 5:6-8; Proverbs 4:23. (Pratte)

Indeed, just as the command is to "be not drunk with wine," is also the command to be "Filled with the Spirit." These two commands are not complementary but in opposition to each other. Instead of being intoxicated with the flesh, one should be intoxicated with the Spirit. Instead of strong drinks controlling one, the Word of God should be what controls the Spirit-filled person. Paul likely used this comparison and contrast to vividly express that alcohol has a controlling effect and causes the person under its influence to do things they would not normally do. Likewise, a person under the control and influence of the Holy Spirit will do things they would not normally do in a very Spiritual way. Also, the Holy Spirit empowers people to be strengthened as they minister their gifts to further the Gospel. The following verses show evidence of the Spirit-filled life. (Vv. 19-21)

19 *Speaking to yourselves in psalms and hymns and spiritual songs, singing and making melody in your heart to the Lord;* This should be the inward language of the Spirit-filled person who cannot contain what lies inside of oneself when such is so but must be expressed verbally and publicly as though to say, "One cannot contain himself." The first evidence of a Spirit-filled person is that there will be a "Silent Joy." This means that within the Spirit-filled person, there is an inward joy that Spiritually affects the heart. Instead of a spirit-filled person being filled with "doom and gloom," he will radiate the song in His heart that comes as the Book of Colossians parallels a state of letting the Word of Christ dwell in one richly. People get high on alcohol and drugs because something is desperately missing in their lives. They are trying to escape from something or to find something better. They generally have no genuine contentment. They unknowingly pursue a counterfeit peace and joy that is not real. The Christian, filled with the Spirit, has found the true meaning of life, and his peace and joy will be in proportion to the Word of God dwelling in His heart. Some commentators believe singing Scriptural songs is how a person is filled with the Spirit. Instead, I think that the singing of Spiritual songs is the result of being filled with the Spirit, which is a result of letting the Word of Christ dwell in you richly. When one is obedient and hungering after God's filling and satisfying that appetite with the Word of God, the Holy Spirit richly abides in such a person, resulting in that person being Spirit-filled.

From such a heart environment, the songs should be sung, and for the songs to have deep Spiritual value, they must be Spiritual songs not geared to the flesh but to the Spiritual, inward man. Some of the most cherished songs throughout history were birthed in great trial and adversity, and the person writing the song was writing it in ways that showed how the Scriptures brought great personal comfort. When they were writing to comfort themselves, they brought others along with them and continue to do so as their songs still live and have meaning in some cases many years after their decease.

CHAPTER TWELVE

Ephesians 5:20-33

Love and Submission

VERSE SUMMARIES 5:20-33

20 *Giving thanks always for all things unto God and the Father in the name of our Lord Jesus Christ*; One's heart should be a heart of gratitude, and having gratitude especially back to the Lord knowing from whom all blessings originate. That gratitude should also spill over to others as a spirit of gratitude which characterizes your being Spirit-filled.

21 *Submitting yourselves one to another in the fear of God*. Submission should indicate a sacrificial rather than a selfish existence. This spirit indicates having a fear of God without pride.

22 *Wives, submit yourselves unto your own husbands, as unto the Lord.* By Paul wording this way to the Church at Ephesus, he may have had a concern thinking that there were wives who were living lose not being completely faithful to their own husbands, but this could also be a general statement of truth to Gard against such.

23 *For the husband is the head of the wife, even as Christ is the head of the church: and he is the saviour of the body.* In regard to Spiritual authority, Paul is saying that the husband is the Spiritual head of the wife, which includes the responsibility of being such in a protective sense where he is to care for his wife, even as Christ is "the saviour of the body."

24 *Therefore as the church is subject unto Christ, so let the wives be to their own husbands in every thing.* Paul continues to use very strong parallels that teach us even as the church is in subjection to Christ, then, in like manner, the wives should also be to their husbands.

25 *Husbands, love your wives, even as Christ also loved the church, and gave himself for it;* The same unselfish love that Christ had for the church should pattern how the husband loves his wife. Practicing this will make it easier for the wife to respond in submission.

26 *That he might sanctify and cleanse it with the washing of water by the word.* The sanctifying and cleansing that comes to the church is in proportion that each member embraces the Word. When members of the church seem to be growing when others are not, it could be that they are those who are giving more attention to the Word and prayer.

27 *That he might present it to himself a glorious church, not having spot, or wrinkle, or any such thing; but that it should be holy and without blemish.* The continuous washing of the Word allows God to present the church to Himself without spots or wrinkles. The emphasis Paul places on cleansing is directly proportional to obedience to the Word of God. A glorious church is not a tribute to the church as it is to Him who brings about the ultimate glorification.

28 *So ought men to love their wives as their own bodies. He that loveth his wife loveth himself.* This could be the "kingpin" that brings about most of the marriage failures when there is an absence of love. There is no real marriage connection if you remove the kingpin of love or it is not there. Love suffereth long and like a strong hinge pin should continue strong. Many marriage issues could be resolved if as in this example, the husband would love his wife as himself while having a fear of God at the same time. Yet, even among professing Christians, this is often sadly lacking.

29 *For no man ever yet hated his own flesh; but nourisheth and cherisheth it, even as the Lord the church*: As one strives to care for himself, he does not purposely try to destroy himself unless he is mentally deranged, or under the influence that removes his natural tendencies and allows him to take care of himself. Likewise, this statement includes the two becoming one and shows how we should do towards our wives as Christ does towards the church.

30 *For we are members of his body, of his flesh, and of his bones.* Another strong statement of truth pertains to our saved relationship with Christ and is kin to the statement when Adam was first introduced to his wife and recognized she was bone of his bone and flesh of his flesh.

31 *For this cause shall a man leave his father and mother, and shall be joined unto his wife, and they two shall be one flesh.* This speaks wonderfully of the miracle of marriage ordained by God and called Holy Matrimony. For those who really experience what God designed to the fullest and even greater when both marriage partners are saved believers, the marriage oneness can not be experienced the same in any other way.

32 *This is a great mystery: but I speak concerning Christ and the church.* Paul skillfully interrelates the marriage of the husband to his wife and the church to its groom. While Paul uses this comparison, he also reminds the Church at Ephesus that everything Paul is saying is to ultimately concern the church and its benefits by having its membership in harmony and excelling in the world as they let their light shine through their obedience to the world.

33 *Nevertheless let every one of you in particular so love his wife even as himself; and the wife see that she reverence her husband.* This seems to be a challenging summary statement of how the marriage order should be. The two focus points for each should be both a description of their sacred roles toward each other and a means for protecting both marriage partners from marriage collapse.

The Beginning of the Commentary 5:20-33

Wives in Submission to Their Husbands

20 *Giving thanks always for all things unto God and the Father in the name of our Lord Jesus Christ.* One's heart should be a heart of gratitude and having gratitude, especially back to the Lord, knowing from whom all blessings originate. That gratitude should also spill over to others as a spirit of gratitude. The second notable evidence of a Spirit-filled person is having "A Spirit of Thanksgiving." This is not just thanking God directly for all those things we should be thankful for from Him, but *a spirit of thanksgiving that should prevail in our very being to every person who benefits us in any manner.* A person should be truly thankful for every action directed positively towards them, including every gift given them. Also, I have made it my practice for many years (my dad taught me this) when I listen to a preacher of the Word to go and personally thank him after he finishes preaching. I cannot remember but a time or two that I did not. I believe there may be a similar ratio of people today who do not offer thanks when they should, as in this example from the ten lepers. When Jesus healed the ten lepers, only one returned after such an enormous event. Occasionally, I will attend meetings and give a commentary or book I have written to all the preachers in attendance. When I do so, there are just a few who make an effort to say

"Thank you." I am not saying they do not appreciate my giving it to them; it is just a tendency we have, and we all probably need to work on it. But being Spirit-filled should make it much easier not to forget if we have a spirit of thanksgiving within us.

21 *Submitting yourselves one to another in the fear of God.* Submission should indicate a sacrificial rather than a selfish existence. This spirit indicates having a fear of God without pride. The third indication of being filled with the Spirit is: "Submitting one to another." Some have the spirit of arrogance, "It is my way or the highway." The Scriptures also indicate this spirit of submission by saying in Romans 12:10, *"Be kindly affectioned one to another with brotherly love; in honor preferring one another."* Ephesians 4:2 speaks of having humility, meekness, long-suffering, and forbearing one another in love, which will contribute to having a reverential respect of God, which then causes one to have a spirit of self-denial that will help in one's submitting to one another. This spirit is essential for there to be strength among those in the Christian community. That same spirit will be apparent in the church, the home, and human government, which are the God-ordained three institutions. The way we all should respond to authorities is noted in Romans 13:1-5 as follows: **1** *Let every soul be subject unto the higher powers. For there is no power but of God: the powers that be are ordained of God.* **2** *Whosoever therefore resisteth the power, resisteth the ordinance of God: and they that resist shall receive to themselves damnation.* **3** *For rulers are not a terror to good works, but to the evil. Wilt thou then not be afraid of the power? do that which is good, and thou shalt have praise of the same:* **4** *For he is the minister of God to thee for good. But if thou do that which is evil, be afraid; for he beareth not the sword in vain: for he is the minister of God, a revenger to execute wrath upon him that doeth evil.*

5 *Wherefore ye must needs be subject, not only for wrath, but also for conscience sake.*

What Paul said to the Romans is in complete agreement with what he said to the Ephesians regarding submission but is on an extended scale which includes all authorities. Christians should be obedient with respect to all authorities. To be otherwise would be rebellion against those authorities and constitute them being law breakers. The only exception is when those authorities call upon you to do something against God's law. The punishment of the lawbreaker is a means to build fear in the hearts of the one breaking the law. Romans 13 also tells us that the lowest level of obedience is fear. It is followed by conscience, love, and then obeying for "Christ's sake."

Although the English term "submit" is viewed in a pejorative way today and is often seen as a sign of weakness or as something one should resist at all costs, it should not be seen in such negative terms here. In general, the verb (ὑποτάσσω) is widely used for the proper social ordering of people, as, for example, warriors giving their allegiance to their commander (e.g., 1 Chr 29:24). Similarly, people living in a certain political jurisdiction are obliged to respect the authority of (ὑποτάσσεσθαι) their local governor. This carries with it the responsibility to live in an orderly manner and not to be seditious or rebellious (Josephus, Ant. 17.314). The following show some of the ways this is accomplished in our relationships:

22 *Wives, submit yourselves unto your own husbands, as unto the Lord.* By Paul wording this way to the Church at Ephesus, he may have had a concern thinking that there were wives who were living lose not being completely faithful to their own husbands, but this could also be a general statement of truth to Gard against such. The preparatory command is given to the woman who is under the man's authority as husband. In each of these commands, that is the pattern. The one who is under authority is spoken to first. The seriousness of the submission is given with the wife's respect to the man being submitted to in the same way that one would submit to the Lord. It is not tyrannical submission nor in any way demanded by the husband. It is love-based and to be reverently performed as the husband likewise is to love his wife respectfully. He should also submit to her if she is correct and he is wrong. That would fall under the command to submit one to another when it is appropriate to do so. The woman is not to submit to another man or husband in the same way as she would her own husband. This Biblical requirement is resisted by the feminists, among others, who, most recently, are demeaning the white male. This is an outright attack on God's plan and His way of ordering his creation. Many of the resistant movements go against God's order and design. They are not against man as much as they seem to be as they are against God.

23 *For the husband is the head of the wife, even as Christ is the head of the church: and he is the saviour of the body.* Regarding Spiritual authority, Paul is saying that the husband is the Spiritual head of the wife, which includes the responsibility of being such in a protective sense where he is to care for his wife, even as Christ is "the saviour of the body." Since the time of the Reformation, Bible scholars have referred to Paul's instructions to wives and husbands, children and fathers, and slaves and masters as a "household code." The expression was first coined by Martin Luther, who referred to it as a *Haustafel* (a table of instructions for the household). It is important to note that there was no identifiable literary form that we can call a "household code" in ancient literature. Although Aristotle mentions the same social groups addressed in Colossians and Ephesians, nowhere else in Hellenistic or Jewish literature do we see each of these groups addressed in succession as we do here. Some interpreters have attempted to argue that there was an identifiable source for the tradition of the household codes in Stoicism (e.g., Epictetus, Diogenes Laertius, and Hierocles).3 But this has ultimately failed since there are no precise parallels in form, and key features of the content of the Stoic exhortation to family members are decidedly different than what is found in Colossians and Ephesians. (Arnold)

Some of the ideas that Luther addressed went back to Plato and Aristotle four centuries before Paul wrote to the Ephesians. Paul injects into their teachings both removing and adding some things to line it up with the mind of the Lord. Nowhere else in either Hellenistic or Jewish literature do we see the order that Paul shows in this section. Peter also listed the family requirements and order as Paul also did in the Pastoral Epistles when we notice how Paul speaks of the Head of the wife, which has been understood historically as him being the authority figure according to God's order and design. In the 1970s and 1980s, some theologians tried to change the word *head* to mean source. These seem to be an attempt to bring the Bible in line with society's view. To do so caused too many contradictions of how the word would have to be similarly used to describe other things that would make using it that way awkward. You would not say that cows are the "head" of milk. You would use the word source. The word head is also a metaphor that is part of Paul's greater metaphor: the body. In such a case, Christ is the *head* of the *body*. Paul uses well-known illustrations to help clarify deeper truths.

24 *Therefore as the church is subject unto Christ, so let the wives be to their own husbands in every thing.* With Paul wording this verse in this manner, he shows how serious this kind of order is necessary in the home. So many homes do not have this kind of leadership, and without embracing and following God's order, the homes are severely affected and may become dysfunctional. The *every thing* expression shows that the way the wives submit is not like a smorgasbord where she picks and chooses at her own discretion and according to her own whims. Yet, in our declining culture, this has sadly become commonplace. There are weaknesses on the part of modern-day husbands and wives that make their responsibilities to each other more overwhelming. It may be traced back to an unwillingness to be Spirit-filled. When this is true, their attitudes are more selfish or self-serving, with no self-sacrificing on the part of one or the other. Therefore, their stability and their intimacy are affected because they are out of the will of God. Paul is teaching the Ephesians and the extended Christian families how to prosper in their relationships instead of being Spiritually impoverished.

Husbands Love Your Wives

25 *Husbands love your wives, even as Christ also loved the church and gave himself for it.* The same unselfish love that Christ had for the church should pattern how the husband loves his wife. Practicing this will make it easier for the wife to respond in submission. Even as the preparatory command was given to the wives, the husbands also had their responsibilities in their God-given relationships. Paul gives them a lofty challenge that every married believer should strive for. It is not suggesting how much, for that is not possible. But Paul does give a pattern or example of how we are to love our wives just as Christ loved the church. Then, there should be a sacrificial love like Christ also had for the church. As He sacrificed His life on the cross, we should be willing to sacrifice our lives if need be. If never called on to sacrifice in a crisis situation, we ought to sacrifice a portion of our lives continuously if that is needed; if it means working two jobs to provide for her and the family's needs, the husband should do so. That may not be the ideal, but having that spirit as a provider may mean such. This would be a way that the husband has a love for his wife, which may mean this in one's giving.

The command entails the husband's responsibility regardless of his wife's behavior, health condition, appearance, or any other potential deterrent. The fact that Christ loved the church—even in her most unlovely and unbecoming state—defines the love commitment that Christ expects from a Christian husband. His love should be unconditional. (Arnold) So many have walked away from their marriages when the first storm or conflict comes, which ought not to be so. This is attributed to no commitment and a lack of love. Any marriage should be worth fighting for and committing to work through marriage issues when possible. To do otherwise often brings ongoing troubles that will have to be dealt with for a lifetime, never with any resolution.

26 *That he might sanctify and cleanse it with the washing of water by the word.* The sanctifying and cleansing that comes to the church is in proportion that each member embraces the Word. When members of the church seem to be growing when others are not, it could be that they are those who are giving more attention to the Word and prayer. Paul speaks of the sanctity of the church as being cleansed with the washing of water, with the water being understood as the Word of God, though some tie it back to water baptism. Water baptism has no sanctifying agent about it. Still, in a pictorial sense, it pictures the death, burial, and resurrection of our Lord and Savior, Jesus Christ, which does not diminish its purpose and value at all. Reformed theology refers to baptism as a sacrament, whereas Baptist theology refers to it as an ordinance. Here is a typical statement of what Baptist churches believe about baptism (as found on the Web site for the Canadian Convention of Southern Baptists): "Christian baptism is the immersion of a believer in water in the name of the Father, the Son, and the Holy Spirit. It is an act of obedience symbolizing the believer's faith in a crucified, buried, and risen Saviour, the believer's death to sin, the burial of the old life, and the resurrection to walk in the newness of life in Christ Jesus. It is testimony to his faith in the final resurrection of the dead." Being a church ordinance, it is a prerequisite to the privileges of church membership and to the Lord's Supper. Baptism is not a means by which God conveys grace but is a testimony of a person who has believed. It is a sign, but not a seal. Where sacraments revolve around what God does, ordinances revolve around what man does and what God did. (Challies)

Water is used in physical and ceremonial cleansing, but water in and of itself does not clean Spiritually, whereas the Word of God does, and Water pictures the Word and, at times, the Holy Spirit. The Bible uses water as a type depending on how the water is mentioned. Moving water pictures the Spirit of God, and still water pictures the Word of God. Notice these passages in John 3:5: *"Jesus answered, Verily, verily, I say unto thee, Except a man be born of water and of the Spirit, he cannot enter into the kingdom of God."* John 4:13-14: "**13** *Jesus answered and said unto her, Whosoever drinketh of this water shall thirst again*: This refers to the actual drinking of water, which is necessary for one's physical survival. In this next verse, the Lord says, **14** *But whosoever drinketh of the water that I shall give him shall never thirst; but the water that I shall give him shall be in him a well of water springing up into everlasting life."* This is a way that the Lord used water as a metaphor to convey the Spiritual lesson of how necessary water is for one's physical well-being, but how Spiritual water is necessary for the imparting of life eternal.

In John 7:37-39 37, *"In the last day, that great day of the feast, Jesus stood and cried, saying, If any man thirst, let him come unto me, and drink.* **38** *He that believeth on me, as the scripture hath said, out of his belly shall flow rivers of living water.* **39** *(But this spake he of the Spirit, which they that believe on him should receive: for the Holy Ghost was not yet given; because that Jesus was not yet glorified.)"* The type presented here shows flowing or moving water as a type or picture of the Holy Spirit.

27 *That he might present it to himself a glorious church, not having spot, or wrinkle, or any such thing; but that it should be holy and without blemish. but that it should be holy and without blemish.* The continuous washing of the Word allows God to present the church to Himself without spots or wrinkles. The emphasis Paul places on cleansing is directly proportional to obedience to the Word of God. A glorious church is not a tribute to the church as it is to Him who brings about the ultimate glorification. Some theologians describe the church as without *"spot or wrinkle,"* picturing the marriage garment or wedding dress as without wrinkles or any soil or blemish. This way of picturing a glorious church is not at all wrong, but understanding the meaning may involve going back further into their culture and time frame. I received this way of interpreting this thought many decades ago and do not know the source; I only remember who shared it with me. *In the earthly sense*, Evangelist C.L. Roach said that this pictures how a father would select a maiden to be his son's wife and the mother of his grandchildren. He would look for a young fair lady without having spots. There were skin conditions that would cause one to have blemishes, which could be described as spots.

Pellagra was a disease that would give such blemishes as defined here: "A deficiency disease caused by a lack of nicotinic acid or its precursor tryptophan in the diet. It is characterized by dermatitis, diarrhea, and mental changes and is often linked to over-dependence on corn as a staple food, which would also be a poor man's food."

This condition is caused by malnutrition, which means the health has been compromised. The father would keenly be looking for such to avoid having a wife for his son, being plagued by weakness, which could affect the ongoing marriage and may even weaken their offspring or cause her to be unable to bear children. When Paul made a Spiritual parallel to this, he said that a malnourished church will be sorely affected and may not even be able to have Spiritual offspring. The wrinkle that is spoken of could have described the father looking for a young girl without wrinkles. Wrinkles are okay for an older person but should not be prevalent in a young person. To have them could mean that she is prone to worry. Therefore, using these two examples, it seems that Paul wanted to give the idea of the church being a glorious church fed on the Word of God and exercising faith, meaning that it is not malnourished or faithless. The glorious church will be a faith church and a fed church!

Then, in the ultimate or the eternal sense, Christ will sanctify and present the church to Himself as a glorious church with no spot or wrinkle or any such thing and never will again. The believer should long for this: to be with Him and enjoy the final glorification. The Church of the Firstborn will be such that everyone will enjoy the same and complete glorification.

28 So ought men to love their wives as their own bodies. He that loveth his wife loveth himself. This could be the "kingpin" that brings about most of the marriage failures when there is an absence of love. There is no real marriage connection if you remove the kingpin of love or it is not there. Love suffereth long and like a strong hinge pin should continue strong. Many marriage issues could be resolved if as in this example, the husband would love his wife as himself while having a fear of God at the same time. Yet, even among professing Christians, this is often sadly lacking. The parallel thought is to Christ's pattern in loving His bride; the husband should do the same towards his bride, so much so that his love for the wife should exceed his love for himself. Self-love to the extreme is selfishness. Many marriages collapse because of a lack of love for either or both mates. When one mate begins to focus on the weaknesses or the deficiencies of the marriage partner, there is the temptation to leave and find some improvement. Yet, statistically, this does not usually happen; the problems are compounded. The only leaving mentioned in the Scriptures that God sanctions is when the man and the woman leave their parents and cleave to each other. Cleaving is a very endearing term that shows how much their oneness should be.

    I recall an illustration of what the word cleave is like. If one compared the marriage to two blocks of wood glued together and pulled apart with much force, the splintered wood would leave many jagged edges. This *tearing* found in a marriage breakup should be avoided at all costs... The level of commitment between them should be irrevocable and strengthened by love with the imperative given to the man to love his wife and the wife likewise. This kind of love is the love of the will, accompanied by the love of emotion or passion. If the emotional love or passion begins to wane, that is a clear signal that there should be a spirit of reconciliation where the two strive to become friends again or more friendly towards each other. If that is not accomplished, loving one's mate should sustain one until one can resolve the "Ooey-gooey" part of marriage or the sweet, sentimental relationship we enjoy.

Christ Our Example

29 *For no man ever yet hated his own flesh; but nourisheth and cherisheth it, even as the Lord the church*: As one strives to care for himself, he does not purposely try to destroy himself unless he is mentally deranged, or under the influence that removes his natural tendencies and allows him to take care of himself. Likewise, this statement includes the two becoming one and shows how we should do towards our wives as Christ does towards the church. In stark contrast to hating one's body is caring for it, and Paul expresses the manner of this care with two colorful verbs. "Nourishes" is a word that appears throughout the Bible for the kind of care parents provide for their children. Paul uses it in the following passage to instruct fathers on the care they should give (6:4; see also 1 Kings 11:20; Job 31:18; Hosea 9:12). The second verb originally had the idea of providing heat. It was used, for instance, of a mother bird brooding over her nest (Deuteronomy 22:6). It was also used metaphorically to give nurturing care and cherish someone. Paul uses forms of both terms when he describes his compassionate care for the Thessalonians while he was ministering to them during his first visit: "But we were gentle among you, even as a nurse cherisheth her children:" (1 Thessalonians 2:7). Once again, the pattern and example that husbands are to follow is that of Christ. Husbands are to consider how Christ presently cares for his church and follow his lead in tenderly caring and providing for their wives. It is through the ascended Christ that the whole body receives all it needs for building up itself in love (4:16; see also 1:23; 4:7–12; 5:14; 6:10). (Arnold)

Once again, Paul gives Christ as the exemplar or example,

for He is the perfect Model. He is greatly to be praised as the husband honors his wife. If you neglect to do so, you may forget how special she is and instead become critical and even bitter towards her, which is prohibited in the Scriptures. (Colossians 3:19) 19 *"Husbands, love your wives, and be not bitter against them."*

30 *For we are members of his body, of his flesh, and of his bones.* Another strong statement of truth pertains to our saved relationship with Christ and is kin to the statement when Adam was first introduced to his wife and then recognized she was bone of his bone and flesh of his flesh. Paul also uses the body by using three metaphors that we are all familiar with to show our identification and relationship with the lord. Paul makes no mistake in relating the husband to his wife, as Christ is to His bride, the church. Paul may be using this analogy, which seems to tie back to Adam's statement upon receiving his bride from the Lord as found in Genesis 2:23,24: *"And Adam said, This is now bone of my bones, and flesh of my flesh: she shall be called Woman, because she was taken out of Man. 24 Therefore shall a man leave his father and his mother, and shall cleave unto his wife: and they shall be one flesh."* This description is a very wonderful and tender expression to show, in both cases, the infused relationship they were both able to enjoy.

31 *For this cause shall a man leave his father and mother, and shall be joined unto his wife, and they two shall be one flesh.* This speaks wonderfully of the miracle of marriage ordained by God and called Holy Matrimony. For those who really experience what God designed to the fullest and even greater when both marriage partners are saved believers, the marriage oneness can not be experienced the same in any other way. The verse has the idea of a man and woman coming together in a close and intimate relationship that encompasses every aspect of their beings—emotional, physical, and spiritual. It certainly includes the physical relationship since Paul uses a cognate verb to speak of the bonding that occurs between a man and a prostitute when they engage in sexual intercourse (1 Corinthians 6:16), but the bonding in marriage goes far beyond a physical union. Hoehner pushes the imagery further, asserting that two items glued together are not the same as an alloy (a mixture of metals) "because in that case, the distinctiveness of each person would be lost." He correctly asserts that each object maintains its distinctive features; thus, husbands and wives do not surrender their personalities or unique traits when they marry. (Arnold).

The imagery of leaving and cleaving shows how one's primary affection for one's parents becomes the primary affection rendered to one's marriage partner. This does not mean that there is no continual love for the parents; it just means that the environment has changed for a new family to be birthed into existence, which has been the pattern for millenniums. The leaving indicates a strong departure, and the cleaving represents a strong arrival into another relationship. That relationship is welded together to become one.

32 *This is a great mystery: but I speak concerning Christ and the church.* Paul skillfully interrelates the husband's marriage to his wife and the church to its groom. While Paul uses this comparison, he also reminds the Church at Ephesus that everything Paul is saying is to ultimately concern the church and its benefits by having its membership in harmony and excelling in the world as they let their light shine through their obedience to the world.

Paul is saying that all of this is a great mystery, or how he likens the two together is new to them. Still, for the Church at Ephesus, he is telling them that he is showing not only the fidelity of marriage but also in addition to strengthening the marriage by offering the parallels; he is ultimately, within the context of the Letter, wanting the Church of Ephesus to become and be stronger.

33 *Nevertheless let every one of you in particular so love his wife even as himself; and the wife see that she reverence her husband.* This seems to be a challenging summary statement of how the marriage order should be. The two focus points for each should be both a description of their sacred roles toward each other and a means for protecting both marriage partners from marriage collapse. Paul said, though he directed the main thoughts towards the church, don't forget your relationship one to another. When Paul describes the relationship of the children to their parents and the slave to his master, he does not compare any of these relationships to the church as he does with the wife and husband. Paul addresses each but always keeps the Church at Ephesus in mind so that it may become stronger as a church.

Then, Paul ends this chapter with this thought. "And the wife see that she reverence her husband." I found that I was wrongly interpreting this part of the verse by calling the reverence mentioned here as being that of having respect, but I learned that such an interpretation does not go far enough. The Greek word for reverence is not just respect but fear and is used not to mean that the husband is one to fear as you would a terroristic threat; the meaning goes beyond respect to have an exceeding reverence for the husband. This is not the kind of terror or fear that one would have for a murderer. Nevertheless, correctly understanding what Paul was saying requires examining the word reverence. The actual Greek word is a word that is common to us all as it is used in different ways. The Greek word is phobéō, from which we get the transliterated word phobia. This word shows a kind of terror they feel towards things. This does not at all mean that this kind of fear is to be directed towards the husband, although the same root word is used. It does, however, elevate the word from having respect for the husband to having an exceeding reverence for the husband. Today, finding one having even a core respect for her husband is becoming more challenging, much less exceeding respect or reverence. The spirit of the way this word is used is seen in I Peter 3:5: *"For after this manner in the old time the holy women also, who trusted in God, adorned themselves, being in subjection unto their own husbands: 6 Even as Sara obeyed Abraham, calling him lord: whose daughters ye are, as long as ye do well, and are not afraid with any amazement. 7 Likewise, ye husbands, dwell with them according to knowledge, giving honour unto the wife, as unto the weaker vessel, and as being heirs together of the grace of life; that your prayers be not hindered."*

To show ways this word is more commonly used as a *fear* word, notice the following list:

- Achluophobia or nyctophobia: This refers to a fear of darkness.
- Androphobia: This refers to a fear of men.
- Autophobia: This refers to a fear of being alone.
- Bacteriophobia: This refers to a fear of bacteria.
- Hydrophobia, or aquaphobia: This refers to a fear of water.
- Necrophobia: This refers to a fear of death or dead things.
- Pyrophobia: This refers to a fear of fire.
- Somniphobia: This refers to a fear of sleep.
- Claustrophobia: Fear of being enclosed.

Though this word does not carry the kind of strength that causes an overwhelming fear that would be satanic or even the kind that appears in the above list, by it having the same root meaning, it does emphasize the intensity of the wife's respect towards her husband for a positive benefit to both her and her husband. This word means, as stressed, more than just casual respect but a holy respect that should be balanced out by the husband's love for the wife. The husband does not take this word as an improper excuse to be dominating or harsh toward his wife. Therefore, the way the wife fears her husband is to reverence, revere, and treat him with deference or reverential obedience, while ideally, the husband loves his wife as Christ loved the church and gave himself for it. Sadly, in so many marriage relationships, this kind of reverence on the part of the wife and love on the part of the husband towards his wife is missing. This passage teaches us that the marriage relationship is holy, and it is no wonder that the feminist groups are vehemently opposed to this kind of rationale and are constantly belittling the role of the male and do not at all embrace the Scriptural teachings of Paul. There is also a human tendency for the wife to not submit to her husband's authority, and she needs to realize how devastating it can be to the marriage, just as when the husband does not correctly love his wife.

CHAPTER THIRTEEN
Ephesians 6:1-24

VERSE SUMMARIES 6:1-24

1 *Children, obey your parents in the Lord: for this is right.* Some New Testament texts, especially the Epistles to the Colossians (Col 3:18-4:1) and Ephesians (Eph 5:21-6:9) as well as 1Tim 6:1-2 and 1Pet 2:18-3:7, contain descriptions of the ideal family according to societal expectations of the time. These so-called "household codes," already begun by Aristotle, depict the relationships of the male head of household with his wife, children, and slaves—an integral part of the affluent household in Roman society. (Osiek) Paul continues a Christian view of the Household Code, introduced by Aristotle and made known mostly by Plato, who was his student, lining it up with how the Christian home should be modeled. He shows that the children are to obey their parents in the Lord. The ancient code before Paul was harsher; with that being said, Paul did not make it weaker but more in line with how Christ adds value to the home when his instructions are followed.

2 *Honour thy father and mother; which is the first commandment with promise*; Paul wisely knew that the home or, as many now would say, the nuclear family should be the starting point for teaching submission to the authorities. If the children grow up as rebels in the home, they will more likely be rebels in society. This may be the reason that God placed a promise on this commandment to help the family and society to be governed appropriately.

3 *That it may be well with thee, and thou mayest live long on the earth.* The word may as used in this verse, signifies that it is not a law but a principle that contributes to general good health and well-being. Even in one's adversity, not having pressures associated with a wicked life will help make it well with those who honor and obey their parents.

4 *And, ye fathers, provoke not your children to wrath: but bring them up in the nurture and admonition of the Lord.* The command is given to the father, who represents the Spiritual head of the home, and in that position, is both answerable to how he raises and orders his home and credited with doing it rightly.

5 *Servants, be obedient to them that are your masters according to the flesh, with fear and trembling, in singleness of your heart, as unto Christ;* The servants mentioned here seem to be a part of the household and are told to be obedient to their masters even as children would be to their parents.

6 *Not with eyeservice, as menpleasers; but as the servants of Christ, doing the will of God from the heart;* It is a most wonderful relationship when the servants are working with a heart attitude of serving Christ as believers. When they do this, they do it in the spirit that Christ is always observing and watching them.

7 *With good will doing service, as to the Lord, and not to men*: When the believing servant realizes he is serving God as he also serves his master, it will contribute to his doing it with the right attitude.

8 *Knowing that whatsoever good thing any man doeth, the same shall he receive of the Lord, whether he be bond or free.* This verse says that the Lord will remember and care for those who do likewise in a kind and generous spirit. The same is indicated in Hebrews 6:10, *"For God is not unrighteous to forget your work and labour of love, which ye have shewed toward his name, in that ye have ministered to the saints, and do minister."*

9 *And, ye masters, do the same things unto them, forbearing threatening: knowing that your Master also is in heaven;*

neither is there respect of persons with him. Do the same with no partiality Paul is writing to the Masters.

10 *Finally, my brethren, be strong in the Lord, and in the power of his might.* People confidently boast in their strength; sickness and aging can remove that kind of confidence, but even as the outward man perishes, the inward should be renewed day by day. (2 Corinthians 4:16) Therefore, we should gain our strength in the Lord.

11 *Put on the whole armour of God, that ye may be able to stand against the wiles of the devil.* Satan is a formidable foe and worthy of respect and not lightly to be regarded, thus one's outfit and equipment should be put on with great respect. His greatness pales in comparison to Christ's greatness, so when you put on the armor of God, you are also putting on Christ.

12 *For we wrestle not against flesh and blood, but against principalities, against powers, against the rulers of the darkness of this world, against spiritual wickedness in high places.* The warfare mentioned is not the fights we have with our fellow humans, but in the region of darkness, which is a way of describing that which is foreign to the Light which is in Christ Jesus. In John 3, we are told that men love darkness more than light because their deeds are evil. That shows a connection to Satan's rule described as principalities.

13 *Wherefore take unto you the whole armour of God, that ye may be able to withstand in the evil day, and having done all, to stand.* The word "Wherefore," as Paul uses it here, is him reiterating the necessity of the armor and why it is so. Standing is an exercise that should occur in both an offensive and a defensive posture.

14 *Stand, therefore, having your loins girt about with truth, and having on the breastplate of righteousness;* The normal use of the girdle is to compress, and the wide belt used by the soldier is to prepare one's body for intense warfare. The thickness of the belt also adds thickness to the midsection more than just the soldier's skin. The wide belt with the breastplate can help reflect the enemies' arrows or darts. The metaphor is given by Paul showing how important the belt of truth is to the Spiritual warrior, as the leather belt is to the soldier in human battle.

15 *And your feet shod with the preparation of the gospel of peace*; Feet and the legs of a soldier are so important, and I am told that the big toe helps one greatly to maintain his balance. For a soldier to have the agility to exercise his warfare, he should protect his feet. In Christian symbolism, Paul says how beautiful are the feet of them that preach the gospel of peace…(Romans 10:13)

"And how shall they preach, except they be sent? as it is written, How beautiful are the feet of them that preach the gospel of peace, and bring glad tidings of good things!"

16 *Above all, taking the shield of faith, wherewith ye shall be able to quench all the fiery darts of the wicked.* The shield of faith has such a prominent part to play in the believer's armor. Paul said "above all," and his saying this related to just how important faith is to the believer's warfare and his total existence. Noticing the shield size that Paul may have been thinking of makes what he is saying more understandable.

17 *And take the helmet of salvation, and the sword of the Spirit, which is the word of God*: The helmet was often decorated and played a part in identifying the soldier and intimidating the enemy soldier. Salvation is a word that is cardinal to our faith, and how it is used here is how we are safe in His so great salvation, and further protected and engaging when holding the Sword of the Spirit.

18 *Praying always with all prayer and supplication in the Spirit, and watching thereunto with all perseverance and supplication for all saints;* **19** *And for me, that utterance may* *be given unto me, that I may open my mouth boldly, to make known the mystery of the gospel,* **20** *For which I am an ambassador in bonds: that therein I may speak boldly, as I ought to speak.* Paul continues to emphasize the value of prayer and his desire to be bold when he speaks, whether he is in chains or not, to preach the mystery of the gospel.

21 *But that ye also may know my affairs, and how I do, Tychicus, a beloved brother and faithful minister in the Lord, shall make known to you all things:* **22** *Whom I have sent unto you for the same purpose, that ye might know our affairs, and that he might comfort your hearts.* Paul lets them know by his signature that what he was writing is true and that Tychicus was the messenger he used to convey to those who read his letter that it was indeed from him. He personalized it by saying in their presence, "Amen", or that all was well regardless of Paul being in Chains.

23 *Peace be to the brethren, and love with faith, from God the Father and the Lord Jesus Christ.* **24** *Grace be with all them that love our Lord Jesus Christ in sincerity. Amen.* Just as these words appear in his salutation as he began the Letter, so do they now appear in his conclusion.

Commentary For Chapter 6:1-24

Children, Parents-Masters, Servants

1 *Children, obey your parents in the Lord: for this is right.* Some New Testament texts, especially the Epistles to the Colossians (Col 3:18-4:1) and Ephesians (Eph 5:21-6:9) as well as 1Tim 6:1-2 and 1Pet 2:18-3:7, contain descriptions of the ideal family according to societal expectations of the time. These so-called "household codes," already begun by Aristotle, depict the relationships of the male head of household with his wife, children, and slaves—an integral part of the affluent household in Roman society. (Osiek) Paul continues a Christian view of the Household Code, introduced by Aristotle and made known mostly by Plato, who was his student, lining it up with how the Christian home should be modeled. He shows that the children are to obey their parents in the Lord. The ancient code before Paul was harsher; with that being said, Paul did not make it weaker but more in line with how Christ adds value to the home when his instructions are followed.

Instead of using the word "submit" as he did of the relationship of wives to their husbands, Paul uses the common word for "obey." "Submit" is not strong enough to express the unquestioning compliance expected from children toward their parents. The Pentateuch warns of the danger of having a stubborn and rebellious son who does not obey his father and mother and will not listen to them when they discipline him. (Deut 21:18). It is the God-given duty of parents to set boundaries for their children and expect them to obey. Failure to do so results in the Lord's displeasure and leads children to rebel against the Lord. God revealed to the priest Eli through Samuel the prophet that he would judge Eli's family because "his sons made themselves contemptible, and he failed to restrain them" (1 Sam 3:13). (Ephesians; Zondervan Book 10, pages 709-710)

"In the Lord" expresses how the Spirit-filled family should be further characterized in the parent-child relationship. The raising of children should be such a wonderful and holy enterprise. To add much credibility to it being a spiritual endeavor on the part of the parents requires a holy allegiance to the Word of God. For this to happen, the parents must endeavor to know what the Scriptures teach and desire to learn so that they may teach. When obedience on the part of the children concerning them being properly taught from the Word of God helps make this so. When the children are obedient, they have been adequately instructed, can be instructed, and choose to be instructed. Since the Scriptures give explicit instructions on how they should obey their parents, it is understood that they are mature enough to receive the instructions. Furthermore, this very first verse teaches that to obey their parents in "the Lord" is right.

2 *Honour thy father and mother; which is the first commandment with promise*; Paul wisely knew that the home or, as many now would say, the nuclear family should be the starting point for teaching submission to authority. If the children grow up as rebels in the home, they will more likely be rebels in society. This may be the reason that God placed a promise on this commandment to help the family and society to be governed appropriately and proper honor given.

The word *Honour* is a word that allows one to fix value on the one who is thus honored. Respectively and reverently, one should revere their parents as a holy command from the Lord with promise. If the children recognize this truth and strive to implement what God is saying should be done, they will discover and see significant benefits from having done so. Our society has so much rebellion and disrespect, even in upper places where there should not be. The absence of such could be linked back to children growing into adults without having any respect for their parents, which results in their having no respect and regard for authorities. They, therefore, will have no respect for one another unless it is for selfish gain, and it is only an act when they seem to show respect, but it is not in such instances coming from the heart.

The home should be the laboratory for building such noble respect as Paul instructs the Ephesians and, thus, all who are Christians likewise. God chose this commandment (the fifth commandment in the Decalogue) to be the first commandment of the commandments to have a promise connected to it. The Decalogue only contains this one promise, but the following commandments are included as those that may also have included promises. Keeping the law or the commandments is given to help maintain and strengthen our government, order, safety, general well-being, etc.

3 *That it may be well with thee, and thou mayest live long on the earth.* The promise is expressed in two parts. First, it will be well with those who keep the law, and as a principle, will contribute to one's longevity. It is not a law but, as indicated, a principle meaning that some reverence and honor their parents who do not live long... some do not honor their parents who live to be very old. However, the benefit of obeying one's parents has many associated values that contribute to a safer and longer life. In contrast, those who do not are more prone to do things that shorten one's life. The word may as used in this verse, signifies that it is not a law but a principle that contributes to general good health and well-being. Even in one's adversity, not having pressures associated with a wicked life will help make it well with those who honor and obey their parents.

4 *And, ye fathers, provoke not your children to wrath: but bring them up in the nurture and admonition of the Lord.* The command is given to the father, who represents the Spiritual head of the home, and in that position, is both answerable to how he raises and orders his home and credited with doing it rightly. During the days of Paul in the Roman government, some were very harsh towards their children, and such harshness would cause the children to cringe and then challenge their father's harshness in their anger while feeling no love in their relationship towards their father or even their mothers. This is also possible for all families of all ages when there is no love or kindness in the home or when the fathers (or mothers) provoke their children to wrath by angry, uncontrolled outbursts. These outbursts can have devastating effects on the children and can scar them and cause them to develop fits of anger as well, and as they have their children, the vicious cycle continues. On the other hand, raising their children in the nurture and admonition of the Lord can yield positive and spiritual results that would add value to their lives for perhaps years to come. Paul is telling the fathers not to provoke their children to wrath. By saying that, Paul prefers that the home be a sanctuary where the entire family can resort and find peace from the tensions and turmoil that are often present in the world. Instead of their being provocation, as it involved the children, there should be admonition.

"Admonition" is more narrowly focused than "instruction" and refers to verbal counsel, including exhortations to proper behavior, warnings, and even rebukes. The term's meaning has remained close to its etymology, which combines the word for "mind" and the verb "to put." It has accurately been described as "the exertion of influence upon the nous [the mind], implying that there is resistance. Using admonition, advice, warning, reminding, teaching and spurring on, a person can be redirected from wrong ways and his behavior corrected." (Zondervan, Ephesians, NT Book 10, P. 716). What better way to be admonished for correction and instruction than for a Spirit-filled Father to teach according to the very Words of God and, like David of old, have the paths of their children lit by the Word of God?

5 *Servants, be obedient to them that are your masters according to the flesh, with fear and trembling, in singleness of your heart, as unto Christ*; The servants mentioned here seem to be a part of the household and are told to be obedient to their masters even as children would be to their parents.

According to the context in which it was written, Paul primarily referred to the household slaves that were common when he wrote these instructions, also known as the household code since it is in the same context as the family. It is not natural to obey while suffering the bondage of slavery, as Paul mentions. Having a good heart of grace, the believing slave should obey in relationship to Christ being his master. That would account for what is meant by having singleness of heart. Suppose the bondage of slavery was very difficult and caused continued despondency? In that case, Paul is telling them to focus on their slavery being within the providential watch care of the Lord and that God offers grace to serve Him well and, subsequently, the strength to endure the bondage with the hope of being ultimately redeemed coming from the Lord.

The Jews and the Romans practiced slavery, and it could vary significantly from situation to situation. The master could realize the value and intelligence of his slave, and he could let his slave be educated to become more valuable to his master. In some cases, the slave and the master had a relationship that could promise the slave's freedom. After his freedom, he could be free to retain a relationship with his previous master as a freeman. He then could even enter into some enterprise that would be profitable to the former slave and master. Then, some were cruel taskmasters and would exact complete and total allegiance from their slaves, which would include harsh punishment if they disobeyed.

Paul seems to speak to both the slave and the master in the context of their being Christians and were to treat each as such. Paul does not deal with the moral and the ethical aspects of slavery. The slaves could have been from any of the different racial backgrounds, and they were sometimes brought into slavery after having been captured during times of war. After being captured, they were brought back to the country and sold as slaves at the mercy of the buyer with the hopes, but not the guarantee, that they would once again recover their freedom. For one to do a study of ancient slavery and how it was practiced would reveal many aspects of how slavery worked. Some slave owners would only own several slaves, and they would be mainly for the purpose of helping in their homes. Then, those who were in agriculture could own hundreds of slaves to raise the food and produce necessary for the people of the land for national survival.

6 *Not with eyeservice, as men-pleasers; but as the servants of Christ, doing the will of God from the heart;* It is a most wonderful relationship when the servants are working with a heart attitude of serving Christ as believers. When they do this, they do it in the spirit that Christ is always observing and watching them.

Many of the slaves were treated as less than garbage, and every day was a terror and horror to them. They served reluctantly, and with no joy, and to lessen the attack by their masters, they would pretend to be serving well and being faithful while they were being watched. Some say that Paul coined the word *eyeservice* to make the masters think they were diligent in their business and labors, but as soon as they knew they were not being watched, they would slack off and not work as they appeared when the master was around. Though most Christians do not face the dread and hardships of being slaves, they are under the authority of their employers and should learn from Paul's instructions to the slaves. I have witnessed those who appear diligent and hard workers when the "boss" is around but slack off when he leaves. This attitude may be what birthed the saying, "When the cat's away, the mice will play." If anyone should have a sterling work ethic and a Godly testimony to go with it, it is the believer. We know Paul addressed this Letter to the believers at the Church in Ephesus, but we also understand that the Ephesians 'Letter is part of the Canon of Truth and is equally intended for us who believe.

7 *With good will doing service, as to the Lord, and not to men*: When the believing servant realizes he is serving God as he also serves his master, it will contribute to his doing it with the right attitude. Paul knew the attitude of the workers could be changed if they would only acknowledge that their service was ultimate to the Lord and the virtue of knowing that should have and be ample for them. Also, it allows us to measure the significance of our own labors when considered the same way. Paul brings into play that the stewardship of God includes that our employment is permitted and is to be regarded as an opportunity from the Lord, even if it is not the most desirable employment. Each responsibility of working is an opportunity to let your testimony be known, and your light shine before men.

8 *Knowing that whatsoever good thing any man doeth, the same shall he receive of the Lord, whether he be bond or free.* This verse says that the Lord will remember and care for those who do likewise in a kind and generous spirit. The same is indicated in Hebrews 6:10, *"For God is not unrighteous to forget your work and labour of love, which ye have shewed toward his name, in that ye have ministered to the saints, and do minister."* Paul shows in this verse that Paul is no respecter of persons, whether a person is bond or free. Paul said each would be rewarded according to their attitude and action as it involves their work and is to be honored and rewarded by the Lord in either case, as they presented and dedicated their labors to the Lord. So should we be mindful of this and likewise challenged.

9 *And, ye masters, do the same things unto them, forbearing threatening: knowing that your Master also is in heaven; neither is there respect of persons with him.* Do the same with no partiality Paul is writing to the Masters. Paul wanted the masters to show mutual consideration to the slaves and do it respectfully and not condescendingly, considering Christ is also our master, and we all are His servants. Paul is telling the masters to forbear having a threatening spirit being patient and longsuffering or slow to thunder, as we have previously studied when examining the word *longsuffering*. Again this pattern should be prevalent in the workplaces where the employers and the employees should respect each other to ensure greater harmony amongst them.

The Believers Warfare 6:10-17

10 *Finally, my brethren, be strong in the lord, and in the power of his might.* People confidently boast in their strength; sickness and aging can remove that kind of confidence, but even as the outward man perishes, the inward should be renewed day by day. (2 Corinthians 4:16) Therefore, we should gain our strength in the Lord.

This verse transitions from the believer's walk to the believer's Warfare. When Paul uses the word, *finally*, it is like him saying, "And furthermore, I have something more to say about what I have said." The very wording of these verses indicates that the Lord does not want our relationships to be weak and constantly threatened by Satan's wiles. Satan is constantly using his devious stratagems to manipulate and control the minds of those believers who are trying to please God. He is an enemy, and apart from God's watch care and strength, Satan would utterly devour us, for he walketh about as a roaring lion seeking whom he may devour. (1 Peter 5:8). The admonition by Paul is to be strong in the Lord and in the power of His might. David cried; this battle is the Lord's (1 Samuel 17:47). When going against Goliath, who is a type of Satan, he would have known the meaning of what Paul was saying. Our victories are not just ours; in Christ, they are

His. It is in Him we find our strength for victory and successful conquests. Such knowledge should help bring the courage needed to face our arch-enemy and adversary with all his tricks.

Western readers might be conditioned to miss the fact that Paul is calling his readers to a relationship of dependence and not urging them to draw on their own internal fortitude and strength. "In the Lord" clarifies that believers must draw on divine power. There is a degree of ambiguity when Paul uses the expression "Lord" since it could refer to the Father or the Son. Here, as elsewhere in Ephesians where the phrase "in the Lord" occurs (2:21; 4:1, 17; 5:8; 6:1, 21), it does refer to the Lord Jesus Christ (see 1:2, 3, 15, 17; 5:20; 6:23, 24). Through their relationship with the resurrected and ascended Christ, believers find empowerment. Paul has repeatedly prayed that they gain a heightened awareness of the vastness of God's power that is presently available through Christ for them (1:19). This power is only available through union with Christ and participation in his resurrection and exaltation (2:6). This power is not mediated through incantations, formulas, or shamanistic or magical rituals. (Arnold)

11 *Put on the whole armor of God, that ye may be able to stand against the wiles of the devil.* Satan is a formidable foe and worthy of respect and not lightly to be regarded, thus one's outfit and equipment should be put on with great respect. His greatness pales in comparison to Christ's greatness, so when you put on the armor of God, you are also putting on Christ. Paul gives the believer instructions to do something that God does not do for us. It is the Christian's responsibility to outfit himself in the armor of God. The purpose of the armor is very obvious in that it is for defense. Good coaches often say the greatest offense is a great defense. They would say, "If the other team cannot score against you, they cannot beat you!" Paul makes and gives the

Church at Ephesus a list of essential armor to sustain a fight and a defense against the wicked devil. Just as having a great strategy is necessary for warfare in a military sense, so is a God-ordained plan of action needed for personal and Spiritual warfare. One of the greatest verses in the Scriptures explaining having a strategy and the need for it is in Proverbs 29:18 *"Where there is no vision, people perish: but he that keepeth the law, happy is he."* The word vision, as used in this verse, *God ordained plan*, strategy, or having a plan of action. The word "strategy" is used here in reference to the Word of God. Fighting Satan always requires God to fight our battles for ultimate success. The ultimate or final battle takes place when we enter into a glorified state where there will be no more battles or Satan.

Paul uses extensive military metaphors throughout this section to convey the idea of spiritual power, such as the complete armor, breastplate, shield, helmet, sword, strapping [a weapon] around one's waist, and putting on shoes. Paul shifts metaphors on one occasion when he uses the term for wrestling, "struggle" (πάλη; 6:12), a word that comes from the sport of wrestling (but could refer to the kind of wrestling a soldier may engage in). (Arnold) The word for struggle is also a word close kin to a word from which we get our word to agonize. Paul is fond of this word and uses it in several of his Letters. As used here, the word wrestle or struggle is only used once in the New Testament. Pertaining to the outfit, there is reason to suggest that, being in Rome, he may have thought of the Roman soldier and how he outfitted himself. If using the Roman example, he leaves out two of the main parts of the Roman armor, the two pila (Javelins) and the (greaves) or leg armor. More likely, he is referring to Isaiah's example; it seems that most of Paul's imagery comes directly from Isaiah (see Isa 11:4–5; 59:17; cf. 1 Thessalonians 5:8).

The wording is "ye may be able to stand against the devil's wiles." Indicates that in such warfare, one may not stand if he is not thoroughly protected, but even that is not enough if the Word of God is left out, as we will soon see.

12 *For we wrestle not against flesh and blood, but against principalities, against powers, against the rulers of the darkness of this world, against spiritual wickedness in high places.* The warfare mentioned is not the fights we have with our fellow humans, but in the region of darkness, which is a way of describing that which is foreign to the Light which is in Christ Jesus. In John 3, we are told that men love darkness more than light because their deeds are evil. That shows a connection to Satan's rule described as principalities. The wrestling described is not as a soldier would engage in warfare against another soldier, but is when one is warring against Satan and the demons, and as one commentator said, "Against Satan's mafia." Each Christian can expect continuous warfare and should constantly be prepared for it. The term principalities carries the meaning of angels and, in this case, the fallen angels whom Satan has instructed to organize attacks against the children of God. For this reason, Paul is giving instructions on how to deal with the devil and his cohorts. It is important to recognize that in such warfare, the weapons are primarily and mostly defensive weapons. They are also to be recognized as powers or demonic authorities who are banned together for their warfare. The warfare is not at all human in its origin but demonic. This is not to say that it does not include humans, for when Satan and his fallen angels influence humans, it may be said that they are controlling those who are human and who are under demonic influence or demons possessed to affect other humans. So if any flesh and blood is involved, it did not originate with the humans, but they became pawns in the devil's hands. Being properly outfitted, believers can resist the devil so that he might flee from them.

Charles Hodge said this about such warfare: "Our conflict is not with man, but against principalities, against powers, against the rulers of the darkness of this world, against spiritual wickedness in high places. The signification of the terms here used, the context, and the analogy of Scripture, render it certain that the reference is to evil spirits. They are called in Scripture demons, who are declared to be fallen angels, 2 Pet. 2, 4; Jude 6, and are now subject to Satan their prince. They are called princes, those who are first or high in rank; and potentates, those invested with authority. These terms have probably reference to the relation of the spirits among themselves. The designation rulers of the world, expresses the power or authority which they exercise over the world. Mankind is subject to them; comp. 2 Cor. 4, 4; John 16, 11. The word is properly used only of those rulers whose dominion was universal. These evil spirits are the rulers of this darkness. The meaning either is, that they reign over the existing state of ignorance and alienation from God; i. e. the world in its apostasy is subject to their control; or this darkness is equivalent to kingdom of darkness. Rulers of the kingdom of darkness, which includes in it, according to the scriptural doctrine, the world as distinguished from the true people of God. The word is used elsewhere, the abstract for the concrete, for those in darkness, i. e. for those who belong to, or constitute the kingdom of darkness, Luke 22, 53; Col. 1,13. Our conflict, therefore, is with the potentates who are rulers of the kingdom of darkness as it now is." (Hodge)

The Believer's Armor

13 *Wherefore take unto you the whole armour of God, that ye may be able to withstand in the evil day, and having done* *all, to stand.* The word "Wherefore," as Paul uses it here, is him reiterating the necessity of the armor and why it is so. Standing is an exercise that should occur in both an offensive and a defensive posture. Paul challenges the Church at Ephesus to total commitment. He expresses the importance of outfitting with God's entire, complete armor. The weapons of our warfare certainly should not be humanly compiled expecting to find victory with the weapons of this carnal world, yet many do. The most important thing a believer can know and do is understand the importance of engaging in Spiritual warfare with Spiritual armor. To do any less spells disaster. The expression stand is used *four* times in this section dealing with warfare. It is essential to keep on fighting the good fight. The good fight involves being equipped for warfare, recognizing the value of doing such, and having the Sword of the Spirit.

14 *Stand therefore, having your loins girt about with truth, and having on the breastplate of righteousness;* The regular use of the girdle is to compress, and the wide belt used by the soldier is to prepare one's body for intense warfare. The thickness of the belt also adds thickness to the midsection more than just the soldier's skin. The wide belt with the breastplate can help reflect the enemies' arrows or darts. The metaphor Paul gives shows how vital the belt of truth is to the spiritual warrior, as the leather belt is to the soldier in a human battle. This also is the fourth use of the word stand in this section, indicating the soldier's posture when the Lord is fighting for you. I like to think of the Lord in front of me, and I am courageously standing in His shadow as though He says, "Keep standing; I have this!" I believe this because everything mentioned is a defensive weapon or armor except for *the Sword of the Spirit, which is the Word of God!* The truth mentioned here is the character of the believer who has as his reason for standing based upon him being saturated with the Truth, making him more than a conqueror if his battle is the Lord's.

Loins Girt About With Truth

To have one's loins girt about speaks of the broad strap that wrapped around the midsection to hold and strengthen the soldier as he fought his battles. Long flowing garments were worn during the time of Paul, and to prepare them for battle, they were to be girded up. For the soldier, a leather and metal belt was used, which was wide and not only protected the soldier but helped strengthen the soldier not to damage his internal organs while engaging in warfare. When I think of this, I think of when I would go to the gym and put a wide belt around my midsection to protect me from rupturing muscles when lifting heavy weights. There seem to be similarities here. About the girdle of Truth, Dr. Martin Lloyd-Jones has some interesting thoughts worthy of being shared in italics with my following comments for each:

The apostle Paul exhorts Christians to put on the whole armor of God to stand against the devil's wiles. Paul did not merely suggest what should make up the believer's armor but clearly declared the putting on of each piece for a specific purpose and intent. The devil is a very cunning and vicious foe who wants to utterly and completely destroy the believer, and without the armor, the believer has no defense. The putting on of the armor is the believer's responsibility to help us stand, and the actual battle is the Lord's. We learn to depend upon Him alone.

The first piece of armor is the girdle of truth. This means having a firm grasp of biblical truth and doctrine. This description should characterize the believer's confidence in the truth of God's Word and how he acts upon it. A person void of the Truth, which has the Word of God as its origin, will be feeble and weak in Spiritual warfare. This is a weakness found among many who are believers when they neglect to study the Word of God. By not studying, they lack, as Proverbs speaks, having Vision, a word for having a strategy that means a God-ordained plan for Spiritual warfare.

The girdle gives a soldier freedom of movement and a sense of security. For Christians, truth gives us freedom from sin and confidence in our faith. There can be no standing or steadfastness in the faith if one lacks the hearing from the Word of God to instruct and monitor us along the way.

There are two aspects of truth: objective (the Bible) and subjective (our understanding and belief). We need both. To function properly means the two must work together just as wisdom and prudence work together. James teaches us that faith without works is dead standing alone. (James 2:20). The use of the Sword of the Spirit, which is the Word of God, is necessary as an offensive weapon, but having the Word working in each of us as we go forth to war gives us the special strength that we need.

The girdle of truth means we have a mastery of the truth and are mastered by the truth. It controls our whole life. The girdle or the special heavy belt clearly indicates that the soldier means business, that he is ready and able to fight a good fight while knowing that his warfare is Spiritual and that he has learned to depend on God for the ultimate victory. It is as though the soldier, when he pulls the belt together and tight, that at any time, the battle may proceed or continue without him having fear, for he has prepared himself by being prepared. The Truth or the Word of Truth is the only weapon that is both offensive and defensive in the believer's armor

Having our loins girded with truth means we have a settled conviction about the truth with no uncertainty or lacking clarity. Truth takes away the uncertainty as nothing else can or will. The reason for having a settled conviction about the truth is that the Word of God is forever settled in heaven...Psalm 119:89 "Forever, O Lord, thy word is settled in heaven." This means the soldier's orders can be depended upon and do not change.

The devil tries to confuse us and lead us into error, so we must know the truth to stand against him. Satan, who is the author of confusion, knows how to confuse. The only way to avoid a confused state is to have the clarity of truth at work according to the Word of Truth.

The New Testament epistles were written to combat error and heresy and teach the truth. The early church councils also defined truth against heresy. The body of Truth became such because of the learned Word of Truth. The Word of God gives us, as individual churches, a common ground where each can be recognized as churches of like precious faith as long as they build their faith upon the Word of God, the Bible. Then, when they meet together, they have things in common.

Without truth, we are like children "tossed to and fro by every wind of doctrine." We must know the truth to stand firm. Apart from the Truth, we are weak and vacillating and cannot know nor have the stability to stand. *Truth is essential for withstanding the devil. We must know what and whom we believe to have victory.* (Lloyd-Jones)

The Breastplate of Righteousness

...and having on the breastplate of righteousness (V. 14b.)

The imagery is of an armed Roman or Israelite soldier prepared for battle. A typical armed soldier wore a breastplate made of bronze or chain mail. It covered the vital organs, namely, the heart, and was fitted with loops or buckles that attached it to a thick belt. If the belt was loosened, the breastplate slipped right off. *"and having on the breastplate of righteousness;"* in allusion to (Isaiah 59:17), meaning not works of righteousness done by men, though these are a fence when rightly used against the reproaches and charges of the enemy, as they were by Samuel, (1 Samuel 12:3), but rather the graces of faith and love, (1 Thessalonians 5:8), though faith has another place in the Christian armor, afterward mentioned; wherefore it seems best to understand this of the righteousness of Christ, which is imputed by God, and received by faith, is a guard against, and repels the accusations and charges of Satan, and is security from all wrath and condemnation. (John Gill)

When Paul compares the armor of God with military gear, each piece represents a part of God's strength that He extends to us when we become His children. The breastplate of righteousness refers to the righteousness purchased for us by Jesus at the cross (2 Corinthians 5:21). At salvation, a "breastplate" is issued to each repentant sinner. God specially designed it to protect our hearts and souls from evil and deception. Our own righteous acts are no match for Satan's attacks (Isaiah 64:6). The breastplate of righteousness has Christ's name stamped on it, as though He said, "Your righteousness isn't sufficient to protect you. Wear mine."

We are instructed to "put on" this armor, which implies that we do not *automatically* wear it all the time. Putting on the armor of God requires a decision on our part. To put on the breastplate of righteousness, we must first have the belt of truth firmly in place. Without truth, our righteousness will be based upon our own attempts to impress God. This leads to legalism or self-condemnation (Romans 8:1). We choose instead to acknowledge that, apart from Him, we can do nothing (John 15:5). We see ourselves as "in Christ" and that, regardless of our failures, His righteousness has been credited to our account.

We "put it on" by seeking God and His righteousness above everything else (Matthew 6:33). We make Him and His ways our dwelling place (Psalm 91:1). We delight in His commands and desire for His ways to become our ways (Psalm 37:4; 119:24, 111; Isaiah 61:10). When God reveals an area of change to us, we obey and allow Him to work in us. At the point where we say "no" to God, we open a little crack in the armor where Satan's arrows can get through (Ephesians 6:16).

As we wear Christ's breastplate of righteousness, we begin to develop a purity of heart that translates into actions. Wearing this breastplate creates a lifestyle of practicing what we believe in our hearts. As our lives become conformed to the image of Christ (Romans 8:29), our choices become more righteous, and these godly choices also protect us from further temptation and deception (Proverbs 8:20; Psalm 23:3). (Got Questions) There could be no righteousness without Truth, and it is fair to say that there is no Truth without righteousness, which further indicates that they both depend upon each other and the metaphors used by Paul are indeed wonderful ways of expressing the believer's warfare and how he is to be outfitted spiritually. It is important to know that the armor is to be completely, not partially, adorned. Each part has critical significance and must be completely worn to be safe. Just as the helmet of salvation is likened to a helmet that protects the brain or mind, the breastplate of righteousness protects a vital portion of the soldier that is necessary for life: the alive, beating heart. As a metaphor, it pictures liveliness in Christ as a Christian warrior.

Feet Shod With the Preparation of the Gospel of Peace

15 *And your feet shod with the preparation of the gospel of peace.* Feet and the legs of a soldier are so important, and I am told that the big toe helps one greatly to maintain his balance. For a soldier to have the agility to exercise his warfare, he should protect his feet. In Christian symbolism, Paul says how beautiful are the feet of them that preach the gospel of peace...(Romans 10:13) "And how shall they preach, except they be sent? as it is written, How beautiful are the feet of them that preach the gospel of peace, and bring glad tidings of good things!"

The first record of shoes was described in Egypt as being sandal-like and protecting the bottom of the feet. The shoes for the soldier had to be skillfully made to prepare him to run and keep his balance in conflict with metal studs like a football player would depend upon his cleats. This verse indicates that the soldier was striving for peace through power, not simply detente. There is no room for compromise with Satan or his forces, but there is a desire to fight for a kind of peace that comes only from the Lord by His Holy Spirit without any compromise.

The Shield of Faith

16 *Above all, taking the shield of faith, wherewith ye shall be able to quench all the fiery darts of the wicked.* The shield of faith has such a prominent part to play in the believer's armor. Paul said "above all," and his saying this related to just how important faith is to the believer's warfare and his total existence. Noticing the shield size that Paul may have been thinking of makes what he is saying more understandable. Faith is a shield, and "faith is the substance of things hoped for, the evidence of things not seen." The invisible shield of faith is mighty to defend one from the fiery darts of the wicked...To gain an idea of the way the shield was formed, seen by this ancient description:

"The Roman panoply consists firstly of a shield (scutum), the convex surface of which measures two and a half feet in width and four feet in length, the thickness at the rim is a palm's breath. It is made of two planks glued together, the outer surface is covered first with canvas and then with calfskin. Its upper and lower rims are strengthened by an iron edging that protects it from descending blows and injury when rested on the ground. It also has an iron boss (umbo) fixed to it, which turns aside the most formidable blows of stones, pikes, and heavy missiles in general." (Polybius, Hist. 6.23.2–5)57 Another thing that I find interesting is that when the soldier was able, he would soak his shield in water and soak the canvas and the calfskin to quench or put out the fiery darts or arrows of the enemy. A great lesson that can be learned from this is that with water being a type of the Word of God, it is like saying that we need to be soaked in the Word of God for our warfare.

The following gives another description from several sources concerning the fiery darts] Lit. "The darts, the ignited darts." The metaphor is taken from the fire arrows of ancient warfare. Here, Wetstein gives abundant illustrations from Thucydides, Livy, Vegetius, Ammianus, and many other authors. Ammianus (about A.D. 380) describes the Roman malleoli as arrows carrying a perforated bulb, like a distaff, just below the point; the bulb filled with burning matter; the arrow discharged from a slack bow, lest speed should kill the flame. Another variety was simpler; the shaft near the point was wrapped in burning tow. (Moule) The large shield's protection was vital when multiple arrows were shot during an enemy attack. Josephus portrays just such a situation: "to avoid the multitude of the enemy's missiles, they should bend down on their knees, and cover themselves with their shields, and that they should retreat a little backward for a while, till the archers should have emptied their quivers" (Jos., J.W. 3.259). For the combining of *faith and shield, it should be the soldier's reminder that he needs* to have the confidence that Christ is with him in his battles and can trust God to take care of him, "come what may!" His faith should not be in himself but in Christ Jesus alone.

17 *And take the helmet of salvation, and the sword of the Spirit, which is the word of God:* The helmet was often decorated and played a part in identifying the soldier and intimidating the enemy soldier. Salvation is a word that is cardinal to our faith, and how it is used here is how we are safe in His so great salvation, and further protected and engaging when holding the Sword of the Spirit. The helmet protects the head and the brain, as used in rough contact sports like football. If one had to leave off his shoulder pads or helmet in an intense game, choosing just one, he should wisely cover his head to protect himself from brain injury. Damage to one's brain could very easily prove fatal, just as the brain is central to all that goes on in the human body; even so, salvation is central to one's spiritual life. The helmet was often the first thing recognized in a soldier's uniform and armor. The first thing recognizable in a Christian ought to be his relationship to God or his salvation in Christ Jesus. Then, the Sword of the Spirit should dominate the Soldier's presence just as his helmet. The sword is a metaphor with the sword picturing the Word of God, which is sharper than a *two-edged sword*—the Sword of the Word, the Helmet of Salvation, and the Breastplate of

Righteousness are three metaphors that help make the soldier's armor and should stand out and be present when the soldier is engaged upon (as when thinking of the Roman soldier as an example). All armor pieces are necessary, but these seem to stand out to me, perhaps more dominantly, as I visually think of the Roman soldier. As mentioned earlier, Paul may have been thinking of the soldiers pictured in Isaiah. The main thought concerning the believer's warfare is that the key to victory is Christ Jesus and His Word while being outfitted as a true soldier of the Cross, facing each battle that comes His way aggressively, and not being cowardly or timid when facing the adversary having God's help.

Conclusion To the Ephesian Letter

18 *Praying always with all prayer and supplication in the Spirit, and watching thereunto with all perseverance and supplication for all saints*; Paul concludes his Letter by stating that prayer is essential to the Spiritual walk and warfare, knowing that the believer is so greatly blessed with the exceeding riches of Christ Jesus to enjoy in ones walk and in his warfare. There is no aspect of having Christ with us and in us, as we also are in Him. Paul also states that he does not casually accept his responsibility but does it with all perseverance and, indeed, with diligence.

19 *And for me, that utterance may be given unto me, that I may open my mouth boldly, to make known the mystery of the gospel.* Paul is praying for the Ephesians, but also desiring they pray for him that he may utter the sacred words of God with boldness and not let the chains affect his ministry at all. He wants to increase his effectiveness to do even more to reveal the mystery of the gospel.

20 *For which I am an ambassador in bonds: that therein I* *may speak boldly, as I ought to speak.* Paul knows who he is and his job and wants to do so as he ought to. He refers to himself as an ambassador in bonds, and the foreign country that he represents is heaven!

21 *But that ye also may know my affairs, and how I do, Tychicus, a beloved brother, and faithful minister in the Lord, shall make known to you all things*: Paul had entrusted Tychicus with a very important mission. He was to deliver the Epistle to the Ephesians, that is, "the circular letter" to the churches in proconsular Asia, to which it was sent, giving a copy of it to the church in Laodicea. He was then to proceed to Colosse, with the Epistle to the church there. In Colosse, Tychicus would plead the cause of Onesimus, who accompanied him from Rome. "Under his shelter, Onesimus would be safer than if he encountered Philemon alone" (Lightfoot, Commentary on Colossians, 314) There were those such as Timothy, Epaphroditus, and here Tychicus who were so helpful and devoted to serving Paul who gave us good examples of how a servant is to serve a servant who all are to serve The Servant.

22 *Whom I have sent unto you for the same purpose, that ye might know our affairs, and that he might comfort your hearts*. Paul, as he did also in his other Epistles, wanted those to whom he was writing to know how he was doing so that they would not be overtaxed with worry.

23 *Peace be to the brethren, and love with faith, from God the Father and the Lord Jesus Christ*. Paul is offering the promise of peace, love, and faith as coming from God the Father and the Lord Jesus Christ.

24 *Grace be with all them that love our Lord Jesus Christ in sincerity. Amen.* In this closing statement, Paul wants to make sure that all who are in the faith loving the Lord Jesus Christ sincerely, have the grace that he speaks of.

So ends the Letter to the Ephesians written in antiquity,

but it is still as fresh as the morning dew to those of us who now read this Letter, a part of the completed Canon of Truth. Thank you, Brother Paul, for being so faithful. Thank you, Lord, for raising him up to speak yet to us…

Completed February 21, 2024; began November the 1st. 2023

BIBLIOGRAPHY

Zondervan,. *Ephesians (Zondervan Exegetical Commentary on The New Testament series Book 10)* (p. 132). Zondervan Academic. Kindle Edition.

Hoehner, Harold W.. *Ephesians: An Exegetical Commentary* (p. 246). Baker Publishing Group. Kindle Edition.

Zondervan,. *Ephesians* (Zondervan Exegetical Commentary on The New Testament series Book 10) (p. 216). Zondervan Academic. Kindle Edition.

Yandian, Bob. Ephesians: *A New Testament Commentary* (p. 58). Empowered Life. Kindle Edition.

Hoehner, Harold W.. *Ephesians: An Exegetical Commentary* (p. 422). Baker Publishing Group. Kindle Edition.

Hodge, Charles. *Commentary on Ephesians*. Kindle Edition.

Pratte, David. *Commentary on the Letter to the Ephesians*: Bible Study Notes and Comments (pp. 64-65). Kindle Edition.

Crews, James K.. *A Commentary on Ephesians*: A Resource for Teachers (and Students) (pp. 92-93). Kindle Edition.

Pratte, David. *Commentary on the Letter to the Ephesians*: Bible Study Notes and Comments (pp. 76-77). Kindle Edition.

Made in the USA
Columbia, SC
09 June 2024